AUTOCAD 2002 INSIDE & OUT

Second Edition

Lynn Allen

CMP Books
Lawrence, Kansas

CMP Books
CMP Media LLC
1601 West 23rd Street, Suite 200
Lawrence, Kansas 66046
USA
www.cmpbooks.com

Editor: Rita Sooby
Managing Editor: Michelle O'Neal
Layout Production: Tim Knapp and Rita Sooby
Cover art: Damien Castaneda

Distributed in the U.S. and Canada by:
Publishers Group West
1700 Fourth Street
Berkeley, CA 94710
1-800-788-3123
www.pgw.com

ISBN 1-57820-075-X

CMP**Books**

To all of my readers

Table of Contents

Introduction. . . . .**xi**
Thanks and Kudos xi

SECTION 1   NO STRESS 1

CHAPTER 1   **Feeling at Home in AutoCAD 2002** **3**
The AutoCAD 2002 Pull-Down Menus 4

CHAPTER 2   **The World of Object Snaps**. **9**
Object Snaps. 9

CHAPTER 3   **Display Commands — What You See Is
What You Get!** **15**

CHAPTER 4   **Grip Me Baby!** **19**
Starting Simple. 20
One More Grip Tip 22

CHAPTER 5   **Modifying Object Properties** **25**
The New Properties Dialog. 25

CHAPTER 6   **Words, Words, Words** **29**
dtext 29
text 33
Control Codes 33

CHAPTER 7   **The Magical World of Mtext** **35**
Line Spacing 36
Changing Case 39

CHAPTER 8   Text Styles and Other Text Tips! **43**
Text Fonts versus Styles. 43
Changing the Current Text Style 45
Miscellaneous Text System Variables 45
New AutoCAD 2002 Text Features 46

CHAPTER 9   Hatch It! **49**
Flooding 49

CHAPTER 10   Clever Construction Commands. **53**
Construction Lines 53
Rays. 55
Divide and Measure 55

CHAPTER 11   More to Offer with Multilines **59**
Multiline Styles. 59
Making Multilines 62

CHAPTER 12   Diving Down into AutoCAD
DesignCenter **65**
DesignCenter Toolbar. 66
The Bottom Line 69

CHAPTER 13   The Quintessential Selection Set **71**
Select Objects. 71

CHAPTER 14   Going in Circles with the New array
Command **75**
Polar Array 76

SECTION 2   LOW STRESS 79

CHAPTER 15   **External References** **81**
Attaching an External Reference 82
Nesting External References (and Circular Xrefs) 83
Overlaying External References. 84
Detaching or Binding an External Reference. 84
Changing the Path and Reloading External References 85
Digging Deeper into the Xref Manager 85

CHAPTER 16   **Editing and Clipping External References** . . . **91**
Clipping your External References. 91
Editing your External References. 94

CHAPTER 17   **A New Dimension** **99**
The New Dimstyle 101

CHAPTER 18   **Demystifying Dimensioning Tabs**. **105**
Tab 1: Lines and Arrows. 105
Tab 2: Text 107
Tab 3: Fit. 109
Tab 4: Primary Units. 112
Tab 5: Alternate Units. 115
Tab 6: Tolerances 116

CHAPTER 19   **Cool Tricks in AutoCAD**. **119**
Cool Trick #1: The Power of the Age-Old change Command 119
Cool Trick #2: A Hidden Option in the array Command 120
Cool Trick #3: Easily Select Objects That Are Too Close Together . . . 120
Cool Trick #4: Make Sure the Open Dialog Searches Your
    Drawings Directory 121
Cool Trick #5: Controlling the Default Profile Setting (and Other
    Switches). 121
Cool Trick #6: Creating New Layers at Lightning Speed 122

Cool Trick #7: Seeing the Scale Factor or Rotation Angle of a Block
Before You Pick the Insertion Point 122
Cool Trick #8: Groups 123
Cool Trick #9: lengthen 125
Cool Trick #10: Automatic Dimensioning 126
Cool Trick #11: The Displacement Option in the copy and move
Commands 126
Cool Trick #12: Removing Objects from a Selection Set 127
Cool Trick #13: Intersecting with appint 127
Cool Trick #14: Did You Know ...? 128

CHAPTER 20   Excellent Changes to Everyday Commands in AutoCAD 2002 . . . . **129**

trim and extend Commands Combined 129
Smarter fillet and chamfer Commands 130
Enhancements to the pedit Command 130
properties Command Updated 131
Speed, Speed, Speed 133

CHAPTER 21   Splines and Ellipses **135**

Ellipses 135
Splines 137

CHAPTER 22   Cool System Variables (aka setvars) **141**

CHAPTER 23   Finding Your Way In Paper Space **151**

Viewports 152
Paper Space Viewports 155
The mview Command 156
The XP Option 158
The Viewports Toolbar 161

CHAPTER 24   Dimensioning in Paper Space **163**

Layers in Layouts! 166
One Final Tip 167

CHAPTER 25   **Taking a Tour Through Options** **169**
The Files Tab. 169
The Display Tab 172
The Open and Save Tab 177
The System Tab 181
The User Preferences Tab 184
The Drafting Tab. 185
The Selection Tab. 187
The Profiles Tab 189

SECTION 3   BRING ON THE ASPIRIN. 191

CHAPTER 26   **Are Your Blocks Smart?** **193**
Mode. 193
Attribute 194

CHAPTER 27   **Editing Your Attributes**. **197**
Global Editing. 197
Edit One at a Time 198
Updating Block Definitions Before AutoCAD 2002 199
Awesome Attribute Editing in 2002 200

CHAPTER 28   **The Down-and-Dirty Basics of
Customizing** **205**
Menu File Types 205
The Anatomy of a Menu File 206

CHAPTER 29   **Button Menus and Accelerator Keys** **211**
Button Menus. 211
The Awesome Accelerators 214

CHAPTER 30   **Toolbar Customization**. **217**
Transparent Commands. 220

CHAPTER 31   **Customizing Your Pull-Down Menus** **223**

Creating a Pull-Down Menu 223

CHAPTER 32   **The Long-Lost Image Tile Menus** **227**

Create the Slide File 227
Create the Image Menu 229

CHAPTER 33   **Customizing Your Keyboard in**
AutoCAD 2002 . . . . **235**

Accelerator 235
The Keyboard Tab 238

CHAPTER 34   **Limitless Linetypes** **241**

CHAPTER 35   **Calculating Geometries** **245**

Mathematical Expressions 245
Units and Angles Format 246
Finding the Radius of an Arc or Circle 247
Shortcut Functions 250

CHAPTER 36   **The Top Secret Filter Command** **251**

Selecting the Filter 252
AND, OR, and NOT 254

CHAPTER 37   **The World of Raster** **257**

What is a Raster Image? 257
The AutoCAD Image Manager 258
Editing Those Raster Images 262
Modifying Your Image 262
Bonus! 264

Index **267**

Introduction

It's hard to believe it's been nearly four years and nearly 50 columns since my first book came out. You'll find this book is most useful for the AutoCAD 2000 to 2002 user, regardless of your level of expertise. It has been broken into three different sections: *No Stress*, *Low Stress*, and *Bring on the Aspirin!* As would be expected, I start out with simple applications and gradually make my way up the guru ladder. The *No Stress* section covers the basics, although even the pros might find some meaty productivity tips. The *Low Stress* section cranks up the dial a bit and wanders into slightly more advanced territory. The *Bring on the Aspirin!* section is not for the faint of heart or the new user. Be sure to get some hours in your back pocket before making the leap to the final chapters.

This book is not intended to help you learn AutoCAD from scratch. For that, I strongly recommend instructor-led training (my 13 years with the Autodesk Training Center program kicks into gear here), or find a good A-to-Z book and be patient because AutoCAD is a complex program with many different aspects.

Remember, this book is a compilation of my columns over the past eight years, not a book I sat down and wrote from start to finish. Consequently, by the very nature of its design it might feel a bit disjointed. Nonetheless, I've tried to put the columns in a logical order to help it flow well. I've also selected those topics I felt would be of the most value and interest to you, regardless of your skill level. I recommend reading this book as needed: If you're having a rough time with Paper Space, by all means jump to the chapter that focuses on Paper Space. If you're learning how to customize your menus, there's nothing that says you have to read the first two sections before going to the more advanced section on customization.

Thanks and Kudos

My AutoCAD life has changed so much in the past four years. Now I spend most of my time on the road sharing AutoCAD tips and tricks with users throughout the world. I don't find I have as much time to answer the e-mail of troubled AutoCAD users as I used to (which makes me sad), but I do get to meet many of you face to face. I'm always amazed at the reception I get wherever I go in the AutoCAD community — please know that it is much appreciated. I often feel so unworthy of all the attention I get because I'm just like you: I'm trying to find better ways to get my AutoCAD jobs done.

On a personal note, I'd like to thank my children, Joshua and Ashley, who have shared me with the AutoCAD community for as long as they can remember. My traveling has taken a toll on them and causes me to frequently question my priorities. I also need to thank my mother, who minds the fort while I'm gone and, more importantly, spoils my children and dogs. None of this would be possible without the ongoing support of Autodesk, who has kindly permitted me to run around the world spreading the AutoCAD gospel on their dime.

I'd also like to thank a few others, starting with Randy Kintzley, Express Tools programmer extraordinaire. He has always been willing to take the time to share his incredible insight into the world of AutoCAD, as well. I've worked with some amazing people over the past few years, including Kevin Merritt and Rebecca Bell, who've made my everyday life at Autodesk so much better; Kathi Fox and Nancy Maul, who are two truly amazing managers who have stood by my side; Renee Swenson, who helps me keep the Autodesk University flag flying high; Heidi Hill, my editor at *CADENCE* magazine for her infinite (and I mean infinite) patience with me; and Arnie Williams, editor in chief of *CADENCE*, who continues to give me a place on the *CADENCE* team.

And a great big huge thanks to all of you — for reading my columns in *CADENCE*, for attending my presentations, for sending awesome e-mail, and for saying the kindest words to me. Every time I think I can't possibly get on one more plane, one of you will come along and tell me how much I've helped you, and suddenly it all seems worthwhile.

SECTION 1

NO STRESS

Welcome to the first and easiest section of *AutoCAD 2002, Inside and Out*. Here, you'll find a friendly overview of the AutoCAD 2002 User Interface for those of you who are making the jump from Release 14 to 2002. I also cover some of the more basic concepts, such as Object Snaps and Text, in this section. I've included a variety of tidbits within each chapter that will appeal to even the most advanced AutoCAD user, so don't discount this section because you're a veteran! Realizing that users of all levels read my column, I try to insert tips and tricks that will benefit all levels of technical expertise. For you newbies, I hope my words will make sense to you as you begin to discover the many aspects of AutoCAD. Be patient with yourself because there is so much to learn!

CHAPTER 1

Feeling at Home in AutoCAD 2002

I always feel trepidation about new releases of AutoCAD. What changes will be made? Will they be for better or worse? Will the learning curve be high or low? For those of you who have followed my column through the years, I'm sure you've read these words before when Releases 13, 14, and even 2000 came out. Because I was such an avid DOS user, Release 13 was a shock to my system, and it took months before I felt I knew my way around the product. Release 14, on the other hand, was an easy transition thanks to the improved stability and well thought-out enhancements. But what is AutoCAD 2002 like? Because many of you will make the leap from

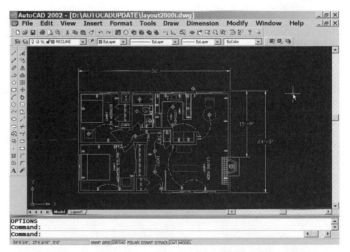

Figure 1.1 An overall view of the AutoCAD 2002 drawing editor.

Release 14 to 2002, I will cover some of the basic transitions you'll come across.

Figure 1.1 shows the standard, out-of-the-box view of the AutoCAD 2002 drawing editor. You'll notice the Model and Layout tabs in the lower left-hand corner of the screen along with the new line weights and the plot-style drop-down list that was added to the Object Properties toolbar. Notice the clearly distinguishable drawing name in the upper left-hand corner of the drawing area. Hitting the maximize button (the one within the drawing area) gives you a tad more drawing room and pushes the drawing name to the upper left-hand corner of the drawing editor, right next to the

AutoCAD 2002 program name. You can see that the full drawing path is displayed — a delightful addition for those of you who use the same drawing names from different directories.

Note   If the full path doesn't display, turn this feature on in the `options` command.

I'll start at the top of the drawing editor and work down, starting with the pull-down menus.

The AutoCAD 2002 Pull-Down Menus

I'm still convinced the pull-down menus are one of the most popular modes of AutoCAD transportation. It can be very frustrating to load a new release, only to find that the pull-down menus are completely rearranged. To Autodesk's credit, the company's developers left the main structure of these menus alone in AutoCAD 2002 (for you Release 14 users). A first glimpse shows only one major change: the new Window pull-down menu accommodates multiple document interface (MDI) functionality (the number-one AutoCAD wish list item for about four years), which permits you to open more than one drawing at a time. This added capability comes with viewing decisions, such as tiling or cascading. You'll also find new features and commands sprinkled among the appropriate menus, along with a few double cascades, which I don't really care for because they make me feel like I'm getting a workout.

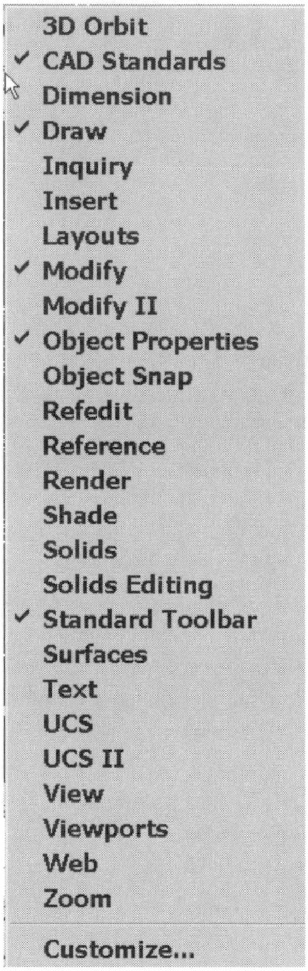

Toolbars

It has taken me a while to warm up to toolbars, but I'm slowly becoming a fan. I strongly recommend you check out a couple of new toolbars. To display all of the toolbars available, right-click on any existing tool. This brings up the menu shown in Figure 1.2. You no longer right-click on a tool to bring up the Toolbar dialog for customizing; now, you select Customize from this new menu to bring up the Customize dialog.

A couple of cool new additions to the toolbar world includes the updated Dimension toolbar, which makes it easy to switch from one dimension style to another, as shown in Figure 1.3. It also includes the awesome new `qdim` command introduced in AutoCAD 2000. Figure 1.4 shows the new Viewports toolbar, which makes it super-simple to assign scale factors to viewports in Paper Space (which is about a million times easier than setting the XP factor in the `zoom` command). You'll also find the new Polygonal option in the Viewports toolbar. The new

- 3D Orbit
- ✓ CAD Standards
- Dimension
- ✓ Draw
- Inquiry
- Insert
- Layouts
- ✓ Modify
- Modify II
- ✓ Object Properties
- Object Snap
- Refedit
- Reference
- Render
- Shade
- Solids
- Solids Editing
- ✓ Standard Toolbar
- Surfaces
- Text
- UCS
- UCS II
- View
- Viewports
- Web
- Zoom

Customize...

Figure 1.2 Right-clicking an existing toolbar button brings up the toolbar shortcut menu.

Shade toolbar (Figure 1.5) makes it easy to turn on the persistent shading options now available for those of you who are into 3D drawing, and the new 3DOrbit toolbar lets you play with the ultimate fun 3dorbit command (Figure 1.6). Even if you are not into working in 3D, you really must spend a few minutes playing with the Continuous Orbit option! It is pure fun, and when you spend so much time using AutoCAD for mundane purposes, you owe it to yourself to have a little CAD fun every once in a while.

The look and feel of toolbars is a tad different as well. You'll notice that the individual tools now have a flat appearance, and they lift as you move your cursor over them. Also notice the new separator lines, which serve the obvious purpose of separating, and the new grab bars, which make it much easier to grab docked toolbars and move them around on the screen.

Figure 1.3 The Dimension toolbar in AutoCAD 2002 also displays the current dimension style.

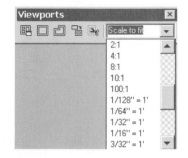

Figure 1.4 The updated Viewports toolbar makes it easy to set viewport scale factors.

Some new toolbar additions surfaced in AutoCAD 2002. The Modify II toolbar has the new Attribute commands that are absolutely fantastic, and the new AutoCAD Standard toolbar contains the commands that help you keep your drawing standards up to snuff. The Object Properties toolbar has the awesome new Layer Previous tool, which allows you to recall your previous layer settings (be sure to try it — you won't know how you survived without it).

Figure 1.5 The Shade toolbar contains the various persistent shading options.

Figure 1.6 The 3DOrbit options are found on the 3DOrbit toolbar.

Moving on to the Model and Layout tabs in the lower left-hand corner of the drawing area, I suspect the main goal behind adding these new tabs to the drawing editor is to encourage those who haven't ventured into the world of Paper Space to take that first step. No longer do you need to know the magic tilemode command to wander back and forth between Paper Space and Model Space because now it's just a tab away. One reader asked me why Autodesk felt the need to put Excel into AutoCAD, which you might think is the case. I can assure you, it's not Excel, just a simple new mechanism to go from one space to another. By default, any new drawings come complete with one Model Space tab and two Layout tabs (named Layout1 and Layout2). It is easy to rename, delete, and add new tabs by right-clicking on any of the tabs. If you like to use the screen slider bars to pan and zoom, you'll find you can expand the slider bar right over any of the tabs you create. Should you do this, you can use the arrows next to the Model tab to move through the Model and Layout tabs.

The Status Bar

A few additions to the AutoCAD 2002 Status Bar other than the standard coordinate display (Ortho, Snap, Grid, and Osnap) and the Model Space/Paper Space toggle are the new Polar, Object tracking (Otrack), and lineweights (lwt). You'll also find the Tilemode option has been removed now that you have the new Layout tabs.

The coolest thing about the Status Bar in 2002 is it only takes a single click to toggle versus the double click that Release 14 required. It is a simple little change, but those clicks add up!

I'll run through a quick summary of the new Status Bar additions here then revisit them in more detail in future chapters. The new Polar option turns on the new polar snap facility. This is a nice addition to Ortho that permits you to easily snap to a user-defined angle. Say I needed to draw a rectangle at a 45-degree angle; I could set my polar angle to 45, and I'd find an auxiliary angle-snapping capability that could snap to 45-, 135-, 225-, and 315-degree increments.

Object tracking takes tracking (introduced in Release 14) to the next level. AutoCAD 2002 displays visual tracking lines, making it easier to work off of object snaps from other objects.

The new Lineweight option turns off the visual display of line weights. When off, your objects display without taking line weight information into consideration, so they'll most likely use a Lineweight of 0.

My only beef with the new status line is that I sometimes have a hard time telling if my toggles are on or off. I felt the differential was much clearer in Release 14 (or maybe I just need new glasses). I find myself hitting the option just to see if it's on or not.

For those of you who still use function keys to toggle most modes on and off, I've included the latest function key settings in Table 1.1

I'd also like to mention the new command syntax. I've always felt AutoCAD didn't do well with consistency in command structure; however, with AutoCAD 2002, this has changed. Look at the new command sequence for the `circle` command.

```
Command: Circle
Specify center point for circle or [3P/2P/Ttr (tan tan radius)]:
Specify radius of circle or [Diameter]:
```

Can you see a difference in the way the commands are laid out? The default (which in previous releases was always displayed in angle brackets, <>) is now spelled out. The default for `circle` is Specify center point for circle. Additional options are displayed within the square brackets. If you draw a circle and re-enter the command, you'll still see the radius of the last circle drawn within angle brackets, as shown here.

```
CIRCLE Specify center point for circle or [3P/2P/Ttr (tan tan radius)]:
Specify radius of circle or [Diameter] <1.1404>:
```

This isn't a huge change, but one you should take note of. Instructors will be grateful because now all the AutoCAD commands follow a similar structure, which should make it easier for new users to learn AutoCAD. Mind you, this doesn't change the way you use the commands themselves, just the way they're displayed on the screen.

In addition to these changes to the user interface, you'll find a ton of new right-click menus. Depending on where you right-click, you'll get completely different results. If you right-click over the drawing area while in a command, you'll get a shortcut menu that contains the command options (along with a few other things). For example, if you right-click over the drawing area when you're not in a command, you'll get a completely different menu. The AutoCAD engineering team was quoted as saying, "When all else fails, right-click!" I strongly recommend trying out the many different right-click menus. I have found some magical options that I can't seem to find anywhere else. When in the Mtext editor, a right-click displays an option that allows you to easily change the case of text. A right-click on a viewport gives you the option of locking a viewport scale factor so you don't accidentally botch it up with a misplaced zoom.

Also notice that Ucsicon was put on a diet for AutoCAD 2002. You can modify it to your liking by selecting the Properties option in the `ucsicon` command. There, you'll find the new dialog box shown in Figure 1.7.

As you work your way through all the ins and outs of AutoCAD 2002, keep in mind that these changes are meant to make your AutoCAD life easier.

Table 1.1 The new function key settings.

F1	Help
F2	Flip Screen
F3	Osnap
F4	Tablet
F5	Isoplane
F6	Coords
F7	Grid
F8	Ortho
F9	Snap
F10	Polar
F11	Object Tracking

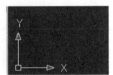

Figure 1.7 The new Ucsicon went on a diet!

CHAPTER 2

The World of Object Snaps

Using object snaps is an integral part of AutoCAD. Drawing without them would be tedious, inaccurate, and painful. But are you using them to their fullest potential? Do you truly understand all the object snaps and their complete functionality? Are you just using the ones you think you need?

This chapter will cover each object snap in detail. I will tour the different methods of grabbing them and their proper implementation. Although object snaps appear to be simple, be sure you're maximizing their usage.

When using an object snap (often referred to as an osnap), you're simply snapping to a specific geometric point on an entity. Object snaps are always accurate and much easier to use than finding the desired point yourself. You can use them anytime you need to indicate a point within your drawing. Osnaps will not grab objects that are not visible or between the dashes of a noncontinuous linetype.

Whether you've learned to grab them from the Cursor menu or a toolbar or just by keying them in, you've seen the extensive listing of object snaps. You can use object snaps temporarily or set a running object snap mode. I tour object snaps as they appear in the Cursor pull-down menu (shift + right-click). The minimum command-line interface is included in parentheses for those of you who still enjoy typing.

Object Snaps

From (fro)   The fro osnap permits users to select a point of reference before selecting their final point. Many of you have used the ID command for this purpose or moved the UCS (universal coordinate system) for quick reference. The From osnap makes this process much simpler. For example, I might want to insert a door symbol four inches from the corner of a room. From the Insertion Point option in the insert command, I can use fro to select the corner of the room. I follow this up by @4<90 (polar coordinates) and my door snaps right into place. I can use relative or polar coordinates, but I must use the @ or AutoCAD will reference absolute coordinates. If you wanted to place a tooling hole two units over and up from an existing part of a drawing, fro would be a good choice.

Endpoint (endp)   Used frequently by AutoCAD users, endp grabs the closest endpoints of objects such as lines, arcs, elliptical arcs, mlines, rays, splines, 3D faces, 3D solids, regions, and polylines. The Endpoint osnap also snaps to the vertices of polylines (which naturally include polygons, rect-angles, etc.) and grabs the closest vertex of each individual object or solid and region.

The keyboard equivalent to the Endpoint osnap is end, as opposed to endp; however in the past, should you accidentally key in end, you'd find yourself at the command prompt, rather than within a command, and on your way to exiting AutoCAD. The end command was terminated in AutoCAD Release 14, but the legacy abbreviation remains.

Midpoint (mid)   This osnap grabs the midpoint of a line, arc, polyline segment, spline, elliptical arc, solid (from the solid command), region, or bhatch segment. You can't grab the midpoint of a ray despite what the help function and manual claim. Logically, mid finds the midpoint of the sides of some 3D solids. If an arc or line has an extrusion thickness, you can snap to the midpoint of the extrusion.

Intersection (int)   The Intersection osnap is a popular tool that grabs imaginary or real inter-sections. By definition, an intersection is where one or more objects cross. An imaginary intersec-tion is where one or more objects would cross if extended in the same direction. (Release 13 very generously modified int to accept these imaginary extended intersections.)

The Intersection osnap contains one additional modification: the ability to individually select two objects so AutoCAD can find the intersection. When the osnap aperture doesn't find an inter-section after the first pick, it prompts you for another object. This capability is great when it's dif-ficult to get into tight places.

Although some of you are Intersection junkies, you should be aware that it takes AutoCAD just a little bit longer to calculate the intersection algorithm and might not be the fastest object snap. When grabbing corners, although int would work functionally, I strongly recommend the faster and easier Endpoint osnap. Because int is only accurate to a certain degree, for the sake of speed, I suggest you use this option only when no other object snap will do. If you've ever tried to trim objects constructed with int and were told you couldn't, int is to blame.

Apparent Intersection (appint)   The appint osnap is extremely important for users who work in 3D. It lets you snap to two objects that intersect in the current viewing plane, although they don't actually meet in 3D space. appint works just like int, but the objects have to cross or meet in the current viewing plane. It will also graciously extend the objects to an imaginary intersection. The objects can also be selected individually, as in int.

Extension (ext)   The ext osnap was added to AutoCAD with Release 2000. It allows you to snap to the phantom extension of an arc or a line. Simply hover over the endpoint you want to work from and the extension displays as a dotted line so you can snap to it.

Center (cen)   The cen osnap snaps to the center of arcs, circles, nurbs, ellipses, and some 3D sol-ids.

Quadrant (qua**)**   This often forgotten object snap snaps to the nearest quadrant of an arc, circle, ellipse, and some 3D solids. If an arc isn't large enough to have a quadrant, you'll receive an error message.

Perpendicular (per**)**   The per osnap snaps to a point perpendicular to the selected object. A reference point is usually selected first. You can snap perpendicular to most 2D and some 3D geometry.

Tangent (tan**)**   The tan osnap snaps to the tangent of an object. Similar to per, a reference is usually selected first. To create a circle tangent to three lines, you could use tan combined with the 3P option in the circle command. Perpendicular and Tangent osnaps won't let you break the rules of geometry.

Node (nod**)**   The nod osnap snaps to points created in the point command. Points can prove invaluable in the divide and measure commands, where snapping to them is the next logical step. Be sure pdmode is set to a decent value (3, for example) to ensure you can see your points. The Point Style dialog box is in the Format pull-down menu.

Insertion (ins**)**   The ins osnap snaps to the insertion point of some text, a block, or an attribute. You can also snap to the nearly extinct shapes in past releases. This option can be useful when you want to add another line of text directly below an existing text string while maintaining consistent spacing. Snap to the insertion point of the existing text with the dtext command. When prompted for the new text string, you'll notice the Dtext box resides on the previous line of text. Hit the space bar (so AutoCAD records something other than null input) and hit an extra <Enter> to drop to the next line. Your new text string will line up directly with the previous string of text.

Nearest (nea**)**   The nea osnap snaps to the nearest point of just about any AutoCAD object, but it doesn't pay attention to text or attributes. It is defined by the point closest to the center of the aperture.

None (non**)**   Have you ever had a running object snap get in your way for one or two quick operations? Did you turn your running osnap off completely, then turn it back on when you completed those operations? If so, you're doing too much work. non turns off the running object snap for one operation only.

When using osnaps, AutoCAD treats polylines and blocks as individual entities. The object snaps do not like blocks not uniformly scaled and do not always provide the correct geometric location.

I have now covered all of the object snap settings. There are two methods of implementing any of these osnaps: temporarily or running. When you pick an osnap from the AutoCAD toolbar, the Cursor menu, or Tablet menu, you're using temporary object snaps. The desired object snap setting is valid for one step, and then it's gone. This setup easily permits you to use many different object snap settings during one drawing session.

One of my favorite options is the osnap button to the Status Bar. When a running object snap mode is set, clicking on the osnap button toggles the running object snap modes on and off. It can even be used transparently within a command. For those of you who don't care for the Status Bar, the <F3> function key gives the same results.

Clicking on the osnap button for the first time (before running object snaps have been set) will send you into the Drafting Settings dialog box, as shown in Figure 2.1. You can also get there by right-clicking on the osnap button and selecting Settings... from the Cursor menu. Here, you'll find all the object snaps are available except From (which is logical). I will focus on the Object Snap tab in the Drafting Settings dialog. At first it might take you a while before you're familiar enough with each of the object snap symbols to know which one it represents.

The main goal of running object snaps is to set up one or more defaults that AutoCAD will find automatically. For example, in dimensioning, it's handy to set a running object snap mode of Endpoint. Before Autosnaps, you

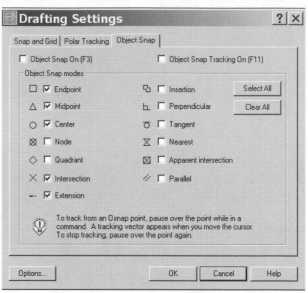

Figure 2.1 The Drafting Settings dialog box.

wouldn't catch me setting several running object snaps at one time. Setting too many would just confuse me as to which object snap mode AutoCAD was grabbing at any given time, especially when selecting one related to the same type of object, such as Center and Quadrant. Because of graphical representation, it's no longer an issue — I have a minimum of four set at all times.

As you enter a drawing command, you'll see the object snaps appear automatically on your drawing. The symbol indicates which object snap AutoCAD is using. If you aren't sure which symbol indicates which object snap, holding the cursor still for a moment will display a tooltip, as shown in Figure 2.2. You can still override running object snaps by selecting an object snap manually, and if they get in your way, it's easy to toggle them on and off by way of the Options button in the Drafting Settings dialog box (Figure 2.3).

Figure 2.2 An AutoSnap tooltip.

If you decide you don't care for Auto-Snaps — you can toggle them off by selecting the Marker option (but why?). You'll also find that AutoSnaps have that same magnetic quality that grips have. When Magnet is on, it locks your cursor onto the snap point. If you don't care for that feature, you can toggle it off as well. After you've progressed to the point where you can identify each of the markers, you may choose to turn off the snap tips if they bug you.

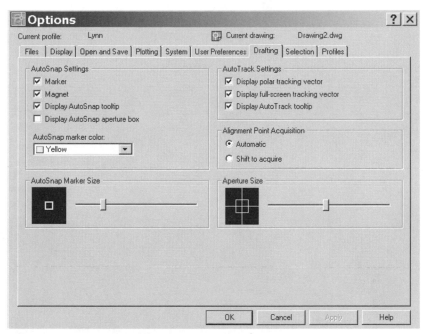

Figure 2.3 The AutoSnap settings can be changed in the Drafting tab of the Options dialog box.

I would expect (and hope) you to leave all of those toggles on and give AutoSnap a chance. Should you choose to resort to standard object snaps, be sure to mark the checkbox for Display AutoSnap aperture box.

The Drafting tab in the Options dialog also allows you to control the size and color of the markers. In a drawing filled with yellow objects, it might be easier to see the AutoSnaps if they were changed to another color.

Note This is the hottest tip in the chapter. If you find yourself in a position where AutoCAD isn't grabbing the object snap you need, you can use <Tab> to cycle through all of the object snaps set for that particular object. This process is very important should you choose Quadrant and Center. AutoCAD will just about always find only the Quadrant object snaps — only the <Tab> key will force it to find the Center object snap, too.

You can also get to the Drafting Settings dialog box by selecting the last option in the Cursor menu, as shown in Figure 2.4. For the pull-down menu fans, you'll find it in the Tools menu. Those of you who choose to use the osnap command will find that it launches the dialog box in AutoCAD 2002. To use the command-line interface osnap command, simply put a dash in front of the command (-osnap). For setting a single running object snap mode, the command-line interface is probably still the fastest method.

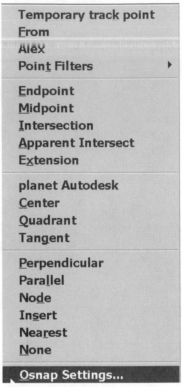

Figure 2.4 Selecting the last item in the Cursor menu takes you to the Osnap Settings dialog box.

CHAPTER 3

Display Commands — What You See Is What You Get!

Any CAD user can tell you that controlling the display of your drawing is incredibly important to the design process. AutoCAD provides many different means of viewing your drawing, some more efficient than others.

If you're fortunate enough to have an Intellimouse, you've no doubt already noticed the great Zooming features of the magical wheel. Rolling the wheel up and down zooms in and out, holding the wheel down kicks into panning mode, and a double click of the wheel performs a zoom extents (my personal favorite). Zooming uses the crosshairs to determine the center point of the display, which gives you more control over the final display, the next topic of rtzoom.

Note   If you're completely bored in the office and would like to have some extra fun, try holding down the <Ctrl>key while holding down the wheel ... you'll feel like you're playing Asteroids!

Those of you without the Intellimouse can get similar results using the real-time zoom and pan commands (rtzoom and rtpan) if you squint. They are accessed easily from the View pull-down menu under Zoom or from the Standard toolbar icons as shown in Figure 3.1.

Figure 3.1 AutoCAD Rtpan and Rtzoom toolbar buttons.

Selecting the Rtzoom tool displays a magnifying glass in your drawing area. Notice the + in the upper right-hand corner and the – in the
lower left-hand corner of the icon. If you hold the Pick button down
while moving the cursor up, you increase the magnification of the display (zooming in). Similarly, if you hold the Pick button down while
moving the cursor toward the bottom of the display, you decrease the
magnification of the display (zooming out). To continue to zoom in
after moving all the way to the top of the drawing area, pick the input
device up, place it at the bottom of the display, and continue as before.
Continue this procedure until you've zoomed in far enough (or until
you've burned off enough calories). If you zoom in too far, the + sign
disappears, indicating that you've reached the maximum zoom depth
stored in memory. Consequently, if you zoom out too far, the – sign disappears, indicating that you've reached the minimum zoom depth
stored in memory. You have to do some serious zooming before you encounter either of these two
situations. Also notice that Rtzoom zooms in on the center of the display, which is often not desirable.

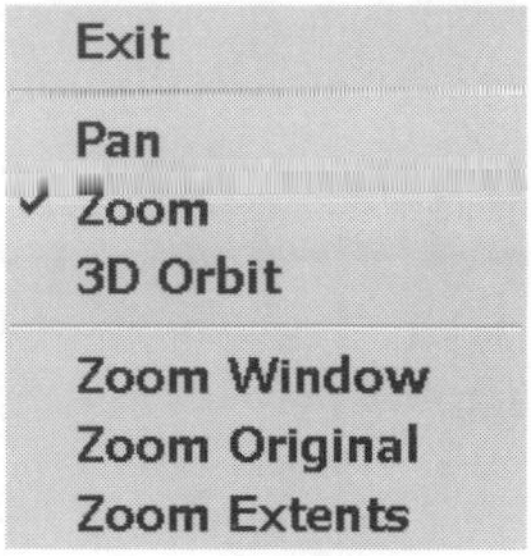

Figure 3.2 Right-clicking while in Rtzoom brings up the Cursor menu.

The command-line prompt for rtzoom follows.

Command: RTZOOM

Press <Esc> or <Enter> to exit; right-click to activate the pop-up menu.

Either <Esc> or <Enter> kicks you out of the command and leaves you at your current display.
The pop-up menu makes Rtzoom more usable. You seldom want to zoom in on the center of the
display, so it's important that you can switch over easily to Rtpan mode. Right-click while in
rtzoom, and you'll see the Cursor menu, as shown in Figure 3.2.

Selecting Pan puts you in the rtpan command, and an icon of a hand displays on the screen.
Holding down the Pick button while moving your cursor around on the screen dynamically moves
the display around without changing the magnification. If you need to change the magnification,
it's easy — right-click and return to Rtzoom. Notice that the old pan command has been replaced
with rtpan. Take a look at the other options in the right-click menu in Table 3.1.

Table 3.1 Options in the Rtpan right-click menu.

Exit	Guess what that does!
Zoom Window	Puts you into the popular Window option of the zoom command.
Zoom Previous	Returns you to the last display on the screen before entering the rtpan or rtzoom command.
Zoom Extents	Zooms out so that all objects are displayed on the screen.

Also notice that rtzoom is the newest of an onslaught of defaults in the ever-popular zoom command. So how many different defaults can a command have? The zoom command takes the cake
with three different defaults.

```
Command: ZOOM
Specify corner of window, enter a scale factor (nX or nXP), or
[All/Center/Dynamic/Extents/Previous/Scale/Window] <real time>:
Press ESC or ENTER to exit, or right-click to display shortcut menu.
```

If you pick from the screen, the zoom command assumes you are choosing a window (no W required). If you key in a number, AutoCAD assumes you're indicating a scale factor (X or XP), and if you hit <Enter>, it launches you into Rtzoom. In the rest of this chapter, I'll run through a quick summary of the other options for those new to AutoCAD or AutoCAD LT.

What's the difference between Zoom All and Zoom Extents? Zoom Extents zooms out until all objects on the screen are displayed. If you have a small circle on the screen and you perform a Zoom Extents, AutoCAD zooms in on the circle, despite how your limits are set to calculate the display of a Zoom Extents. Zoom All, on the other hand, zooms out to the extents of the objects or to the limits — whichever is larger. As a reminder, the limits comprise the area of your drawing covered by the grid. The Help file indicates that Zoom All always performs a regeneration, but I no longer find that to be the case. The Help file also indicates that you cannot execute either Zoom All or Zoom Extents transparently (from within another command), and that's not true either. I had no problem performing either transparently. To further confuse you when working in 3D, a Zoom All actually zooms to the extents of the drawing.

Zoom Center zooms in relative to a center point that you select. You will be asked to supply a magnification factor or a height. A smaller value for the height increases the magnification, and a larger value decreases the magnification. This usually requires too much work (and thought) for me, so I'm apt to stick to zooming via a window.

I marvel that Zoom Dynamic still exists now that rtzoom has been added to the command palette. When Zoom Dynamic first came out, it was such an exciting addition to the product, but I don't know anyone who still uses it. Zoom Dynamic uses a view window similar to that seen in the Aerial Viewer to determine the final display. The Pick button controls the size and the position of the view window. The view window is moved to the proper location, and an <Enter> executes the zoom (although you'd think a final pick would do so). I could zoom many windows in the amount of time it takes to use Zoom Dynamic. Previously, I used Zoom Dynamic to avoid those painful, time-consuming regenerations, but that's not really an issue with AutoCAD 2002.

With Zoom Previous, you can go back up to 10 previous zooms, should you be able to remember what was on the screen 10 zooms ago.

Zoom Scale has three different options, depending on the syntax you use. If you key in a straight value, such as 2 or 4, AutoCAD uses that scale to zoom relative to the drawing limits. For example, a value of 1 zooms to the limits of the drawing. A value of 2 changes the magnification·of the zoom lens you look through to twice the value. A value less than 1 pulls away from the drawing. AutoCAD uses the center of the drawing limits as the center of the final display.

You can also add an x to the end of the specified value, which zooms in relative to the current display rather than the entire drawing. For example, zoom 2x zooms in two times the current display, and zoom 4x zooms in four times. It's not uncommon to see an AutoCAD pro using a zoom of .8x to pull the current display out just a tad. This practice was especially popular when Zoom Extents zoomed out to the edge of the drawing display.

Those of you proficient in Paper Space know that the Zoom XP option is the key to dimensioning success. Rather than launch into a painful dissertation on Paper Space (you'll find that in Chapters 23 and 24), I'll summarize. One of the advantages of using Paper Space is the ability to have more than one scale factor per drawing. Zoom XP sets up these scale factors within your viewports. Table 3.2 compares some of the XP settings to scale factors.

Essentially, you'll be taking the value shown on the left (in units) in Table 3.2 and dividing it by the value on the right. For example: 1" = 1 foot is the same as 1 = 12; 1 divided by 12 equals $1/12$, hence 1/12XP. You can also use the decimal equivalent.

Table 3.2 Zoom XP scale factors.

1" = 1 foot	1/12XP
$1/2$" = 1 foot	1/24XP
$1/4$" = 1 foot	1/48XP
1 = 100	1/100XP
2 = 1	2XP
4 = 1	4XP

If you set up your viewport scale factors using Zoom XP and set the `dimscale` factor to 0 (or select the Scale to Paper Space option in the Dimension Style dialog box), your dimensions will display at the size you've specified. AutoCAD looks at the XP factor per viewport to ensure that all your dimensions will display at the same size.

You astute AutoCAD wizards will realize that in Release 2002, two Zoom options are no longer listed but nevertheless still work: Left and Vmax. Both of these options are accepted if you key them in, but I wouldn't count on them being supported in future releases. Left selects the lower left-hand corner of the intended view followed by a magnification or a height (similar to Center). Vmax zooms out to the maximum zoom possible without doing a regeneration.

Zooming is basic to designing in AutoCAD; hence, it's very important that you thoroughly understand it. So many different methods of controlling the display in your drawings exist. Be sure you're using the best one!

CHAPTER 4

Grip Me Baby!

Grips are one of the most powerful editing tools available in AutoCAD (and AutoCAD LT) to date. You might not agree, instead seeing grips as those annoying blue boxes that appear when you least expect them. If so, chances are you may not fully understand them. However, with a little patience, an open mind, and a little help from this chapter, I hope you'll see the light and be on your way to faster, more efficient editing habits.

Grips permit fast and effective editing in the following areas: Move, Copy, Rotate, Stretch, Scale, and Mirror. Grips eliminate the tedious steps you're used to and throw in some automatic object snaps as well.

Be sure your grips are on by using the `options` command, clicking the Selection tab, and selecting the Enable Grips box as seen Figure 4.1. You also can key in the `grips` command and set it to 1. If you think you have modified the grip colors or size, use the Grips dialog box to change Unselected grips to Blue and Selected grips to Red. Blue is a good color for

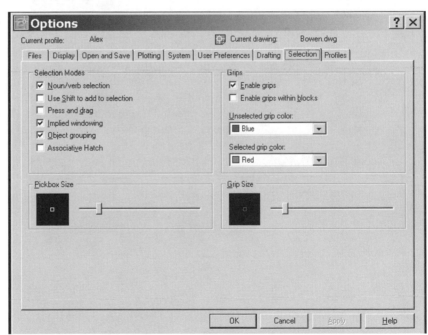

Figure 4.1 The Selection tab in the Options dialog box.

grips because it doesn't distract from the selected drawing objects. The size of the grip boxes should be large enough to see easily but not so large they overwhelm (about one-third of the slider bar should do).

Starting Simple

Draw three objects: a line, an arc, and a circle. Grips live at the command prompt. They cannot be used while in an existing standard AutoCAD command. As soon as you enter a standard AutoCAD command, all your grips disappear from the screen. While at the command prompt, pick the line with your input device. Three blue boxes show up on the line: one at each endpoint and one at the midpoint.

There are three different types of grips: hot, warm, and cold. When grips are warm, they're ready to be edited. Notice as you move your cursor within the range of any grip how you're pulled in, as though a magnet resided at each grip point. Pick one of the endpoint grips, and see that the grip has turned red. You guessed it — this is a hot grip. Selecting a hot grip enters the Grip mode, and you're ready to pick the editing mode you desire.

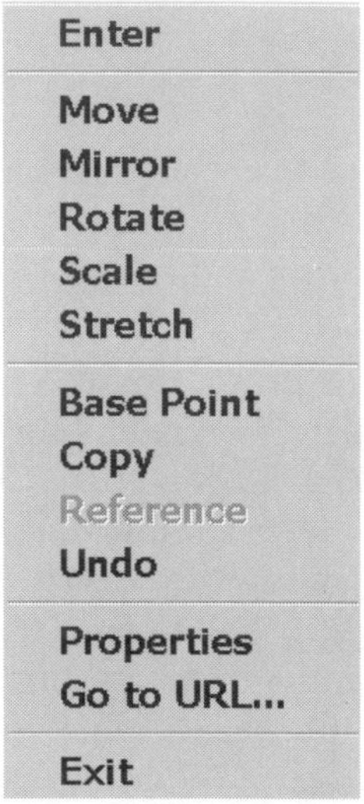

Review the graphics screen and notice the word *Stretch* in the command prompt area. Notice as you pull the cursor around that you stretch the line (turn Ortho off for greater flexibility). Hit the space bar and that Stretch is replaced with Move. As you move the cursor, you're in Move mode; hit the space bar again, and you're in Rotate mode. Continue hitting the space bar to try Scale and Mirror and then you can return to Stretch. Grip mode will loop until you select an option. While in Stretch mode, pick where you'd like the new endpoint to go. After picking, you're back at the command prompt and back to warm grips.

To make your grips go away, hit <Esc>. (If you're still in AutoCAD 2000, you'll need to hit <Esc> twice to get rid of the grips.)

Grip options display in the following order.

- Stretch
- Move
- Rotate
- Scale
- Mirror

If you know you want to Mirror and don't want to page through each option to get there, you can proceed directly to Mirror by keying in mi. Keying in the first two characters of any option takes you to your desired mode. Don't try this unless you have already selected a hot grip. You also can use the great right-click shortcut menu to select the mode of your choice, as shown in Figure 4.2.

| Enter |
| Move |
| Mirror |
| Rotate |
| Scale |
| Stretch |
| Base Point |
| Copy |
| Reference |
| Undo |
| Properties |
| Go to URL... |
| Exit |

Figure 4.2 The object grips right-click menu.

Now, pick the arc on your display. While at the command prompt, pick the edge of the arc to display the three grips. Make a hot grip out of the midpoint grip by picking it. Space through the options to see the different results of each editing selection. Return to the Rotate option. Notice in the command prompt area the several options available within the Rotate option.

```
<Rotation angle>/Base point/
Copy/Undo/Reference/eXit: C
```

All editing options have additional selection parameters available. Key in C for Copy (or pick Copy from the screen menu shown on the right). Now, as you pick while rotating the arc, you'll get multiple copies of the arc, as shown in Figure 4.3. This method is similar to using the Polar option in the array command. When you've made several copies, hit <Enter> to return to the command prompt (or x to exit). Only the original arc has warm grips. Hitting the escape key again will make the grips disappear.

At the command prompt, pick the circle and notice the five grips that appear: one at each quadrant and one at the middle. Make a hot grip in the middle and page through each option, finishing at the Scale option. Scale the circle down by a factor of .5.

Figure 4.3 The arc was copied by selecting C at the prompt and rotating the arc.

What if I wanted to move the left grip of the circle to the right endpoint of the line? If I want to edit (move) the circle and use the grips on the line to do so, I'll need both warm and cold grips. The line will need cold grips (I don't want to move the line), and the circle will need warm grips.

Pick the line and the circle so they both have grips. To make the grips on the line cold, hold down the <Shift> key and pick the line (but not on a grip). This selection turns the line cold. Now the circle remains as the only object that will be edited.

Make the grip at nine o'clock on the circle hot by picking it. Hit the space bar to change to the Move option. Move your cursor until the circle locks into place at the end of the line. The quadrant at nine o'clock on the selected circle falls at exactly the endpoint of the line. All this is done with no object snaps!

Make all the grips disappear and reselect the circle. Make a hot grip on one of the quadrants. While in Stretch mode, hold down <Shift> while picking a point on the screen. The <Shift> key assumes the Multiple mode (like picking C for copy) and emulates the offset command. The shift key used with any of the grip editing commands places you in Multiple mode.

Grips appear at different points on different objects. Because a polyline is one continuous object, the grips appear at each vertex. Stretching the individual vertices of a polyline is much easier with grips than using any of the standard AutoCAD commands. There's no faster method of manipulating a spline curve than with grips. Grips leave the pedit command in the dust!

Draw a vertical dimension. Returning to the command prompt, select the dimension to display its grips. The grip selected as the hot grip will make all the difference in the world with dimension objects. If you select one of the dimension line grips, you'll only move the dimension line location. Picking an extension line grip permits relocating the selected extension line, which would modify the dimension value as well. If you want to move the dimension text, pick the grip on the text and move it to the desired location. Editing dimensions with grips is flexible and efficient.

Returning to the Options dialog box, pick the checkbox labeled Enable grips within blocks. Insert a block, and display its grips. Many grips will display, and any of these can be used as your hot grip. Don't be fooled into thinking that you can edit the individual objects of the Block without exploding them. Grips don't permit breaking any standard AutoCAD rules. I would suggest turning this feature off — all those grips get very confusing.

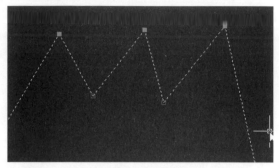

Figure 4.4 Holding the shift key down when selecting grips allows you to choose more than one.

Sometimes the hot grip is not the desired base point for the object you edit. All the grip editing modes provide the additional option of Base Point as a selection. For example, if I want to Mirror a library symbol, Grip mode assumes I want to mirror around the hot grip. The axis I want to mirror around is not near the hot grip. I can use the Base Point option to change the first point of the mirror axis to suit my needs.

Grips permit stretching off of one hot grip at a time. Sometimes you may need to stretch at two or more different locations within the same stretch procedure, which would require more than one hot grip. Holding the shift key down while selecting existing grips allows you to select more than one hot grip, as shown in Figure 4.4.

One More Grip Tip

Grips are smart enough to remember and repeat preselected angles, distances, and scale factors. Returning to the line you've already drawn displays the grips. Make the midpoint grip hot and go to Rotate. Pick the Copy option (notice the command prompt indicates **COPY (multiple)**. You are going to explicitly key in 20 for a 20-degree rotation angle. The magical <Shift> key comes into play one more time. Holding it down and moving the cursor around the two lines, causes an auxiliary snap to occur at 20-degree increments. Pick while holding down <Shift>, and you'll find yourself making evenly spaced copies of the line as you move around in a circular fashion.

The <Shift> key also remembers distances while copying or mirroring. Say I want to make five copies of a desk block, each eight feet apart. I would pick the desk, make a hot grip, and use the Move, Copy option to input the first distance of @8'<90 (eight feet up at an angle of 90 degrees). After the original distance is set, I can use <Shift> to copy the remaining desks into place — all at eight-foot increments.

The shift key is important and provides four functions:

- It places you into Multiple mode while editing (same as copy).
- It repeats the last distance or angle while editing.
- It permits the selection of more than one hot grip for stretching.
- It turns warm objects cold.

All grip editing functions provide an Undo option to undo the effects of the last step. An undo at the command prompt undoes the editing that took place in the last grip mode, so be careful. Realize also that you didn't execute a standard AutoCAD command at the prompt to get into grips. Don't make the mistake of hitting <Enter> at the command prompt to get back into grip mode. It will repeat the last standard AutoCAD command instead of entering Grip mode, and most likely, all your grips will disappear. The only way to enter grip editing mode is to select a hot grip.

If you're dealing with a standard AutoCAD setup, the pickfirst variable will be on (which is the only way your grips will display). If you also have objects with grips highlighted when you go into the erase command, AutoCAD will assume the grip objects are the ones you want to erase. Soon those valuable objects will vanish. Always get rid of your grips (<Esc> key) before entering a standard editing command.

Experiment with grips; force yourself to use them. Even if you're not willing to invest the time to become a grip expert, there's no effort required to quickly move blocks or text objects around on your drawings using the simplest of grip fundamentals. AutoCAD provides many roads to the same end — some faster than others. Using grips is just another road along the route to efficient editing.

CHAPTER 5

Modifying Object Properties

I doubt that too many of you will disagree with me when I say you spend more of your time editing in AutoCAD than you do drawing in it. Hence, editing functions are critical to your success as an AutoCAD operator, so you want them better, faster, and easier to use with each new release. I'll be the first to admit that I loved the Properties button in AutoCAD Release 14. I used to joke that the paint was partially rubbed off of my Properties toolbar button, I used it so often. As a quick refresher, the Properties button in AutoCAD Release 14 executed a LISP routine called AI_Propchk. If one object was selected, AI_Propchk would execute the ddmodify command. If more than one object was selected, it would execute ddchprop. ddmodify allowed you to change just about anything you wanted to change in an object — height, rotation angle, location, and so on. ddchprop only allowed you to change object properties such as layer, color, and linetype. This functionality was somewhat limiting in that even though you selected similar types of objects, you could only edit their properties. For example, you couldn't use this command to change the size of four circles in your drawing to a specific radius unless you executed the command four times.

The New Properties Dialog

Enter AutoCAD 2002's new Properties dialog. This modeless, sizeable dialog can come and go at the touch of a few keys. There are several different ways to grab it (my personal favorite is hitting <Ctrl-1>). By default, this places the new Properties dialog on the left side of the screen, as shown in Figure 5.1. You can also select the new Properties tool from the Standard toolbar, as shown in Figure 5.2. It's located in two pull-down menus: Tools–Properties or Modify–Properties. For those of you who prefer using the command line, the properties command gets you there, too. You can also select the objects desired, right-click, and pick Properties from the shortcut menu.

If no objects are selected, you'll find the dialog displays, as shown in Figure 5.1. An indicator at the top tells you there are no selected objects. The general properties of the current drawing and viewport are displayed — the current layer, color, linetype, plot style, UCS, and so on. You also can use this mode to change anything that isn't grayed out, so technically, you could use this dialog to change the current layer, turn off the Ucsicon, and so on. You'll also notice two tabs on this dia log: You can choose to have the information displayed by category or alphabetized, whichever works better for you.

The true power of the command is demonstrated when objects are selected. Follow along with me by randomly drawing some circles, lines, polylines, and so on. Be sure to include a few different layers to work with as well. Now, change the radius of multiple circles to .5.

I start by selecting the circles (do yourself a favor and work with pickfirst set to 1). Notice at the top of the dialog that it tells you how many circles you've selected. Unlike the old properties command, I can modify any properties these four objects have in common. Because they're all the same type of object, I can modify the radius, diameter (in case you can't multiply by two), and center point, as well as the total area of each circle along with the standard object properties (layer, color, linetype). I can double-click over the existing radius value and input a new one. An <Enter> or action taken in any other box forces the selected objects to update. Figure 5.3 shows the dialog after modifying the radius of the circles. Notice it indicates at the top of the dialog that four circles in the selection are set.

Now it gets even better. Put a crossing window around all of the objects in your drawing. Notice that the options available for editing are dramatically reduced to just the general properties. The top of the dialog indicates that the entire selection set (All) consists of X objects. But here's my favorite part. Pick the drop-down list, and you'll see that all of the objects are broken down by object type, as shown in Figure 5.4. You can now select just the text, just the circles, or just the polylines.

Have you figured out the possibilities yet? Suppose you're handed someone else's drawing. Also assume that this person has never heard of CAD standards, and objects are sprinkled all over the place on random layers. Your goal is to put the proper objects on the proper layer. Ugh! Now it's much easier with the Object Properties dialog. Put a window around the entire drawing, select Text from the drop-down list, and put all the text on the text layer. Continue by putting the dimensions on the dimension layer and so on. Maybe you prefer to be lazy while drawing (I can relate). Now it's easy, after the fact, to put the objects where they belong, although you'll probably give your CAD Manager a heart attack.

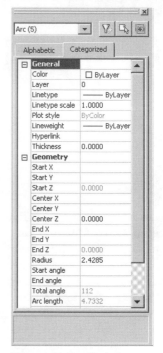

Figure 5.1 <Ctrl-1> displays the Properties dialog.

Figure 5.2 The Properties button is located on the Standard toolbar.

You can change the text height, obliquing angle, or the text using this method. You can change any dimension variable for a particular dimension as well.

Right-click on the dialog, and you'll see the shortcut menu shown in Figure 5.5. If you don't want the dialog to dock, turn Allow Docking off. You can turn off the dialog by choosing the Hide option, selecting the × in the upper right-hand corner of the dialog, hitting another <Ctrl-1>, or executing the propertiesclose command. The Description option in the shortcut menu controls whether the Description section at the bottom of the dialog displays. If you are fairly familiar with the different properties of an object, you might prefer to hide the description and use the extra room to display more properties (thus scrolling less). The final option in the shortcut menu, Undo, is self-explanatory: It undoes the last event performed within the dialog.

One point of confusion is the lack of arrows in the dialog to indicate a drop-down list. For example, to change objects from one layer to another, you pick once in the layer box to display the arrow indicating there's a drop-down list. It takes another pick to get the drop-down list and one final pick to select the desired layer. That's one more click than the Object Properties toolbar requires (and every click counts!). I've also found that many users believe that because no arrows are displayed in the box, there must not be a drop-down list associated with that item. I suspect that if the box was filled with the drop-down list arrows, it would look too complex or confusing; hence, they were left out.

There are a few tricks to navigating through the dialog using keyboard keys. The <Home> key always takes you to the top of the Properties list, and <End> takes you to the end of the Properties list. For those of you who are extremely coordinated, you can also navigate to a specific property by hitting <Control-Shift-the first character of the property you want to jump to>. For example, <Control-Shift-H> jumps to the Hyperlink property. You might decide it's not worth the extra work and just stick to using your cursor.

The Quick Select command icon is also in the upper right-hand corner of the dialog. This sends you to a light version of the filter command, as shown in Figure 5.6. This dialog makes it easy to further define a specialized selection set. For example, if you need to select all of the circles with a radius larger than 2.5, Qselect is the perfect path to take. Here, you can select a specific filter, such as radius, and apply it to the current selection set.

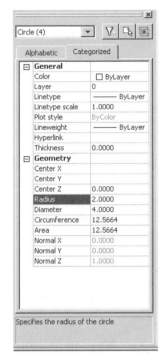

Figure 5.3 The Properties dialog displays the object properties of four selected circles.

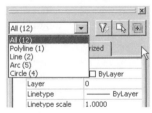

Figure 5.4 You can modify objects by object type.

If you want all the blue circles and the red lines, use the Quick Select filter twice. The first time you use it, indicate that you want all the blue circles, exit then reenter Quick Select. Now, specify that you want the filter to be red and then pick the option at the bottom to Append to current selection set. This gives you a selection set of blue circles and red lines. For those of you comfortable with the more robust `filter` command, you'll find this dialog a breeze to figure out.

AutoCAD 2000i added the ability to pass a selection set to the command. This means you can now use the standard selection options such as previous, all, fence, crossing polygon, remove, and so on. When the dialog was first implemented, you could only use pick, crossing window (right to left), and regular window (left to right). You could also just use the <Shift> key to remove objects from the selection set. Simply pick the Select Objects button from the right-hand corner of the dialog and create your selection set. Follow this with an <Enter>, and those objects pass to the dialog and are ready for editing.

The last button (also added in AutoCAD 2000i) controls the `pickadd` system variable, which only permits one active selection set at a time. This was included to permit you to make many changes to different select sets quickly. You select objects, change them, and when you select the next group of objects, the first set is automatically dismissed. This is difficult to explain, so I suggest you try it for yourself.

In the end, even though I occasionally miss `ddmodify`, I've grown to love and appreciate this new, more robust command.

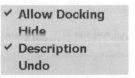

Figure 5.5 Right-clicking in the Properties dialog displays this shortcut menu.

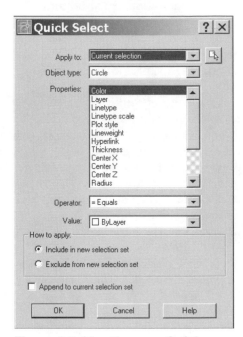

Figure 5.6 Use the new Quick Select dialog to filter objects further.

CHAPTER 6

Words, Words, Words

No matter what you do for a living, you can't get away from text. Some applications require laborious amounts of notes, whereas others require just a few text strings here and there. In AutoCAD, you're faced with a decision. Which of the three text commands should you use? What are the pros and cons of each command? What about future edits? Should you do it the old way or should you try the new Release 2002 method?

In this chapter, I deal with the age-old text commands `text` and `dtext`, as well as the `mtext` command. I hope you will gain some insight and learn some tricks you didn't know about. If you're a veteran user of AutoCAD, forget old habits and open your mind (you might find some time-saving tips).

The `text` command has been in AutoCAD forever. Its interface is not too friendly. It is command prompt–driven — no charming dialog box; no visual display on the drawing of the text you're inputting. When dynamic text (`dtext`) was introduced to AutoCAD, few users resisted switching to this much friendlier command, which was capable of displaying the text in the drawing area and using the correct font to boot. Paragraphs were easier to create. Even though `dtext` could be temporarily confusing when using the Fit or Aligned option, it was a great improvement over `text`.

Then came `mtext`. A far cry from `dtext`, multiline text provides the look and feel of a text editor built right into AutoCAD. The ability to control the color, font, and size of individual words was something never permitted in AutoCAD before Release 13. Top that off with a spell checker, and you could hardly ask for more (though, of course, you do).

I'll step through the text progression, elaborating in more detail on the `text` and `dtext` commands. They each have their proper place in drawing annotation, but I'll make sure you know where.

dtext

`dtext` is still the most frequently used of the text commands and is the obvious choice for single lines of text (as opposed to paragraphs). The text is stored in strings; editing the properties of individual words is impossible. The user can select the style, position, height, and angle of text within the `dtext` command. The `dtext` options are as follows.

```
Command: DTEXT
Justify/Style/<Start point>:
Height <0.2000>:
Rotation angle <0>:
Text: Sample
Text: Test
Text:
```

First, dtext asks you to select a starting point for the text. By default, you select a lower left-hand corner justification for your text. Should you desire a different justification, you can get a listing by keying in J.

```
Justify/Style/<Start point>: J
Align/Fit/Center/Middle/Right/TL/TC/TR/ML/MC/MR/BL/BC/BR:
```

Justify

The 15 Justify options are overwhelming. You'll probably use three or four in your CAD lifetime. Tables 6.1 and 6.2 show explanations for some basic options. Align and Fit are quite different from the others. They are actually a little easier in the text command; they tend to be deceiving when using dtext.

Table 6.1 Vertical justification abbreviations.

L	Denotes the startpoints of text (justify to the left).
C	Denotes the center line of text. AutoCAD calculates the center by dividing the distance between the start- and endpoints of the text in half.
R	Denotes the endpoint of text (justify to the right).

Table 6.2 Horizontal justification abbreviations.

T	Denotes the top line of text. AutoCAD assumes uppercase letters, even if your text string doesn't include any.
M	Denotes the middle line of text. Middle is calculated by dividing the distance from the top to the baseline (not bottom) in half.
B	Denotes the bottom line of the text string. Bottom is calculated using any descenders (text characters that fall below the baseline: y, j, q, p, g).
baseline	Denotes the baseline of the text string, excluding descenders. Five options work via the baseline: Default (left justified), Center, Right, Align, and Fit.

Align   Select the start and endpoints of your desired text string (relative to the baseline). You will not be prompted for text height or angle. After keying in the text string, AutoCAD calculates the appropriate height to squeeze the text between the two endpoints. The fewer the characters, the larger the text height. The angle is also calculated by the angle between the two endpoints. The Align option has a few pitfalls.

- You select the two endpoints in reverse order, and your text appears upside down.
- dtext doesn't calculate the final text height until you hit the final <Enter> and terminate the command. What you see on the screen is definitely not what you get (so don't let it confuse you).

Fit   Similar to the Align option, with one additional prompt: Height. You control the start and endpoint of the text and indicate the desired text. This option is great for title blocks, where height should remain consistent, but you're often squeezing text to fit into a small area. The Fit option could also modify the width factor of the characters. For example, if the start and endpoints of your text string are far apart, the text height is quite small, and you use only a few characters, you'll get short, squatty letters. Conversely, if you put the endpoints close together and give a large height with many characters, the letters are quite tall and thin. Once again, you don't really know what the final result is until you hit the final <Enter> and end the command.

Justification quiz   What's the difference between Middle and MC (middle center)? MC calculates the insertion point horizontally from the baseline to the top. Middle calculates the insertion point from the bottom (where the descenders live) to the top.

Time-saving tip   When specifying a justification, it's not necessary to input J to specify the desired justification. You only enter J when you need to list the options.

```
Command: DTEXT
Justify/Style/<Start point>: TC
Top/center point:
```

Style

You can change the current text style to another pre-existing text style (you can't create them in this option). You can also list any or all existing text styles by inputting a question mark, as shown here.

```
Command: DTEXT
Justify/Style/<Start point>: S
Style name (or ?) <SIMPLEX>: ?
Text style(s) to list <*>:
Text styles:
Style name: SIMPLEX Font files: ROMANS.SHX
```

```
Height: 0.0000 Width factor: 1.0000 Obliquing angle: 0
Generation: Normal
Style name: STANDARD Font filer: txt
Height: 0.0000 Width factor: 1.0000 Obliquing angle: 0
Generation: Normal
Current text style: SIMPLEX
```

A Generation of Normal indicates that the style is not upside-down or backwards.

Height   After specifying the justification and insertion point, you'll be prompted for text height (unless you picked the Align option). The height can be shown by selecting a point on the screen, or it can be input manually.

Rotation angle   The Rotation angle can also be selected on the screen or input manually. The Rotation angle is calculated relative to the current angle 0. If you've moved angle 0 (perhaps to North) in the units command, the text will be measured relative to this new setting. The Rotation angle option doesn't appear if you justified using Align or Fit.

Text   By the time you get to the Text option, a vertical bar should appear on your screen. This bar is the size you indicated as the text height. As you key in characters for your text string, the bar will move across the screen. If you backspace, the characters disappear one step at a time. Pressing <Enter> takes you down to the next line (for paragraphs of text). You can move the text bar anywhere on the screen by moving the crosshairs to another location and picking on your screen. This setup permits placement of multiple lines of text all over your drawing without having to re-enter the dtext command. When you've input all the desired text, hitting <Enter> twice completes the command. The first <Enter> takes you down to the next line, and the second returns you to the command prompt.

dtext always displays left-justified until you hit the final <Enter>, after which, the text will be as you designed. This option can be confusing to the unsuspecting user, but be patient, and eventually the text will position itself correctly. Keep in mind that the text on the screen is temporary and isn't stored within your drawing until you hit the final <Enter>. Should you issue a cancel to exit the command, all of the text on the current line disappears. You must exit the dtext command using <Enter> to keep all of the input text.

You can also drag and drop text from a text editor using these simple steps.

- Create and save your tex file.

- Enter the dtext command and answer all the prompts until the Text option.

- Drag and drop the text file (you can use File Manager to grab the file) into AutoCAD.

The text appears on the screen using the current Text style. If you drag and drop without entering the dtext command, AutoCAD brings the text in as an Mtext entity. You can also use the clipboard with the mtext command using <Ctrl-V>.

- Highlight the desired text in your text editor.
- Copy to the clipboard (<Ctrl-C>).
- Enter the mtext command, and when you enter the Mtext dialog, execute a <Ctrl-V>.

This method allows you to bring in partial files.

text

By far the most primitive, the text command is still invaluable when programming AutoCAD. I'd venture to say that a good portion of your customized menus and LISP routines are using text behind the scenes to do their magic. Unbeknownst to many, you can create paragraphs with text (a good tip for LISP routines). The command looks identical to dtext, but I'll step through it to show you how to create paragraphs.

```
Command: -TEXT
Justify/Style/<Start point>:
Height <2.6602>:
Rotation angle <0>:
Text: Plain old
Command:TEXT
Justify/Style/<Start point>: enter
Text: AutoCAD text
```

To force text below the previously drawn text string, hit an extra <Enter> at the startpoint. This method can also be used in dtext, in case you accidentally leave the command and want to pick up where you left off.

Note In AutoCAD 2002, you need to place a dash in front of the text command to get the true text command.

Control Codes

Both text and dtext use special control codes to input those oft-needed characters not found on the keyboard. Control codes can also be used to underline or overscore your text strings. Six predefined control codes are available, as

Table 6.3 Special character control codes.

%%o	Toggles overscore on/off.
%%u	Toggles underscore on/off.
%%d	Draws degree symbol (°).
%%c	Draws a center/diameter symbol (Ø).
%%p	Draws the plus/minus tolerance symbol (±).
%%%	Forces a single percent sign (believe it or not).

shown in Table 6.3. All control codes begin with %% to inform AutoCAD you're issuing a special code. It doesn't matter whether the following character is upper- or lowercase.

Developers at Autodesk chose two percent signs as a control code indicator, believing it was highly unlikely that anyone would need that unusual combination. If you insist on using two percent signs in your text strings, you can use three percent signs to force one (%%% = %). Six percent signs would be needed to get two (%%%%%% = %%).

To indicate to AutoCAD that you want to write the text strings 98° and 5±.001 while in the text or dtext command, enter the following, respectively.

`Text: 98%%d`

`Text: 5%%P.001`

Underscoring and overscoring are slightly different because they are toggles. The first instance of the control code toggles the under/overscoring on, and the second instance toggles it off. If there is no second instance, the entire line of text is underscored (not the entire paragraph). <u>AutoCAD</u> is created using the following code.

`Text: %%UAutoCAD`

If you want to underline just part of a line, as in "<u>AutoCAD</u> is a great tool," use the following code.

`Text: %%uAutoCAD%%u is a great tool.`

When using dtext, the control codes don't display in their final state until you complete the command (so don't panic when all these percent signs show up on your screen).

CHAPTER 7

The Magical World of Mtext

All applications annotate their drawings in some way. I've already explored the text and dtext commands, their pros and cons, and their place in the text world. text and dtext have been available for countless releases and are still often the favorites of veteran AutoCAD users. Multiline text (Mtext) provides many annotation advantages you just can't get in single-line text.

Each line of text in the text and dtext commands is considered one object, in the form of a text string. Although dtext permits paragraph creation, each line is still an individual object. Not so with the mtext command. Multiline text is exactly that — text with many lines. All the lines together constitute one object. All the lines move together, copy together, and so on. However, because of the advanced nature of Mtext, you can edit individual lines, words, and even individual characters. Mtext permits changing such properties as color, font, or height down to the character level. Text entities of the past have never had such capabilities.

Mtext can be accessed by typing T at the command prompt or by selecting Draw–Text –Multiline text from the menu. You can also access Mtext from the Draw toolbar, selecting the button in the lower right-hand corner marked with an A. Although the toolbar buttons say Text, they execute the mtext command. Autodesk is really pushing Mtext to be the standard for drawing annotation. The Dimension text objects are all Mtext objects.

Mtext starts with a command-line interface, then launches into a dialog box (it is one of the only commands to do so). I'll review the command-line options first.

```
Command: mtext
Current text style: STANDARD. Text height: 0.2000
Specify first corner:
Specify opposite corner or [Height/Justify/Line Spacing/Rotation/Style/Width]:
```

Mtext uses a bounding box to determine the placement of text. You define a rectangle, and AutoCAD uses this rectangle to determine the insertion point and line width. Text is permitted to spill out of the rectangle. The direction of the spill is controlled by the justification (or attachment) and is indicated with an arrow. I'll tour each of these options.

Height   This option specifies a new text height, which can also be changed within the Mtext dialog box.

Justify   Justify selects the justification options (equate this to the Justification option in Dtext). Mtext uses Top Left justification by default. Not all of the Dtext justification options exist in mtext. They aren't all necessary because Mtext uses a bounding box to define text placement. Should you select the Justification option, you'll receive an additional prompt of justification options.

TL/TC/TR/ML/MC/MR/BL/BC/BR   These abbreviations are the same as those in the dtext or text commands (Table 7.1).

Figure 7.1 shows the abbreviations as they relate to the Mtext bounding box. All Top justification options spill downward out of the bounding box. Middle justification options spill up and down evenly. Bottom justification options spill upward out of the bounding box. For example, TL stands for Top Left. The text is justified from the upper left-hand corner, and extra text spills downward. MR stands for Middle Right. The text is justified by the middle-right side of the bounding box. Text spills up and down. After selecting an attachment option, the mtext command returns to the original options, allowing other modifications.

Table 7.1 Justification options.

T	Top
M	Middle
B	Bottom
L	Left
C	Center
R	Right

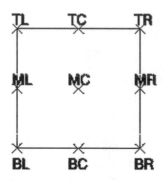

Figure 7.1 Command abbreviations as they relate to the Mtext bounding box.

Line Spacing

As you draw your Mtext window, you'll see the new prompt, Line Spacing, along the command line. No longer are you forced to live with single-line spacing. Now, you can increase your line spacing up to a value of 4X.

```
Command: mtext
Current text style: "Standard" Text height: 0.2000
Specify first corner:
Specify opposite corner or [Height/Justify/Linespacing/Rotation/Style/ Width]: L
Enter line spacing type [At least/Exactly] <At least>:
Enter line spacing factor or distance <4x>:
```

There are two types of line spacing in mtext: At least and Exactly. At least looks at the height of the largest character in the line of text and spaces accordingly. Those lines of text with taller characters will have added spaces between the lines to compensate, so technically, you could end up with unevenly spaced lines, depending on the characters used from line to line. I found this option difficult to control.

Exactly is much easier to use because it forces the line spacing to be *exactly* the same for all lines of text regardless of character height. If you plan on using Mtext in any type of tables, be sure to use Exactly.

Regardless of which type of line spacing you select, you'll be prompted for a line spacing factor or distance. Line spacing is the vertical distance between the baseline of one text string and the baseline (or bottom) of the next. You can specify spacing increments in multiples of single-line spacing by adding an X to the value. For example, 3X would mean you want triple spacing, or three times the standard single-line spacing. This is much like going down three lines on a typewriter (some of you do remember typewriters, right?).

You can also specify an absolute value. It's helpful to know that single spacing is 1.66 times the height of the text characters. AutoCAD restricts you to a line spacing between .25 times your current line spacing and four times your line spacing. This can get very

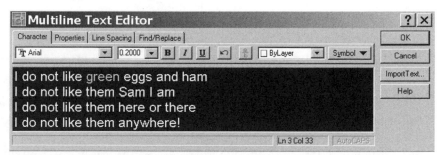

Figure 7.2 The Mtext Editor dialog box contains many options not found in Dtext.

confusing. As a simple example, say your current text height is set to 1. The absolute values you'll be able to key in range from 0.4167 (0.25X) to 6.6667 (4X).

Rotation   Select this option if you want to change the rotation angle for the text. Unlike text or dtext, the mtext command always resets the rotation angle back to zero after the command is executed.

Style   Use this option to change to another existing text style. It does not let you create a new style.

Width   Specify the Mtext object width by keying in the numeric answer or picking on the screen.

Other corner   Pick the opposite corner of the rectangular bounding box. It doesn't matter whether you pull the box up or down, you're only specifying the width at this time. Remember, Mtext will spill outside of the bounding box.

The Mtext Editor dialog box contains many options not found in dtext, as seen in Figure 7.2. You can change the fonts, color, height, and much more of individual sentences, words, or characters. Many of the buttons send you to other dialog boxes. Notice that the Mtext dialog box is made up of four tabs: Character, Properties, Line Spacing, and Find/Replace.

The Mtext dialog box works the same way your favorite text editor does. If you've selected a True Type font, you'll be able to bold, italicize, and underline by highlighting the desired text and selecting the appropriate button.

The Undo button lets you undo your previous operation. It's followed by the Stack/Unstack button (primarily for fractions). Although stacking is confusing at first, it's easy to do when you understand how it works. Stacking is controlled by the forward slash or the carat (^) symbol. Using the forward slash stacks the characters and separates them with a bar. The carat symbol stacks them without a bar, as shown in Figure 7.3.

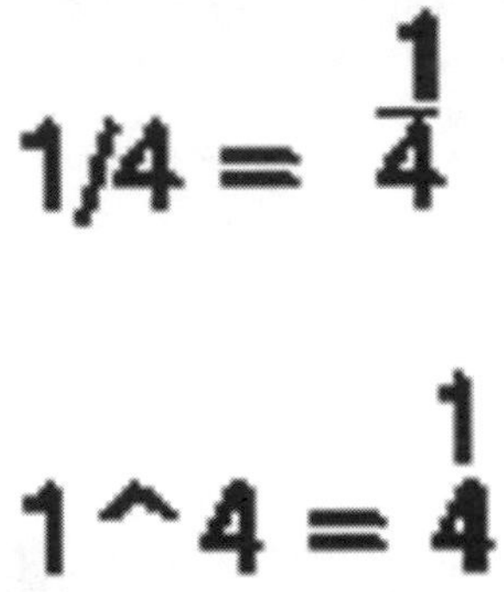

Fractions were dramatically improved with a new feature called AutoStack in AutoCAD 2000. In all releases since 2000, whenever you key in a set of numbers remotely resembling a fraction (such as 1⁄16), AutoCAD displays the dialog shown in Figure 7.4.

Within the AutoStack Properties dialog is basic fraction control, such as whether you want to remove the extra space between the whole number and the fraction, do you want horizontal or diagonal fractions, and so on. For those of you who aren't afraid of commitment, there's an option at the bottom of the AutoStack dialog that says, "Don't show these options again, use these settings." This will rid you of the dialog if it bugs you. Let me warn you though, it's a chore to bring back, but I will show you how later on in this chapter.

Figure 7.3 Examples of stacked fractions.

You have even more control over your fractions when you highlight the fraction and right-click. In this right-click menu, you can unstack the fraction as well as go to Properties. Properties bring up the more detailed fraction dialog, as shown in Figure 7.5.

Within the Stack Properties dialog, you can control the size of the fraction relative to the text height, you can position the fraction above or below the baseline, and you can control the style of the fraction. Hidden within the Style option is the ability to set it up to display tolerances, where AutoCAD displays the upper and lower tolerance with no line in between. Should you need to bring back the AutoStack dialog that you banished by accident earlier, you can do so by selecting the AutoStack option here. After arranging your fractional settings to your liking, save these settings by picking Save Current Settings. Failure to do so will apply the changes to the currently selected fraction only.

Notice the color option (which defaults to ByLayer) followed by the Symbol pull-down menu. The Symbol pull-down makes it easy to insert your favorite character. Selecting Other will send you to the Windows character map, where you can pick from a wide selection of characters (especially in Wingdings).

The Import Text button brings in an external text file. This option sends you to the Import File dialog box so you can select the file to bring into Mtext. (Text can also be copied to the clipboard and pasted into Mtext using <Ctrl-C> and <Ctrl-V>.) Release 14 supports Rich Text Format (RTF) files.

Figure 7.4 The AutoStack Properties dialog lets you stack fractions diagonally or horizontally.

Properties tab   This tab contains the overall property settings for your text, as shown in Figure 7.6. These are the same options available to you when you first entered the `mtext` command.

Line Spacing tab   You can also control the line spacing from within the Mtext dialog. It is a little easier to understand because you can get away with simply selecting the line spacing from a drop-down list, as shown in Figure 7.7. By default you'll find only single, 1.5, and double in the drop-down list, but you can key in your own values (following the upper and lower limits described above). At Least is the default, so be sure to change that if you want all of your Mtext line spacings to match or if you plan on using Mtext inside of tables. Another minor annoyance is that Mtext doesn't display the line spacing until you exit the dialog. It might be nice to be able to see the results before exiting and possibly having to undo it.

Find/Replace tab   This tab acts much the same as in a word processor. Select the words to find and replace, and AutoCAD does the rest. You can specify case-sensitive and whole-word searches.

Changing Case

Another big wish list item was the added ability to change text from lower- to uppercase. If you highlight the text you want to change and right-click, a right-click menu pops up that allows you to change case, as shown in Figure 7.8.

Another nice option added to Mtext is the ability to combine paragraphs. Simply select all the text you want to combine into one paragraph, right-click, and select the Combine Paragraphs option from the right-click menu.

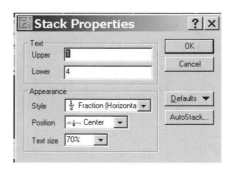

Figure 7.5 The Stack Properties dialog offers more advanced options.

Also notice the new AutoCAPS toggle in the lower right-hand corner of the Mtext dialog, which you can double-click to toggle CAPS on or off. You can, of course, also use the Caps Lock button on your keyboard as well (consequently, I'm not too sure what the big benefit here is).

Note   Heads up! If you cancel out of the Mtext dialog box, all text will be lost.

All of the text created within one `mtext` command is one object to AutoCAD. When editing the text, you will do so by editing the entire object. The `ddedit` command is probably the fastest method for modifying an Mtext object because it quickly

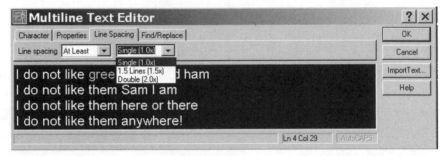

Figure 7.6 The Line Spacing tab offers a drop-down list with three spacing options.

pulls up the Mtext dialog box for editing. The Modify pull-down menu has an Object–Text–Edit option you can use to execute the `ddedit` command (but what a workout!). You can also use the Properties toolbar button to edit Mtext. These commands permit editing of all the features in the original Mtext dialog box.

Note   You can quickly edit any of your text by double-clicking on it.

Mtext and grips work well together. If you've ever needed to change the width of a paragraph in Dtext, you know how difficult it is. It's easier to erase the text and start all over. With Mtext, it's simple. Select the Mtext object at the command prompt to activate grips. Make one of the outer grips hot by selecting it. Notice how you can stretch the rectangle? Try changing the size of the rectangle and see how the text rewraps to accommodate the new size.

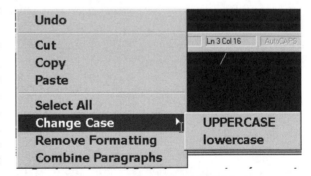

Figure 7.7 You can now change between upper- or lowercase in the Mtext right-click menu.

For those of you who indulge in customizing, Mtext can be accessed via the command-line interface (no dialog box) by executing the command with a dash in front of it.

Figure 7.8 The Properties tab in the Multiline Text Editor dialog.

Command: -MTEXT

Mtext is a valuable tool; it's almost like having a word processor built right into AutoCAD. Be sure to leave Dtext aside periodically and familiarize yourself with the new Mtext dialog box. It takes minimal practice to feel comfortable working in this new environment. You can expect to see even more functionality in Mtext in the future.

CHAPTER 8

Text Styles and Other Text Tips!

Now that you've mastered Mtext, it's time to ask yourself the following questions. What's the difference between a style and a font? Can I temporarily change my slow TrueType fonts to a faster font while in production mode? What do all those text variables actually do? In this chapter I take your base knowledge even further by discussing many aspects surrounding text.

Text Fonts versus Styles

A text font defines the shape of the text characters. AutoCAD supports TrueType fonts and its own SHX fonts. The early releases of AutoCAD read only those text fonts based on shape files, which have no fill capabilities. TrueType fonts permit not only the use of TTF fonts that come with AutoCAD, but of all other TrueType fonts (including the Windows Wingdings font).

The `text` and `dtext` commands do not allow you to use font files directly — you must create a style with them first. The `mtext` command uses the current text style as you initially input the text but permits overriding selected characters with a different font. A text style sets up many parameters for your text, such as an obliquing angle, fixed text height, and, of course, the text font of your choice. Many text styles can use the same text font. One style might have an obliquing angle (or slant) of 30 degrees; another style might have an obliquing angle of 45; however, both use the same font.

The Text Style dialog box command can be found in the Format pull-down menu (Figure 8.1).

Style Name   Text style names can contain letters, numbers, and some special characters, such as the dollar sign ($), underscore (_), hyphen(-), and so on. The name of text fonts, on the other hand, must be the name of existing text fonts AutoCAD can find through the usual search process. To create a new style, select the New option and key in the desired name. By default, AutoCAD uses the names Style1, Style2, and so on.

Font Name   To set a type style, select from the drop-down list in the Text Style dialog box. This dialog box searches for SHX and TTF files (AutoCAD and TrueType fonts). After selecting a font, the character preview set updates. You can also apply font styles, such as bold or italic, to TrueType fonts.

Height   You may choose to set a fixed or variable text height. When a style with a fixed text height is used, the `mtext`, `text`, and `dtext` commands no longer prompt you for text height. If you want to use a variety of text heights with the same text style,

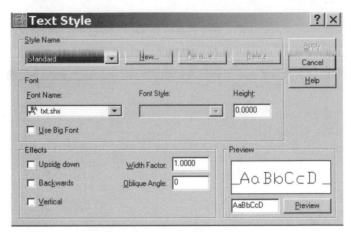

Figure 8.1 The Text Style dialog box allows you to use the text font of your choice.

leave the height at the default value zero (0.0000). It is a frequent mistake of new users to immediately place a fixed text value in the `style` command. This mistake is followed by frustration when the `dtext` command no longer permits you to change the text height. Set a fixed text height only when you want to assign a specific text height to a style.

Preview   AutoCAD assumes a character preview set of "AaBbCc. . ." To view a particular word or set of characters, you can key in a replacement set over the existing set in the text box. Select the Preview button to view the new set of characters.

Effects   The Effects section of the dialog box allows additional control over your text.

> **Width Factor**   A width factor greater than 1 stretches the characters; a value less than 1 compresses the characters. You might find it useful to set the width factor to a value less than 1 when you need to place many characters in a small area but do not want to change the height.

> **Obliquing Angle**   The obliquing angle option in the `style` command controls the slant of the characters. A positive obliquing angle slants the text forward (to the right), and a negative obliquing angle slants the text backwards (to the left). The angle is an offset from 90 degrees and must be in the range of –85 to +85 degrees. This ability is useful when drawing isometrics, where it's very important that the text lie on a particular isometric plane.

> **Backwards**   The `style` command also can force text to appear backwards (right to left), which creates mirrored text used occasionally in PC design and moldings.

> **Upside down**   Fairly straightforward, this option forces text upside down.

Vertical   By default, AutoCAD creates text in a horizontal orientation. Text can also be placed vertically, one character below the other. Each successive line of text is placed to the right of the preceding line, rather than below the preceding line. When in the various text commands, notice that the default text rotation angle is set to 270 degrees when using a vertical text style. Not all text fonts support vertical orientation.

Delete   The Delete button is an easy way to get rid of unwanted text styles. Heretofore, this could only be accomplished with the `purge` command.

Apply   The Apply button applies all changes to the currently selected style. If you forget to apply and select the Close button to exit, AutoCAD reminds you that you haven't saved the changes and asks you if you want to apply the changes to the current style.

If you change the font or vertical property of an existing text style, all existing text using that style will be updated. Changing the style properties, such as height and obliquing angle, will not affect existing line text (Dtext or Text objects) — only that of subsequent text. Mtext, on the other hand, applies changes to width and obliquing angle to existing text.

Rename   Text styles can be renamed with the Rename button.

Changing the Current Text Style

The current text style can also be changed from within the `text`, `dtext`, or `mtext` commands via the Style option.

```
Command: DTEXT
Justify/Style/<Start point>: S
Style name (or ?) <TITLE>: TEST
Justify/Style/<Start point>:
```

Of course, you can use the `style` command to set a new current style because it sets whichever style you create to be the current style.

Miscellaneous Text System Variables

`textqlty`   `textqlty` controls the resolution of TrueType fonts. The accepted value range is between 0 and 100, with a default value of 50. A setting of 100 sets the resolution to 600 dpi, 50 to 300 dpi, and so on. The higher the setting, the finer the resolution and the slower the regeneration. As you lower the value of `textqlty`, the text appears more jagged (but you'll regenerate faster). If you think your TrueType fonts are really slowing you down, tampering with `textqlty` might help.

`textfill`   `textfill` fills (or does not fill) the TrueType fonts. When set to 0 (default), the text appears in outline form. When set to 1, the text is filled in (after the next regeneration). Filled-in TrueType fonts look great but can really slow you down.

qtext   When qtext (quick text) is set to 1 (or on), the existing text changes to bounding rectangles on the next regeneration. In drawings with a great deal of text, this option could improve your speed dramatically. The rectangles let you view the placement of text without slowing you down.

fontmap   One of the main issues concerning text revolves around regeneration speeds and fonts. A decrease in speed accompanies the addition of TrueType fonts. The fontmap system variable can temporarily map the slower fonts to simpler, faster fonts. Then, when you're ready to plot, you can map the text back easily to its original font. You need to create a font-mapping file first. This file can be created in a text editor (Notepad will work). AutoCAD expects a file with an FMP extension, although it will read whatever file you indicate.

The file content is simple: The existing font is entered first (the slower font) followed by the destination font. The two are separated with a semicolon. Here's an example of a simple map file called example.fmp.

```
swissi.ttf; romans
system.ttf;txt
```

This file maps the swiss.ttf font of your current drawing to the simpler romans font and the system.ttf font to the txt font. The name of the mapping file needs to be saved to the fontmap system variable. You can also input the name in the Options dialog box (Windows) under the Files tab.

When you want to return to the original fonts, simply delete the mapping choice from the Options dialog box or return the fontmap system variable to " . ".

fontalt   fontalt sets a default alternative font. Have you ever opened a drawing to find that you were missing one of the fonts it includes? You had to instruct AutoCAD which font to use as a replacement for the missing font. The fontalt system variable can set a default font for just such instances.

New AutoCAD 2002 Text Features

If you've ever tried to scale multiple instances of text, you've discovered that the scale command just doesn't cut it. Unless you can scale the text to its own base point, the text is going to move while it scales to an undesirable position. Enter the new scaletext command.

scaletext allows you to use standard object selection of multiple lines of text (including text, Mtext, and attributes). You are then asked to select the justification to use for each text string (even if it's not the justification you originally used). Follow this up with the desired final height or scale factor. There's even a Match Object option that allows you to pick an existing text string that has the intended height.

```
Command: SCALETEXT
Select objects: Specify opposite corner: 4 found
2 were filtered out.
Select objects:
Enter a base point option for scaling
[Existing/Left/Center/Middle/Right/TL/TC/TR/ML/MC/MR/BL/BC/BR] <Existing>:
Specify new height or [Match object/Scale factor] <14.0000>: s
Specify scale factor or [Reference] <2.0000>: .5
```

Have you ever wanted to change the justification of text strings? The new justifytext command allows you to do exactly that. Simply select the text and input a new justification.

```
Command: JUSTIFYTEXT
Select objects: Specify opposite corner: 4 found
Select objects:
Enter a justification option
[Left/Align/Fit/Center/Middle/Right/TL/TC/TR/ML/MC/MR/BL/BC/BR] <Left>: r
```

The text strings don't move; they've just been assigned a new justification.

Very few applications squeak by without using some type of text. I hope these minor text adjustments and explanations will help make life annotating your drawings just a little bit easier.

CHAPTER 9

Hatch It!

The `bhatch` command revolutionized the way to crosshatch drawings. There was no longer a need to spend countless hours creating and selecting boundaries in an effort to please the old `hatch` command. Suddenly, the boundaries were miraculously created.

AutoCAD Release 13 brought two new features to cross-hatching: automatic island detection and associative hatching. This powerful new combination eliminated even more tedium.

AutoCAD Release 14 finally added a solid fill pattern to its extensive library list. In addition, the overall cross-hatching capabilities have been improved to produce more predictable results.

There are two types of cross-hatching boundary detection – ray casting and flooding. Ray casting, the more primitive of the two, asks the user to select an internal point near the boundary of the enclosed area to crosshatch. Then AutoCAD sends out four rays in search of a boundary in the positive and negative X, Y directions. The first ray to find an edge starts to formulate a polyline around the enclosed area. End users have been doing this same series of events manually for years, creating ad hoc boundaries with the `pline` command, then using these boundaries to hatch. All other regions within the selected area also need to be individually selected to ensure proper results. These internal regions are called "islands." After selecting the boundary and the islands, you then apply the hatch pattern.

The baggage that comes with ray casting becomes apparent should you need to change the hatch pattern after applying it. The hatch pattern has to be erased and recreated with the modifications. If the boundaries were modified in any way, the cross-hatching remains as it was originally created. The primitive ray casting cross-hatching has no way to adapt to a changed boundary definition.

Flooding

Most users will use the latter technique to create hatch patterns; hence, the emphasis of this chapter is spent on flooding. I'll enter the `bhatch` command from the Draw pull-down menu, which displays the Boundary Hatch dialog box (Figure 9.1). To view all of the available crosshatch patterns, click on the browse button next to the pattern name. You can also select the pattern by name by picking from the Pattern drop-down list.

As you leaf through the listing, note the ISO patterns that were added to meet international standards requirements. Selecting any of the ISO patterns also permits input in the ISO pen width edit box. Adherence to ISO standards is another Autodesk strategy for the globalization of AutoCAD.

Most of the options displayed on the left side of the dialog box are self-explanatory. Under Pattern, User-defined and Predefined options, along with a new Custom option, are offered. Predefined uses the standard hatch patterns shown in Figure 9.2. User-defined lets you define a simple crosshatch pattern of lines on the fly. You determine the angle and spacing between the lines (Spacing and Angle edit boxes) and whether the crosshatch lines are to be double-hatched (the Double option). Toggling on the Double option draws a second set of lines perpendicular to the originally defined lines.

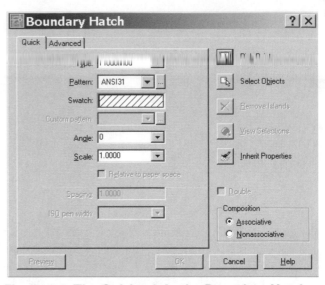

Figure 9.1 The Quick tab in the Boundary Hatch dialog box gets you started hatching.

Selecting a Pattern type of Custom enables the Custom pattern edit box. If you want to use a custom hatch pattern (PAT file) that isn't part of the standard file, you can input that name. The rest of the process proceeds as usual.

Jumping to the right side of the dialog you'll see the Inherit Properties button; it is used to duplicate the settings of an existing hatch pattern. This option is useful when editing another person's drawing with unfamiliar hatch pattern settings. The Inherit Properties button prompts you to select an existing hatch pattern and automatically fills in the dialog box with the proper information.

Notice the Associative toggle. You definitely want to select this option. Selecting Nonassociative will keep your hatch patterns from molding to changed boundaries.

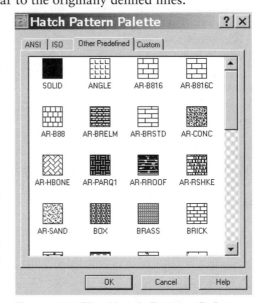

Figure 9.2 The Hatch Pattern Palette dialog box offers many choices.

Select the Pick Points button (assuming you have a drawing to be cross-hatched) and select an area you'd like to hatch. Notice how AutoCAD not only selects the boundary, but the internal islands as well. Should you prefer that AutoCAD ignore one or more islands, you can return to the dialog box and select the Remove Islands button, which allows you to choose the internal regions you don't want crosshatched. The View Selections button permits you to view the currently defined boundaries. The Advanced tab sends you to a subdialog box, as shown in Figure 9.3. This subdialog box allows you to return to the now-primitive world of ray casting by turning island detection off. You can indicate whether you'd like the final boundary to be constructed with polylines or regions, should you choose to retain the bound-aries. You also can define a specific boundary set if you feel the cross-hatching procedure is too slow. Defining a boundary set narrows the realm of entities that AutoCAD takes into consideration when searching for a boundary (speeding up the selection process).

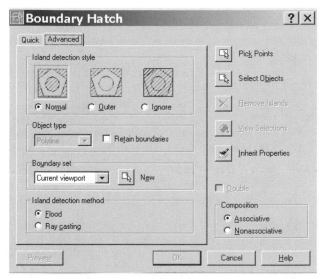

Figure 9.3 The Advanced tab in the Boundary Hatch dialog lets you customize.

The dialog box in Figure 9.3 contains your current style of hatching (Normal, Outer, or Ignore). The default setting is Normal, which hatches every other group of boundaries from the outside in. Outer crosshatches the outermost boundary only, and Ignore crosshatches through everything, regardless of internal boundaries. The Advanced dialog can also be used to toggle Retain boundaries on or off.

Warning   Toggling the Retain boundaries box on greatly inhibits future boundary editing. Leave it off!

When the proper islands have been detected, select the Preview button. If you need to modify the scale factor, angle, or pattern, now is the time to do it. If all looks well, click on Apply to save.

The bhatch command adapts well to blocks and external references (xrefs). There is no need to explode or bind the geometry because bhatch will hatch any closed region easily. Occasionally, a discrepancy occurs when the X and Y scale factors of the block or xref are not the same.

You should try modifying the objects you've used as your boundary (move and scale them) and see the crosshatch adapt to the change. Crosshatch patterns update even if they are on a frozen layer or a layer that is turned off. There is, however, one rule to follow as you edit your boundaries. Don't open the boundary; it will result in a disassociation of your hatching.

You can change your cross-hatching after the fact by using the hatchedit command (Modify pull-down –Object cascade). On entering this command, you'll see a repeat of the original Boundary Hatch dialog box with a few items grayed out. Make your changes and click on OK. It's that simple.

If you delete an island, the cross-hatching reheals itself. You can also turn off all of the hatching by setting fillmode to 0, followed by a regeneration.

For programmers   AutoCAD has a command prompt interface you can use to write script files, menus, or AutoLISP routines. Using a dash in front of the bhatch command (or boundary and hatchedit) executes a command prompt–level interface rather than a dialog box.

There is one final surprise: The old hatch command is alive and well. In fact, it was enhanced to accommodate point acquisition. If you want to crosshatch a section with no existing boundary quickly, don't draw a boundary to hatch; let the hatch command do it for you.

```
Command: hatch
Pattern (? or name/U,style) <ANSI31>:
Sale for pattern <1.000>:
Angle for pattern <0>:
Select hatch boundaries or <Return> for direct hatch option.
Select objects: enter
Retain polyline <N>:
From point:
Arc/Close/Length/Undo/<Next point>:
```

This option lets you to draw an ad hoc area on the screen and crosshatch it. The area doesn't even need to be closed. If you choose to retain the polyline, you'll have a polyline around the edge of the hatch pattern. This hatching is not associative, however, and cannot be modified.

Most applications use cross-hatching of one sort or another. I hope you've found some key concepts in this chapter that will make hatching a little bit easier.

CHAPTER 10

Clever Construction Commands

Those of you with a hand-drafting background probably remember drawing countless construction lines as part of your routine drawing practice. Switching over to CAD doesn't necessarily mean those days are over. I'll cover an assortment of construction commands — some new and some well-hidden old favorites. Many of the commands I address are valuable secrets used by a slim percentage of the AutoCAD world.

Construction Lines

Two types of objects are used for construction lines: xlines and rays, as shown in Figure 10.1. An xline is a line that extends infinitely in both directions. A ray has a starting point and extends infinitely in only one direction. You might immediately fear the consequence of zooming or plotting to the extents of such an object, but don't worry. Neither one of these two new objects affects the drawing limits or extents of a drawing. Xlines and rays can be moved, rotated, offset, and so on. Trimming off half of an xline would leave you with a ray. Trimming off the other half would leave you with a plain old line. If you're going to use xlines or rays specifically for construction purposes, you might choose to place them on their own layer, which allows you to remove the objects from the screen by freezing the layer. Both the xline and ray commands are in the Draw pulldown menu. The menu option for xlines is Construction Line.

```
Command: XLINE
Hor/Ver/Ang/Bisect/Offset/<From point>:
Through point:
```

The default option, From Point, requests a root for the intended xline. This point becomes the conceptual mid-point of the construction line. Because the object extends infinitely in both directions, it can't have a real midpoint. This root point will also be one of the three object grips assigned to the xline. After placing the root, you are prompted for a through point, which indicates the xline direction. You can create as many xlines as needed within the same command, but they'll all use the same root point.

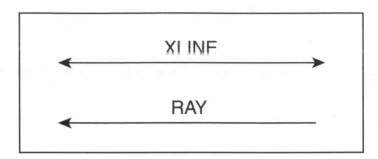

Figure 10.1 An xline Is essentially a line that extends infinitely in both directions. A ray has a starting point and extends infinitely in only one direction.

Hor   The Horizontal option creates horizontal xlines only (parallel to the X-axis of the current UCS). You'll be reprompted for each new root point.

Ver   This option is the same as Horizontal, but the xlines are drawn parallel to the Y-axis of the current UCS.

Ang   The Angle option allows you to specify an angle or reference an existing object (similar to the rotate command).

```
Reference/<Enter angle (0)>: r
Select a line object:
Enter angle <0>: 45
Through point:
```

By default, you only enter the desired angle of the xlines. You can draw many xlines with different root points, but they will all use the indicated angle.

If you'd prefer to reference an existing object and specify an angle from that object, select the Reference option (see the format in the description of the Angle option).

Bisect   Here's one you don't see everyday! The Bisect option creates a construction line that bisects a selected angle. You need to specify three points — the vertex and two points (typically on the lines) — that create the angle, as shown in Figure 10.2.

Offset   Based on the same concept as the offset command, the Offset option in the xline command creates a construction line parallel to an existing object. The existing object can be a line, polyline, ray, or another xline. After specifying an offset distance or a through point, you'll be prompted for the object from which you want to offset. Any eligible object has two sides, so specify the side to offset.

There is a slick use of xlines in relation to the new spline object. Create a spline, enter the `xline` command, and specify the Perpendicular object snap. After selecting the spline, AutoCAD lets you trace the xline across the spline, keeping it tangent all the while. This method works with other objects but is especially powerful with respect to splines.

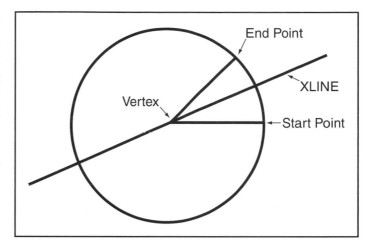

Figure 10.2 The Bisect option creates a construction line that bisects a selected angle.

Rays

The `ray` command is more limited in scope and options than `xline`. I've only seen a couple of real-world situations where I might use the `ray` command while drafting. Projecting center lines up or down in a profile might be a situation where `ray` would come in handy. An obvious reason for creating a ray is to ensure that AutoCAD knows what to generate when you trim off half of an xline.

```
Command: RAY
From point:
Through point:
Through point:
```

Notice that you are not given the wide range of options available in the `xline` command. Select a root point and the direction you want the ray to be drawn.

On a humorous note, the AutoCAD Help function defines a ray as a "Semi-infinite line." Isn't that akin to being kind-of pregnant?

Divide and Measure

The next two commands have been around for ages but are incredibly underused as powerful construction tools. Without proper understanding of these two commands, a user will see them as useless.

Both divide and measure have the same fundamental goal: to place markers at even increments along an object. They're great for quickly creating title blocks, placing effects evenly along another object, and so on. To effectively explore these two commands, you'll need a couple of objects to work on; lines and circles will do.

By default, both of the commands use points as markers. If you don't change the Point Display mode to something visible, you'll think `divide` and `measure` are a waste of time. Remember, by default, points display as minuscule dots, so you won't see them. The Point style dialog box is located in the Format pull-down menu (Figure 10.3). Now, select a different point type — the ✕ works well. If you insist on typing or customizing, setting `pdmode` to 3 also changes the Point style to ✕.

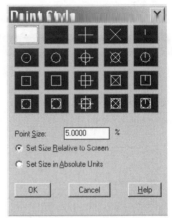

The `divide` command takes the selected object and divides it into the indicated number of equal sections using markers, but the object isn't physically broken. Both `divide` and `measure` are found in the pull-down menu under Draw–Point.

```
Command: DIVIDE
Select object to divide:
<Number of segments>/BLock: 5
```

Figure 10.3 The Point Style dialog box gives you several options besides the plain old dot.

This sequence divides the selected object into five equal segments. The range of segments must be between 2 and 32,767. If the object selected was a circle, AutoCAD begins at angle zero and divides in a counterclockwise direction. Closed polylines have a marker placed at the initial starting vertex. If you'd rather place library symbols (blocks) than points as markers, select the Block option in the `divide` command.

```
<Number of segments>/Block: b
Block name to insert: tooling_hole
Align block with object? <Y>
Number of segments: 3
```

The `divide` command only reads block names currently defined within your drawing. If you plan on using a wblock or another drawing name, you'll have to separately insert it first to store the block definition within the drawing. Aligning the block places the block tangent to or collinear with the selected object. Choosing No (`N`) places the blocks along the object at their normal orientation. Figure 10.4 shows a block of an arc placed on a spline curve.

The `measure` command is similar to `divide`; rather than indicating the number of segments, it indicates the length of the segments. AutoCAD divides the selected object into as many segments as is possible; it is not at all uncommon to have a little extra left over.

```
Command: MEASURE
Select object to measure:
<Segment length>/Block: 1.5
```

The segment length can be keyed in or shown visually by picking two points on the screen. On open objects, AutoCAD starts measuring relative to where you selected the object (so be aware of your pick point). Circles are measured relative to the current angle 0 setting (typically 3:00). The measure command uses radical segments (not chord lengths) when handling arcs or circles.

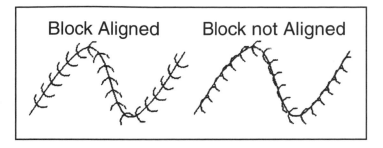

Figure 10.4 A block of an arc is placed on a spline curve.

You easily can snap to the markers placed with these two commands using object snaps. You can snap to points using the Node object snap and to blocks using the Insertion object snap. After placing the markers on an object with either the divide or measure command, AutoCAD places the markers in the Previous selection set, which makes it easy to select them for editing.

Other quick construction methods would include the From object snap or the ID command, which lets you select a new @ reference point that you can use in the following draw command. For example, I might want to place a tooling hole one inch up and over from the lower left-hand corner of a mounting bracket. When prompted for the center of the tooling hole, I would key in @1,1. AutoCAD would use the reference point selected in the ID command.

The From object snap provides the same functionality but is accessible from within the drawing or editing commands. In the same situation, I would forgo the ID command and directly enter the circle command, and when prompted for the center of the hole, I would use the From object snap.

```
Command: CIRCLE
3P/2P/TTR/<Center point>: from
Base point: end
of <Offset>: @1,1
Diameter/<Radius> <0.9351>:.2
```

The From object snap doesn't like some commands, such as the insert command. Being able to quickly construct drawings from scratch is the role of many AutoCAD operators. Time is always an issue, so it's important to know as many short cuts as possible.

CHAPTER 11

More to Offer with Multilines

Multilines (mlines) were added to make it easy to create a series of parallel lines. Although mlines were obviously created with the AEC world in mind, I've seen them used quite creatively in other disciplines. Obvious applications that come to mind are roadways, electronics, piping, HVAC, and, of course, architecture. I'll tour the innermost sanctum of the new multiline objects and the key commands associated with them.

The `mline` command can create up to 16 parallel lines at the same time. Each line of an mline is called an element. You have control of the distance between each element, as well as its color and linetype. In addition to defining each individual element, you have many options that relate to the multiline as a whole. Some of these options include capping, filling, and displaying the miter joints.

Multiline Styles

The three commands directly associated with multilines are `mline`, `mlstyle`, and `mledit`. Before executing the `mline` command, you need to set up a multiline style. Similar to text or dimension styles, it defines the desired end result before drawing the object. The entrance to the `mlstyle` command is located in the Format pull-down menu under Multiline Style (Figure 11.1). Die-hard keyboarders can key in the command.

Consistent with other named styles, you'll recognize the familiar Standard name. This style is fairly simple and made of two elements one unit apart. The following options are available.

Current   This option lists the name of the current multiline style. You can also use it to change the current style to any previously defined style loaded in the drawing. If you have xrefs to other drawings, some externally referenced multiline styles might have come along. Notice that the syntax is the same as other externally referenced named objects.

Name   Use this area to enter the name of a new style you want to add or save.

Description   You can place a multiline style description in this section of the dialog box (optional).

Save   To save a multiline style to a file for future use in another drawing, save it as an MLN file. Acad.mln is the default filename and is stored within the Support directory.

Load   This button loads a previously defined multiline style from an MLN file.

Add   The Add button adds a newly created style to the existing drawing. It also makes the designated style current.

Rename   You guessed it! Use Rename to change the name of an existing style.

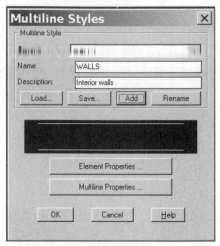

Figure 11.1 The Multiline Styles dialog box.

Element Properties/Multiline Properties   Both   send you to a subdialog box.

Notice a picture of the new style in the image tile. (Note: linetypes, other than continuous, don't display in the image tile.)

Element Properties

The Element Properties subdialog box sets the properties for the individual mline elements (Figure 11.2).

The Elements section of this dialog displays the properties and offset distance of each element. Notice the elements always display in descending order (by offset distance). The following buttons also appear in the subdialog box.

Add   This adds a new element to the multiline style. By default, AutoCAD adds the elements at an offset of 0.

Delete   This button lets you remove the selected element from the style.

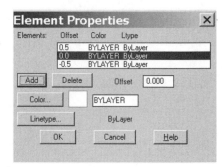

Figure 11.2 Element Properties dialog box lets you set properties for mlines.

Offset   With this edit box, you can change the offset distance of the selected element. Double-click in the box for quick replacement editing.

Color   When selected, this option sends you to the Select Color dialog box (color). The color selected is assigned to the highlighted element. You also can key in the color name or number in the text box.

Linetype   Similar to Color, this option displays the Select Linetype dialog box (ltype), in which you can load and select a linetype. The linetype selected is assigned to the highlighted element. Notice that, unlike Color, you can't key in the linetype name.

Multiline Properties

This dialog lets you define properties of the entire multiline as a whole (Figure 11.3). If you want AutoCAD to display a miter line at the corner joints, toggle the Display joints option.

Caps   You also can cap your multiline from the beginning (startpoint) or at the end with either arcs or straight-line segments.

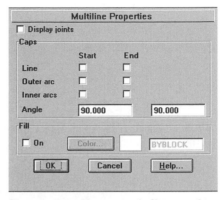

Figure 11.3 **You can define entire multiline properties in this dialog.**

> **Line**   This option lets you cap your multiline with a straight-line segment at the startpoint, endpoint, or both.

> **Outer arc**   Here, you can cap your multiline with an arc connecting the outermost elements.

> **Inner arcs**   If you have a multiline with at least four elements, AutoCAD creates an arc connecting pairs of inner elements. If you have an uneven number of elements, the middle line is not capped. For example, if you have six elements in your multiline, elements 2 and 5 and elements 3 and 4 are connected with inner arcs (Figure 11.4).

> **Angle**   This edit box controls the angle of the capping arc or line. Any value between 10 and 170 degrees is valid. I should warn you, changing the angle of capped arcs yields unusual results.

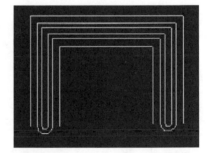

Figure 11.4 **Use Inner arcs to cap inside multiline elements.**

Fill   The Fill panel permits you to turn on a background fill for your multilines and control the Fill color. The Color button within Fill sends you to the Select Color dialog box.

Note   Modifications made to the Fill panel do not display in the image tile in the Multiline Style dialog.

Making Multilines

After you've set your multiline to suit your needs, key in a name for this style (over the existing one in the Name area) and click on Add. If you don't add it to the drawing, your changes will be disregarded. This new style becomes current.

Note If you want to save the multiline for use in other drawings, be sure to use the Save option.

Now you're ready to create your multilines. Under the Draw pull-down menu, you'll see Multiline (or execute the `mline` command manually or from a toolbar). There are three options in the `mline` command: Justification, Scale, and Style. The default option is `<From point>`, as in the `line` command. Using the default, you can begin drawing your multilines using the current multiline style. As you create multiline segments, you'll see the prompt `Undo/<To point>`, which allows you to undo multiline segments if you make an error.

Three Justification options determine how the multiline is drawn between points: Top, Zero, and Bottom. Top draws the multiline below the cursor. The element with the highest positive offset value is at the specified point. Zero draws the multiline relative to the center line (the 0.0 origin point of the multiline). Bottom draws the multiline above the cursor; the element with the smallest offset value is at the specified point.

You can also scale the overall width of the multiline. This scale factor multiplies the values set within the Multiline Style dialog box. For example, if you select a scale factor of 2 and your offsets are .25 and −.25, the end result would be an offset of .5 and −.5. The total width of the multiline doubles.

Mline Trivia (for AutoCAD Jeopardy contestants!) A negative offset flips the order of the offset elements. This change puts the smallest offset on top (probably a negative offset). A negative scale value also alters the scale factor (by the absolute value). I think I'd prefer to create another style — it would require fewer brain cells.

Here's one more for the trivia buffs: A scale factor of 0 actually collapses the mline into a single line. I'm thinking `line` command, myself.

The Style option switches from one existing multiline style to another. The style you specify must already be loaded or defined with the drawing.

Grips and multilines go well together. The Grips appear at the endpoints of the segments based on the justification. You can use object snaps on multilines and the following standard editing commands: `copy`, `move`, `mirror` `stretch`, and `explode`. If you explode a multiline, it turns into ordinary line segments.

Because of the complexity of multilines, you edit them in their own dialog box. Mledit is located in the Modify pull-down menu under the object cascade.

The Multiline Edit Tools (Mledit) dialog box is made up of four columns (Figure 11.5). Each has its own mission. The first column works on multilines that cross, the second on multilines that form a T, and the third on corner joints and vertices. The fourth column cuts or welds a multiline.

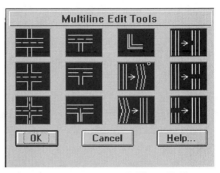

Multilines that cross   The three options are closed cross, open cross, and merged cross. The order in which you select the crossing mlines is very important. The Golden mline Editing Rule states: select the mline you want to end up on top last; the order they're selected is the order in which they'll be placed.

Figure 11.5 The Multiline Edit Tools dialog box offers four distinct multiline groups.

Closed cross   This option (top) creates a closed-cross intersection between two multilines (see example in Figure 11.6). You are prompted for a first and second mline. The second mline will lie on top of the first one. This orientation will force AutoCAD to break the mline underneath and cement the two together. If you find you've selected in the wrong order, take advantage of the Undo option built into the mledit command.

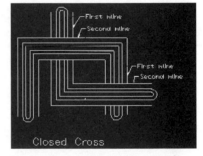

Open cross   With an open cross (middle), the order of selection is still important. An open cross breaks all the elements of the first multiline and only the outside elements of the second multiline.

Merged cross   The order of selection doesn't affect the results of a merged cross (bottom). Both multilines are completely merged together.

Figure 11.6 The Closed Cross option creates a closed intersection between two mlines.

Multilines that form a T   This second column of the Mledit dialog box deals with closed, open, and merged Ts. The Golden Rule for crosses applies to Ts (they are dependent on the order picked).

Corner Joints

The Corner Joint option creates a nicely squared off corner where two multilines meet. AutoCAD will trim (or extend) the first multiline to its intersection with the second multiline. This is another example of being "pick dependent."

Vertices   Say you need to add an alcove to an existing room comprised of multilines. One quick fix would be to use the Add Vertex option within Mledit. You could add four vertices and then use grips to stretch the inner two vertices out to form a nice addition. New vertices don't display a change in the multiline. However, when using grips, you'll see the new additions to the multiline.

It's a simple matter of selecting the Add Vertex option within Mledit and picking the multiline on which you'd like the new vertex.

You can also delete an unwanted vertex. In Mledit, select the Delete Vertex option, and AutoCAD deletes the vertex nearest to the selected point.

Cutting and Welding

If you decide to insert a door within your mline, use `mledit` to cut through one element at a time or all of them simultaneously. The Cut Single option prompts for the two points to cut between. AutoCAD will cut only the element selected.

If you choose the Select All option, AutoCAD cuts through all the elements of the multiline. You are prompted for two points, as with Cut Single.

The opposite of cutting is welding. Should you make a mistake or change your mind after a cut, you can always weld your mlines back together with the Weld All option. Simply pick the two points you want AutoCAD to weld, and your mline will be as good as new!

If you're unable to get the proper results within the Mledit dialog box, `explode` the mlines and use the standard editing commands. Any command that works on lines will now work on multilines.

Mlines have been the victim of bad press ever since they came out. Although there's definitely room for improvement, mlines have much to offer in many different applications. If you find you're creating lots of walls, invest in Architectural Desktop. It puts AutoCAD to shame with its `walls` commands.

CHAPTER 12

Diving Down into AutoCAD DesignCenter

Wouldn't it be nice if you could see pictures of all your blocks before inserting them? Have you ever wanted to grab the layers, dimension styles, or text styles from an existing drawing for use in your current drawing? How many of you have searched through a plethora of drawings, looking for a specific block? Wouldn't it be great if you could drag and drop data from the Internet? Enter the AutoCAD DesignCenter.

DesignCenter originated from the well-received Content Manager in AutoCAD LT. It takes the Content Manager many steps further and works with more named objects. It can access the following types of content.

- Drawings inserted as block references or external references

- Block references within drawings

- Layer definitions, linetypes, layouts, text styles, and dimension styles

- Raster images

- Hatch patterns

- Custom content created by third-party applications

Figure 12.1 The DesignCenter icon resides in the Standard toolbar.

You can access DesignCenter several ways, but I prefer using <Ctrl-2> to toggle it on and off. You also can find it on the Standard toolbar (the icon shown in Figure 12.1) or in the Tools pull-down menu. For those of you addicted to the command line, enter adcenter.

You can keep the dialog on your screen by docking it to one side, but let me warn you that it's big — very big. You won't want to sacrifice your screen real estate for long, although it's really not a problem because you usually jump into DesignCenter, perform your task(s), then jump back out.

Figure 12.2 shows the AutoCAD Design-Center in full view. You can size it up, down, left, or right. You can move it around on the screen, but I prefer mine docked to the left of the screen. Help within the dialog simply doesn't exist; you'll have to execute the `help` command separately and search for Design-Center to find the documentation. In general, the dialog is broken up into two sections: the Treeview listing, which is the directories and files on the left of the dialog, and the Palette, which allows you to view content on the right of the dialog.

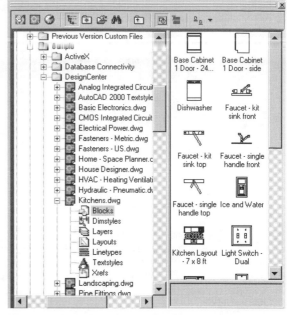

Figure 12.2 The AutoCAD DesignCenter in full view.

DesignCenter Toolbar

I'll start by stepping through the icons across the top of the DesignCenter dialog. To get the list of tools displayed in Figure 12.2, you might need to toggle the Treeview on by selecting the icon shown in Figure 12.3, which displays the file directory on the left side of the dialog box.

Controlling the File Display

The first three tools (Figure 12.4) control the display of files in Treeview. The first icon, Desktop, lists the file directories within your local and networked drives. It works much the same as Explorer (and is my preferred display listing). The second icon, Open Drawings, lists only those drawings open in your current AutoCAD session (Figure 12.5). The third icon, History, lists the last 20 locations you accessed through the AutoCAD Design-Center (Figure 12.6).

Figure 12.3 The Treeview tool toggles the file directory on and off.

Treeview

The Treeview icon, as described previously, displays or hides the tree view of your files. I find the icons to be somewhat confusing because some of them are toggles and some are not. For example, Treeview is a toggle, whereas the first three icons are not.

Figure 12.4 The first three icons in the AutoCAD DesignCenter represent the Desktop, Open Drawings, and History.

Favorites

You can customize DesignCenter by setting up a Favorites folder, as shown in Figure 12.7. This allows you to access quickly the content you use most frequently. The tree view can be difficult to negotiate through, especially if you have drawing files on several different drives or on the network. By adding directories and drawing files to the Favorites folder, you'll be able to avoid undue repetitious scrolling and searching. You can add to the Favorites folder by right-clicking on the desired file or directory (aka folder) and selecting the Add to Favorites option from the shortcut menu (Figure 12.8). You can

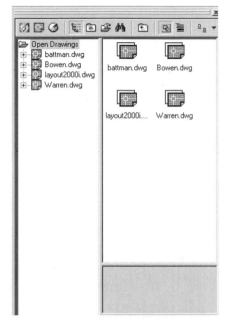

Figure 12.5 The Open Drawings icon displays only those drawings currently open.

Figure 12.6 The History icon displays a listing of the last 20 locations accessed through DesignCenter.

right-click anywhere on the Palette to save content to the Favorites folder as well (Figure 12.9).

Putting files into the Favorites folder doesn't physically move them to another location; it simply places shortcuts into the Autodesk Favorites folder, which is a child to the Windows system Favorites folder. These shortcuts can reference items on your local drive, a networked drive, or even the Internet.

Should you choose to modify the Favorites folder in any way, you'll need to right-click on the Palette and select the Organize Favorites option from the shortcut menu. Right-clicking on any file or folder lets you delete, add to zip files, rename, and so on. When deleting a file from the Favorites folder, you'll see a warning that lets you know it's going to the Recycle Bin. Don't freak out when you see this; it's deleting the shortcut, not the actual file.

Figure 12.7 You can customize DesignCenter using the Favorites folder icon.

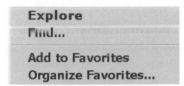

Figure 12.8 Right-click on a file to save it to the Favorites folder.

Figure 12.9 Right-click on the Palette to save content to the Favorites folder.

Load

You might find it easier to manually select the file you want to load into the Palette by using the Standard file dialog box. The Load option (Figure 12.10) allows you to do just that.

Figure 12.10 The Load option lets you manually select the file you want to load into the Palette.

Find

Find (Figure 12.11) is probably the most powerful feature in DesignCenter. It allows you to comb through your many drawings in search of specific content. If you're searching for a specific block (or other named object supported by DesignCenter) and have no clue which drawing it's in, Find will make you really happy.

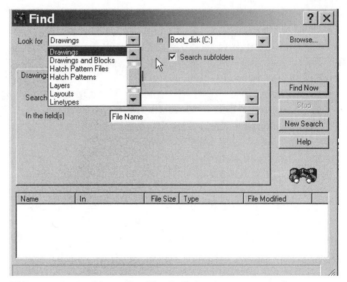

Figure 12.11 Use the Find dialog to search for specific content.

Find works like any standard search utility. Figure 12.12 shows the kind of content for which you can search (dimension styles, drawings, blocks, layers, layouts, linetypes, textstyles, and external references). Simply select the type of content for which you're looking, where you'd like AutoCAD to search, and the name of what you're looking for (wildcards are accepted). You can search multiple path names separated by commas. The Browse button displays a tree view of the directory structure. Begin the search by selecting the Find Now button, and stop the search by clicking on the Stop button. If you added description text to your blocks or drawing files, use the Find dialog to search for description text as well.

If you specify that you are searching for drawing files, you'll get two additional tabs in the Find dialog: Date Modified and Advanced (Figure 12.12). Date Modified searches for content created or modified during a certain time period; Advanced searches for a specific text string in a block name, block or drawing description, attribute tag, or attribute value. You also can search on a minimum or maximum file in the Advanced tab.

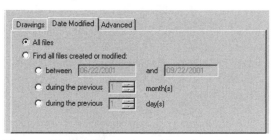

Figure 12.12 When searching for drawing files, the Find dialog adds two additional tabs — Date Modified and Advanced — to further narrow your search.

Up, Preview, and Description

The Up icon moves up one level from the current location along the directory tree. The Preview icon displays an image of an object in the window at the bottom of the Palette. I haven't found this option useful for content other than blocks. If you have a bunch of Release 14 blocks, you could find you're not getting the block previews. Use the `blockicon` command to create bitmaps of all your blocks in the open drawing. The Description icon displays a text description at the bottom of the Palette window if one exists. All three icons are shown in Figure 12.13.

Figure 12.13 The Up, Preview, and Description icons.

Views

You can control the way content displays in your Palette window. I find the Large icons option (Figure 12.14) works best for me, whereas the other options don't really bring much to the table.

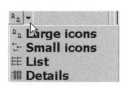

Figure 12.14 The Large icons option enlarges your icons so you can see them better.

The Bottom Line

The real deal with DesignCenter is that you can drag and drop content easily from one drawing to another by dragging and dropping the desired layer, block, and so on from the DesignCenter Palette into your drawing. You can also select the desired content, right-click, and copy it to the clipboard. Follow this up by picking in the destination drawing, right-clicking, and pasting. This procedure takes more time but could be useful if you need to drop the content into multiple drawings. Double-clicking on block definitions executes the `insert` command, which permits you to control the scale factor, rotation angle, and so on. You also get this option if you right-click and drag the content over to the drawing.

What scale factor do you get when you drag and drop blocks over to your drawing? If you look in the `units` command, you'll notice that a new option has been added to the dialog box: Drawing units for DesignCenter blocks. Here, you can specify the units you want AutoCAD to use when inserting blocks by drag-and-drop. Also, if you insert a block containing dimensions, it's doubtful that the dimensions insert true to scale.

AutoCAD DesignCenter has some nice features that can help you spend less time searching and more time designing. I hope this chapter showed you enough features to get you started and get you to invest some time learning to use it.

CHAPTER 13

The Quintessential Selection Set

Are you stuck in a windowing rut? Do you find yourself using several windows to get the exact objects you need? Have you ever wondered what the difference was between Last and Previous? Do you find yourself staring at the Select Objects prompt and thinking, "There must be other options?" If you answered yes to any of these questions, read on!

There are 17 different options for selecting objects (yes — 17!), and most users only know about three or four of them. Back in the old days of AutoCAD, selecting objects was simple. The prompt read: Select objects, Window, or Last. There were three, and only three, options. Over the years, Autodesk has tried to satisfy users' wishes by adding new options. I'm sure you'll find most of these 17 options useful, and I hope they will encourage you to expand your selection set horizons. I've listed 16 of the many different options below (the 17th option is the simple pick to select an object). In this chapter, I'll walk through Auto, Add, All, Box, Crossing, CPolygon, Fence, Group, Last, Multiple, Previous, Remove, Single, Undo, Window, and WPolygon.

I've listed them in the order found in the AutoCAD Help function. Is it just me, or does someone need help alphabetizing? However, I have noticed that AutoCAD LT lists them in the proper order.

Select Objects

Window/Crossing   I predict that most of you selecting objects one at a time and use automatic windowing 90 percent of the time. Automatic windowing refers to the automatic standard and crossing windows that appear when you select a point on the screen where no object resides. Moving the window from left to right creates the standard window, and moving it from right to left yields a crossing window. The standard window is solid; the crossing window is dashed. The standard window selects only those objects found completely within the selection window. A crossing window selects all objects that are completely within the selection window, as well as those that cross the window (Figure 13.1). If one-quarter of a line was within a crossing window with three-quarters hanging out, the line would still be selected.

Selecting objects one at a time is easy. Place the pickbox on top of the desired object and pick. The pickbox can be made larger or smaller using the `pickbox` command. It is measured in pixels. For those of you who are bad shots or lose to your kids at Nintendo, you might find it useful to enlarge the pickbox. Making it smaller can come in handy, as well, when you're trying to squeeze into smaller areas.

Note   If the `pickauto` system variable is not on, you will not get automatic windowing.

Auto/Box   Auto and Box go hand in hand. They've traditionally been used in menus to force the automatic window I spoke of previously. If the user accidentally turns pickauto off, the menu selection would still force automatic windowing.

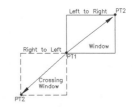

Figure 13.1 The two different types of windows: Crossing and Window

Auto forces the automatic windowing discussed above. If the user picks in a location where no object resides, it goes into the Window/Crossing window mode. If the user picks in a location where there is an object, that object is selected and no window appears.

Box forces an automatic window only, even if the user selected on top of an existing object.

Add/Remove   Add and Remove also work together to add and subtract objects from an existing selection set. Say you want to Move all of the objects in one section save for a couple right in the center. Do you painfully select the desired objects by using multiple windows? No! It is so much faster to select all of the objects in the section and then remove one or two objects from the final selection set. The Remove option is used for this exact reason. When selecting the Remove option, you'll find the familiar Select Objects prompt is changed to Remove Objects. Should you choose to go back to the Select Objects prompt, use the Add option (just type A for short). As you are flipping back and forth between the Add and Remove modes, note that objects verify their selection or deselection on the screen.

Note   If someone has turned off the `pickadd` variable, you will only be allowed one chance to select objects. Because of this, you may see an occasional Add option added to menus to ensure the user has the opportunity to select more than once. It's doubtful that you (or anyone) would intentionally set this value to off.

A few releases ago, Autodesk added the Shift to Remove feature to AutoCAD. This is much easier to use than the Remove option because there's no need to key in R. Simply hold down <Shift> to remove objects from the selection set. While holding down <Shift>, you can also use automatic windowing. In this situation, there is no need for the Add option. This is a great feature that's highly underutilized.

All All selects every object in your drawing. The only objects safe from this option are those on frozen or locked layers. Save this option for really bad drawing days!

Note The AutoCAD Help function is remiss in not mentioning locked layers; however, the LT Help function mentions it.

Crossing Polygon (CP**)/Window Polygon (**WP**)** These options are great, underused selection secrets! The objects you want to select don't always lie conveniently within a rectangular area. Hence, rectangular windows don't always do the trick. The CP and WP options allow you to create a polygonal area with as many sides and whatever shape you want. Rather than creating several windows to get the desired objects, try using these two options. CP selects all the objects within or crossing the polygonal area (Figure 13.2); WP selects only those objects that fall completely within the polygon.

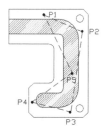

Figure 13.2 Use a Crossing Polygon to select objects in a nonrectangular area.

Both CP and WP must follow one rule: the Polygon cannot cross or touch itself. AutoCAD continually sketches in the last segment to ensure a closed polygon. Notice the Undo option, should you accidentally select an incorrect location for a polygon vertex.

Fence Use the Fence option when it's easiest to draw a series of connected line segments through the desired objects (Figure 13.3). Fences don't need to close, and they can cross themselves. You'll also find the Undo option in the Fence selection, should you pick an incorrect point. The trim and extend commands are great places to use the Fence option, because the alternative is selecting objects one at a time.

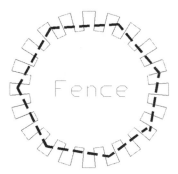

Group Have you ever wanted to save a group of objects for future editing purposes? The Group command lets you do exactly that. You can name a group of objects to be used later as a selection set. You can also use this same group over and over again. Look at the group command if this is one of your design needs. Should you create a group, you can call to that group by using the G option.

Figure 13.3 The Fence option is a valuable method for selecting objects.

```
Select objects: g
Enter group name: desks
```

Note   The `group` command and Group option are not available to LT users.

Last/Previous   These options are often mistaken for each other. Use Last to select the last object created in the database; use Previous to select the previous selection set. If you want to move and array a group of objects, select the objects once for the Move command, and use the Previous Selection option when you enter the `array` command.

Multiple   Multiple is an AutoCAD legacy option. It permits the individual selection of many objects (by picking) without highlighting them. This is intended to speed up the selection process (should you be using a 286). You pick and pick and pick and hope you picked the correct objects. If you pick at an intersection twice, both objects will be selected (although this doesn't always work). When you think you've selected all of the objects, hit <Enter>, and the objects become highlighted. Years ago on slow machines, this was used occasionally, but I don't hear of it being used today.

Single   This option is used primarily in menus. When entered, the user gets only one chance to select objects before the command progresses to the next step. I can think of no reason to use this in your daily drawing routine.

Undo   Undo is obviously popular. Should you select the wrong objects, there's no need to cancel the operation and start over; just Undo to deselect the last object(s) selected. Take the lazy route and don't do any more work than absolutely necessary!

One last point of interest in selecting objects is object cycling. Have you ever tried to pick an object in a crowd but found that AutoCAD keeps grabbing the wrong one? Object cycling to the rescue! If you hold down <Ctrl> while picking, AutoCAD cycles through all the objects that fall under the pickbox as you continue to pick. When the correct object is highlighted, simply hit <Enter>. You don't need to continue to hold down <Ctrl> after the first pick. Try it, it's a great addition to your newly found selection set knowledge.

Are you open to trying some of the other selection set options? You'll have to force yourself to get out of that automatic windowing habit, but I'm sure you'll find the advantages worthwhile.

CHAPTER 14

Going in Circles with the New array Command

If you were to look at the internal departments of Autodesk, you would find two different development teams designing AutoCAD LT and standard AutoCAD. Although these teams work closely together to ensure they're all on the same page, occasionally the LT team wanders down a top secret path and sneaks a few features into LT that standard AutoCAD doesn't have. If these added features are popular enough, you'll often see them surface in the next release of AutoCAD. Content Explorer from LT eventually made it into an even more powerful command called Design-Center in AutoCAD 2000, and I'm happy to announce that three great features made their way down the yellow brick road from LT to AutoCAD 2002. One of them is the new Array dialog box.

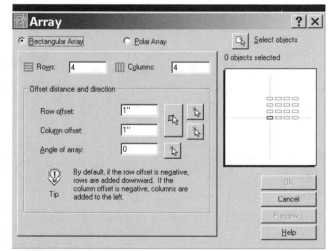

Figure 14.1 The new Array dialog ensures you get the correct results.

Are you among the remote few who always get your arrays correct on the first try? Or are you one of the rest of us who end up taking several trips to the array and undo commands before getting the desired results? If you are of the former, you'd better skip this next chapter. If you're of the latter, then you'll love the new Array dialog.

Found in the Modify pull-down menu and toolbar, the new Array dialog has one of the most beautiful buttons found in AutoCAD: Preview. When this option was added to the Bhatch dialog, you could hear choirs singing in the background. Now you can preview your final array results before it's too late (Hoorah!).

On entering the Array dialog (Figure 14.1), you'll notice the same initial option, Polar (for circular arrays), or the default option of Rectangular (rows and columns). Simply select the number of rows and columns (remembering that rows run horizontally and columns run vertically), select the objects to be arrayed, and the distance between the rows and columns to get the perfect rectangular array. A button permits you to visually select the distance between the rows and columns all at once with a rectangle. Another button manually selects the distance

Figure 14.2 The new Array dialog lets you preview and modify your arrays before exiting.

between the rows only, another button below that permits you to manually select the distance between the columns. A positive distance arrays up and to the right; a negative distance arrays down and to the left. As would be expected, all distances are calculated from center to center.

The Angle of array button is a nice option with which you can specify the angle you'd like a rectangular array to move along (the default is 0). Previous releases required you to set snapang system variable, which incidentally still works, in order to array at an angle other than zero. You can also manually select the array angle using the pick button next to the angle option. For you overachievers, rumor has it the maximum number of copies you can make in a rectangular array is 100,000. Hopefully, you'll find this sufficient!

After setting up your array, it's highly recommended that you Preview the results, just in case! You can choose to accept or modify, or you can cancel the command (Figure 14.2).

Polar Array

Those who've used AutoCAD for a while remember when the polar array was called a circular array (in fact, you can still type a c when prompted for polar or rectangular). The options varied slightly from those you see today. You also might have discovered that, depending on how you answered the various questions in the polar array command, you would be asked different questions relating to your

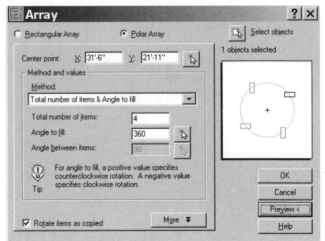

Figure 14.3 The Polar Array option in the Array dialog is used to create circular arrays.

final array. For example, (and feel free to try this in 2000 or Release 14), if you answered the first option, Total number of items, by simply hitting <Enter>, you were in for a surprise question later on. I won't take you through it, but you must promise to try it on your own!

When you select the Polar Array option in the new Array dialog you'll find the various options shown in Figure 14.3. Selecting Method controls which options are available to you. You can choose from three different methods, which are all combinations of the following three options: total number of items, angle to fill, and the angle between items. Total number of items refers to the total number of copied objects. Angle to fill is the total number of degrees you want the objects to fill (For example, 180 would fill half a circle.). Standard AutoCAD operating procedure means that a positive angle will array in the counterclockwise direction and negative angle in the clockwise direction. Angle between items is used when you'd prefer to indicate the degrees between the items and let AutoCAD figure out how many total copies will fit in the given parameters.

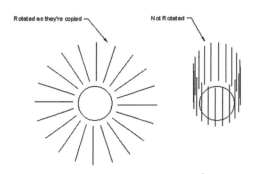

Figure 14.4 You can get different results depending on whether you rotate the objects when copied.

You also need to indicate whether you want the copies to be rotated as they're copied. Figure 14.4 shows you the two very different results you get, depending on your selection.

Look back at Figure 14.3 and notice the More button, which indicates additional hidden options (Figure 14.5). The More button changes to a Less button when extended (now that's amusing!). I can't think of any other dialog AutoCAD has that works quite like this one.

Hidden behind More is a newer option called Base Point (I think it showed up initially in Release 14). It no longer is a mystery what point AutoCAD chooses as the reference point to calculate the array. The base point is the point on the object that always remains equidistant from the center of the array. Figure 14.6 shows the three different results you can get from three different base points.

By default, AutoCAD determines a base point depending on the type of objects being arrayed and how they were originally drawn. Table 14.1 indicates how AutoCAD figures out the default base point.

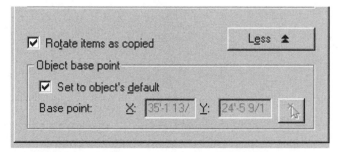

Figure 14.5 The More option controls the object's base point.

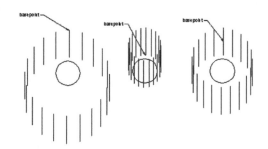

Figure 14.6 Different base points can yield completely different array results.

Aside   I remember the frustration of one of my colleagues, Sharkey Nerren, from 10 years ago. He was irritated because the array command didn't allow you to specify a base point. Every time he taught the array command to his students, he complained about it. Sharkey no doubt found himself smiling when this option was introduced.

On the right side of the dialog, notice that an image tile updates as you make changes to the Array dialog. This is to help guide you through the array-making process.

Should you need to access the command-line interface for the array command, simply key in a dash before the command name (-array). You'll find the new Base option living there as well.

Table 14.1 How AutoCAD determines the default base point.

Object	Base point
Arc, circle, ellipse	Center point
Polygons, rectangles	Starting corner
Donuts, lines, plines, 3D plines, rays, splines	Starting point
Blocks, mtext, dtext, text	Insertion point
Construction lines (xlines)	Midpoints (how do you find the midpoint of an infinite line?)

SECTION 2

LOW STRESS

Welcome to the Low Stress section. I've bumped up the complexity a notch as I continue down the road to achieving maximum productivity. One chapter is dedicated completely to cool tips and tricks, and another chapter that focuses on Paper Space is my most popular column to date. Dimensioning is explored in painful detail as well, so no stone is left unturned. Pat yourself on the back if you've made it this far, and get ready to embark on a journey that takes you further into the caverns of AutoCAD.

CHAPTER 15

External References

External references (xrefs) are vital to capitalize on the power of AutoCAD. Those of you who've never investigated the xref command should ask yourselves the following questions.

- Have I ever wanted to temporarily reference another drawing from within my current drawing?
- Do I insert several detail drawings into one finished drawing?
- Do I create assemblies out of many different drawings?
- Am I constantly updating library symbols in different drawings?
- Do I insert many drawings into one finished drawing only to end up with an incredibly large final drawing?
- Am I in a workgroup situation that strives toward concurrent engineering?

If you answered yes to any of these questions, read on.

If you insert a wblock or block into your current drawing, you will get the entire block reference definition with it, even if you later delete the library symbol. Also, you'll be forced to purge your drawing to rid yourself of that extra garbage, even though you only wanted to use the drawing as a reference. External references to the rescue!

External references are exactly what their name indicates: externally referenced drawings. AutoCAD shoots a pointer out to the externally referenced drawing and brings the file into your current drawing. When you exit your drawing, AutoCAD releases the drawing, discarding all the excess baggage that goes along with the file. When you reenter your drawing, AutoCAD magically knows to go get the external reference again for your use. This process continues until you tell AutoCAD you are no longer interested in the externally referenced drawing. At that point, AutoCAD heartlessly casts it by the wayside.

To top off that great feature, others are welcome to use the externally referenced drawing and make modifications to it. Each time AutoCAD goes out and gets the xref drawing, all the new changes are incorporated within it.

The biggest and best benefit of using external references is being able to attach as many external references to your drawing as you want, without your base drawing getting any bigger!

The Xref Manager (Figure 15.1) is located under the Insert pull-down menu. Follow along and try the various options. You'll need two drawings. One drawing is your base or current drawing; you will xref the other drawing into the base drawing.

Attaching an External Reference

The Attach option officially attaches an external reference to a base drawing. This dialog prompts you for the drawing you want to attach, as well as other parameters such as

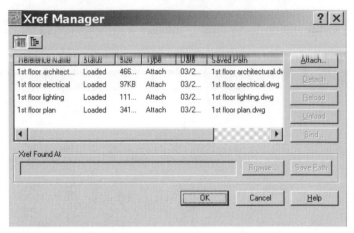

Figure 15.1 The External Reference Manager shows the list view of xrefs.

location. The options displayed are similar to those found in the `insert` command (Scale factor, Rotation angle, and so on). You can key in the parameters or specify it on-screen by checking the toggle button. You'll notice that the insertion point is relative to the origin of the externally referenced drawing (unless a previous base point was selected). Select a drawing to attach to your base drawing, then select an insertion point, X and Y scale factor, and rotation angle to complete the attachment. Hit OK to exit the dialog, and your drawing appears in the Xref Manager. When you exit the Xref Manager, you'll see the referenced drawing within your base drawing.

So, what can you do with this externally referenced drawing? Treat it much as you would a block object. You can hatch it, snap to it, dimension it, use the inquiry commands on it, move it, or copy it. However, you cannot modify or explode it. If you erase the xref, you'll also delete the object from your drawing, but not the external reference definition. You must follow the proper procedure of Detach to officially remove an xref from your drawing.

Look at your layers or your block definitions. Notice that all of the layers from the externally referenced drawing kindly came along for the ride. The same is true for the block definitions and other named objects. Although the naming convention is somewhat long for the externally referenced layers, they're easy to distinguish from your existing layers. If you externally referenced a drawing named Gear, your group of layers would look like the following.

```
GEAR|CONST
GEAR|DETAILS
GEAR|DIM
```

If the xref drawing had block definitions, the definitions would carry the same naming convention. Go into the `-block` command and list your blocks with the ? option.

```
Command: -block
Block name (or ?): ?
```

```
Block(s) to list <*>:
Defined blocks.
   GEAR                    Xref: resolved
   GEAR|SPROCKET           Xdep: GEAR
```

User	External	Dependent	Unnamed
Blocks	References	Blocks	Blocks
0	1	1	4

Dependent blocks came with the xref. You cannot use them unless you bind them to your drawing.

Note Unnamed blocks are usually dimensions or hatch patterns. Also notice that AutoCAD ignores block attributes in xrefs.

You can control the visibility, color, and linetype of an xref's layer, but by default, when you leave the base drawing, those values are reset to the original settings. This situation can be very frustrating if you go to great lengths to set up a particular layering scheme. Here is where the heroic visretain system variable comes to the rescue. When visretain is set to 1 (which is, unfortunately, not the default), AutoCAD remembers all of your settings and stores them, so the next time you enter the base drawing, you'll see the layers exactly as you left them. Should you later decide to detach the external reference, however, all of these layers will vanish from your drawing. You can also set visretain in the Open and Save tab of the Options dialog under Retain changes to Xref layers.

Save and exit your base drawing. Open the referenced drawing and make some obvious modifications. Exit the external reference drawing and reopen your base drawing. Are the modifications you just made reflected in your base drawing? You bet! External references can help ensure you're always viewing the most up-to-date information.

Nesting External References (and Circular Xrefs)

Using xrefs to attach a drawing containing its own xrefs is nesting external references. Technically, you can nest an xref if it contains a second xref that has a third xref that contains a fourth xref within a drawing. I'm sure you get the general idea. A problem does come into play, however, if you create a loop by externally referencing into a drawing that already contains one or more of the nested xrefs. This situation is referred to as a circular external reference and results in a warning message. It's difficult to explain, so I'll look at a simple example.

1. Drawing B has an attached xref called Drawing A.

2. Open Drawing A and use the xref command to attach Drawing B.

This situation creates a circular xref and issues a pleasant warning message.

Overlaying External References

The inability to create circular external references has been a problem for the serious xref user. This issue prompted the creation of a new option called Overlay in the `xref` command. The proper use of the Overlay option can eliminate the circular reference problem altogether. Follow this simple scenario.

1. Drawing B has an attached xref called Drawing A.

2. Attach Drawing B to Drawing C. Will you be able to see the xref Drawing A? Definitely.

3. Attach Drawing C to Drawing D. While you're in Drawing D, you can see Drawing A, B, and C. All of the xrefs follow the base drawing wherever it might go. They are inseparable unless they are officially detached.

However, an overlayed xref doesn't follow the base drawing wherever it goes. It resides in the base drawing only. If the base drawing is attached to another drawing, you won't see the overlayed xref in the final drawing. Another example illustrates this point.

1. Drawing B has overlayed xref Drawing A.

2. Attach Drawing B to Drawing C. Will you be able to see Drawing A? No, you won't. Drawing A stayed behind.

Reflecting back on the circular xref example, if you change the original attachment to an overlay, AutoCAD won't return an error message.

Other than this operation, an overlayed xref has the same properties and functionality as an attached one. You're not missing out on anything by using the Overlay option versus the Attach option. To overlay an xref, select the Overlay option in the Attach Xref dialog box.

Detaching or Binding an External Reference

When you're finished using the external reference, you can detach it from your base drawing (never erase!), which removes its layer and block references as well.

Should you decide to keep an xref for good (perhaps for editing purposes), you can use the Bind option in the Xref Manager. After binding an external reference, it takes on the properties of a wblock. You can now explode and modify the external reference objects. Once you bind an xref, you will no longer see any modifications made in the original xref drawing. The link has been broken.

The layer and block names are somewhat different as well, so I'll look at the new layering name convention.

```
GEAR|CONST
GEAR|DETAILS
GEAR|DIM
```

Change the names of these layers pronto; they're too long and scary looking! If you are going to give drawings containing external references to clients, be sure to bind the xrefs before handing them over; otherwise, your clients will be frustrated when opening your drawings and finding all of the xrefs missing. They're living happily at home on your computer. You can also use the new `etransmit` command to ensure all of your xrefs go with your drawing files.

Release 14 added an additional option that might be preferable to binding. The new Insert option allows you to simply change the xref to a block definition, thus eliminating the lengthy layer names. This option is found in the Xref Manager.

Changing the Path and Reloading External References

When you attach or overlay an external reference, AutoCAD remembers the path and the directory in which it is stored. AutoCAD always looks in this directory first when searching for the xref to load. Should you move the externally referenced drawing to another directory, you really should let AutoCAD know! This step is extremely crucial when you're working in a network environment where individuals may be mapped to different drives. If AutoCAD cannot find the xref drawing in its original directory, it will also search the AutoCAD support path set up using the `acad` environment variable. If you've set up a project in the Preferences dialog box, AutoCAD will search your project directories as well.

Say you're working in an environment where concurrent engineering is prevalent. You could be working on a floor plan at the same time the electrical engineer is working on the electrical system of the building. You've already externally referenced the electrical drawing into the floor plan when they tell you that some changes have been made. The Reload option will go back and get the drawing again, reloading it with the most recent modifications. It definitely beats exiting and reloading the drawing.

This is a fairly high-level explanation of the world of external references. If you want to investigate further, look into clipping external references using the new `xclip` command or `xbinding` any of the named objects that belong to your external reference. For example, the xref you brought into your base object has a great chair you'd like to have access to in your base drawing. You might even want to be able to modify it. The `xbind` command can be used for this very purpose. `xclip` allows you to clip away portions of the external reference you don't want to display.

I remember doing some work with planners for the city of Glendale, California, a few years ago. They had one monster drawing of the city that was so huge, it took about 15 minutes just to regenerate and display on the screen. This enormous map was a combination of about 30 different drawings inserted into one final drawing, resulting in the enormous file size. Not only was it a behemoth, but each time they made a modification to one of the individual drawings, they also had to remember to update the map of the entire city.

Switching to external references made their lives dramatically easier. Their drawing was no longer out of control, and as they updated the individual xref drawings, those changes were automatically made in the final combination map of the city.

Digging Deeper into the Xref Manager

One of the disadvantages of xrefs in the past has been trying to keep track of them within your drawing. You might have xrefs within xrefs (nested). You might have some xrefs that are overlaid rather than attached. You might have some xrefs that AutoCAD can't find. The Xref Manager makes it easy to view all of them within a drawing and understand their relationships to each other.

Figure 15.2 shows the list view of external references within the drawing, providing the specifics of each xref. The tree view, which I'll look at later, makes it easy to view the connections from one xref to another. The list view has six headings of detailed information. As with all MFC-compliant dialog boxes, you can click on the headings to sort the information in ascending or descending order. Each column can be moved to display the information in a way that works for you.

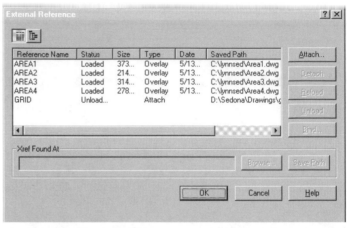

Figure 15.2 The Xref Manager with a list view of xrefs within a drawing.

Reference Name   Reference Name lists the external reference name. By clicking on it, you can change the name of the xref. If you modify the name, all dependent symbols are modified as well. Although the xref name can have more than eight characters, I recommend limiting the number of characters to accommodate the restrictions of the symbol tables.

Status   This column can be confusing because your external references can be in so many different possible states. The following list identifies all the possibilities.

Loaded   The xref was found when the drawing was opened or reloaded. It is displayed.

Unloaded   The xref is currently unloaded from the drawing. It is not displayed.

Not Found   AutoCAD was unable to find the xref using the assigned path. It might have been moved to another location.

Unresolved   AutoCAD found the xref but could not read the file (possibly a corrupt file).

Unreferenced   This is a nested xref that is attached to another xref that is no longer attached to the current drawing; not found or unresolved.

Orphaned   This is a nested xref that is attached to an xref that is unloaded.

As you can see, xrefs can be in a wide range of possible states at any given time.

Size/Type/Date The Size and Date headings are self-explanatory (and read-only). The Type heading indicates whether the xref is attached or whether it is an overlay. You can double-click on the words Attach and Overlay to toggle easily from one to the other. This is a great feature if you decide to change the type after the fact.

Saved Path This column contains the path AutoCAD uses to find the external reference file. If you move the external reference, use the Browse button to relocate the file and the Save Path button to resave the proper path. AutoCAD searches the hard-coded path saved here first and then follows that up by looking in the Project directory. Project names can be created in the Options dialog

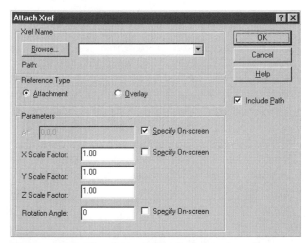

Figure 15.3 The Attach Xref dialog box is easy to navigate.

box. The five buttons on the right side of the dialog contain the real power of the Xref Manager. These buttons permit you to Attach (or Overlay), Detach, Reload, Unload, and Bind new xrefs.

Attach The Attach option sends you to the dialog shown in Figure 15.3. It is easier to Attach or Overlay new drawings with this visual interface. Select the drawing name; determine the type of attachment; and indicate the position, scale factor, and rotation angle of the xref. Selecting the Browse button displays an Explorer-style dialog box, complete with preview images, to help you select the correct drawing (Figure 15.4).

If the Include Path option is checked, AutoCAD saves the full path to the xref in the drawing database. If this option is not selected, you save the xref name only. This selection forces AutoCAD to search for the xref not only in the current project, but in the AutoCAD support file search path as well.

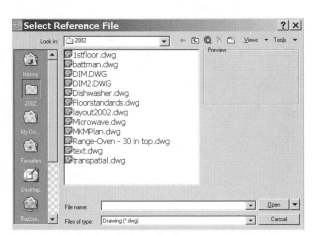

Figure 15.4 The Select Reference File dialog box.

After selecting the external reference file, you can choose to key in the parameters via the dialog or specify the parameters visually on screen (Figure 15.5).

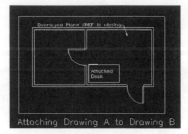

Detach   When you no longer need an xref in your drawing, you can detach it. Erasing the external reference removes the physical object, but not the instances of the drawing from the database. When you detach an xref, it's as though the xref never existed. You cannot detach a nested xref unless you detach the parent. You also cannot detach an xref referenced by another xref or block.

Figure 15.5 Drawing A is attached to Drawing B.

Reload   The Reload option is useful when the original externally referenced drawing has changed during a drawing session. Use Reload to get the most up-to-date xrefs displayed in your drawing. Reload also changes the status of unloaded xrefs back to their original state.

Unload   Less extreme than Detach, the new Unload option removes the physical display of the xref from the drawing but maintains a pointer to it. This feature will improve performance during a drawing session and speed up regenerations.

Bind   When you want to make the xref a permanent part of your drawing, use the Bind option (Figure 15.6).

This dialog presents one of the other cool options to the Xref Manager: the Insert option. You are probably familiar with how binding an xref produces long layer and block names. You get that nice `DWGNAME$#$` in front of all the named objects to distinguish them from those found in the original drawing. The new Insert option can turn your attached xref into a block. It uses no cryptic symbol table names. If it encounters duplicates, it gives precedence to the current drawing.

Figure 15.6 The Bind Xrefs dialog makes xrefs a permanent part of a drawing.

Note   If you change a reference name, you will not be able to bind until you exit the dialog and reenter again.

The above options don't take effect until after you've exited the dialog box. Don't forget the "what's this" help that's available if you need a brief reminder of the features in this dialog. Just click on the question mark in the upper right-hand corner and click the cursor on the area you need to know more about.

Tree View

The tree view lies within the new Xref Manager. By hitting the standard Tree view button in the upper left corner (or <F4>), you get a very different listing of the various external references within your drawing (Figure 15.7).

This new tree view display is a great view of the relationship of one xref to another. Here you can clearly see the parent/child relationship between nested xrefs in hierarchical format. The icons indicate the state of each xref. I personally find that all the icons look the same, and I always resort to the list view for

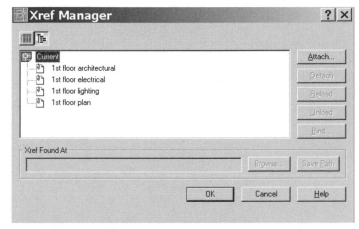

Figure 15.7 The tree view provides a standard tree diagram of xrefs in a drawing.

the friendly text information. Essentially, if there's a little red question mark on the icon, that's a bad thing — something is unreferenced, not found, orphaned, or worse. Any overlaid xref looks as though there are two sheets of paper instead of one.

You can select the list view or the tree view using <F3> and <F4>, respectively. I think you'll find the Xref Manager makes it much easier for you to use and control your external references.

External references are used extensively by AutoCAD power users, so find out why they are vital to so many industry professionals. Give them a try!

CHAPTER 16

Editing and Clipping External References

Clipping your External References

Who needs to clip external references? Anyone who wants to display only a portion of an externally referenced drawing. You might xref in an entire hospital building but only want AutoCAD to display one wing in your current drawing. Not only do you want just the single wing to display, but you don't want to be slowed down by the overhead of the entire hospital drawing. When AutoCAD is set up properly, you'll find that it grants both wishes.

The xclip Command to the Rescue

xclip is found in the Modify pull-down menu under Clip–Xref. It is also the third button across in the Reference toolbar (Figure 16.1).

Figure 16.1 The Xclip tool is found in the Reference toolbar

The xclip command lets you visually clip the display of a selected external reference. It does not affect the original drawing in any way. You can clip to a predefined boundary, or you can define a boundary on the fly. You can also clip many external references at one time. At any given time, you can choose to turn the clipping off and redisplay the entire xref. There's much to the xclip command, so I'll break it up into easily digestible doses. To follow along, open a drawing containing external references or attach a couple of external references to a new drawing for practice. I'll use the drawing in Figure 16.2.

After entering the xclip command, AutoCAD asks you to select the external references you want to include in the clip. All of the standard object selection methods are acceptable.

```
Command: XCLIP
Select objects: Other Corner:
4 Found
Select objects: <Enter>
ON/OFF/Clipdepth/Delete/generate
    Polyline/<New boundary>:<Enter>
Specify clipping boundary:
Select polyline/Polygonal/
<Rectangular>:
```

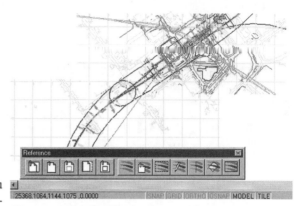

Figure 16.2 Xrefs that are about to be clipped.

After selecting the external references, you need to indicate the next step. In the first example, I'll jump straight to selecting a new boundary (the default). Hit <Enter> to specify a clipping boundary.

Three types of boundaries are accepted in the xclip command. You can use an existing polyline as a boundary or you can create a polygonal (many-sided) or rectangular boundary on the fly. I'll choose the default again and select the two opposing corners of a rectangle, after which, the only xref area displayed on the screen lies within the rectangular area (Figure 16.3).

You also can use an existing polyline as a boundary by entering S (for Select polyline) then picking the desired polyline. AutoCAD also permits you to use open polylines and internally closes the polyline by connecting the starting point with the closing point to determine the final boundary. If connecting the starting point with the closing point causes the polyline to cross itself, an error message displays.

I was able to apply a fit curve and a spline to the polyline without any problems. I noticed the spline accomplished more pleasing final results. The Help menu indicated that only straight pline segments were acceptable, but I found I had no problem using a curve-fitted polyline.

Figure 16.3 The xrefs after rectangular clipping let you see only the part of the xref you need.

I even drew a square with the polygon command and splined it to get an image that was pretty darn close to a circle. Using this image as a boundary, I was able to create a circular clipped xref.

The xclip command also lets you draw a polygonal area on the fly to indicate a boundary. I use this option the most because it makes it easy to isolate irregularly shaped areas.

The xclip command has many options buried within. I'll review the remaining options found at the first prompt.

On When xclip is set to On, AutoCAD displays the clipped external references.

Off When xclip is set to Off, clipping boundaries are ignored, and the external references are displayed in their entirety.

Clipdepth This option sets the front and back clipping planes. It can get confusing if you're not familiar with the process (dview anyone?). You are asked to specify the distance from the front clipping plane and the boundary, as well as the distance from the back clipping plane to the boundary. You also can delete clipping planes within this option.

Delete This option deletes a clipping boundary you don't intend to use again. If you just want to temporarily display the entire external reference, be sure to use the Off option. You can't use the standard erase command to delete a clipping boundary.

Generate Polyline This option turns a clipping boundary into a polyline. It's useful if you need to modify the boundary after the fact. AutoCAD places the polyline on the current layer using the current linetype and color settings. If you use grips, or perhaps pedit, on the new polyline, you need to redefine the new boundary to ensure that the changes take place.

Note You cannot have more than one clipping boundary per xref.

Now that you're only using the portion of the xref you need, how do you make sure AutoCAD only uses the displayed sections versus the entire drawing when it's zooming, selecting, and regenerating? To make sure you're getting optimum performance, return to the Open and Save tab of the Options dialog.

The right-hand side of the dialog contains the three external reference file demand-load options. Setting Enabled or Enabled with Copy ensures you get top performance out of your xrefs.

Enabled AutoCAD's performance is improved by turning on Demand Loading. It should be noted that other users can access, but not edit, the file while it is being referenced.

Enabled with Copy AutoCAD uses a copy of the referenced drawing in your drawing and turns on Demand Loading (thus improving performance). Other users may access and edit the original drawing.

Disabled This option turns off Demand Loading, which means that you are no longer improving AutoCAD performance by displaying only a portion of an externally referenced drawing. Others may access and edit the referenced file. This setting is saved under the xloadctl system variable.

One last step to ensure you maximize your productivity with xrefs lies within the Saveas dialog box. As you save your externally referenced drawings, make sure they are saved with an index type of Layer & Spatial. Ouch, that sounds painful, doesn't it? I'll go through the process one step at a time.

In the Saveas dialog box, select the Options button from the Tools pull-down in the upper right-hand corner. This action takes you to the Saveas Options dialog (Figure 16.4). Select the DWG Options tab to see the Index type drop-down list. By default, this type is set to Layer & Spatial, which is exactly the way you want to leave it. I'm only pointing this out in case someone modified your setup. Layer & Spatial indicates optimum AutoCAD performance because it loads only those layers that are on, thawed, and within a clipped boundary area, which is what you want.

The remaining options are for you future AutoCAD Jeopardy contestants.

None   Neither layer nor spatial indexes are created when you save drawings (translation: you will go very slowly).

Layer   AutoCAD loads only those layers that are on and thawed.

Spatial   AutoCAD loads only the portion of the xref within a clipped boundary.

Do yourself a favor, check this dialog once and forget about it.

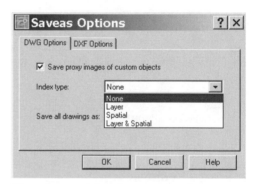

Figure 16.4 The Saveas Options dialog box. The Layer & Spatial Index type loads only those layers that are on, thawed, and within a clipped boundary area.

Editing your External References

In a drawing with an attached external reference, you notice a small change that needs to be made within the xref. When you try to edit the xref, AutoCAD reminds you ever so politely that this is an external reference, and you must go to the original drawing to make the change … doh! What a hassle! Wouldn't it be nice if you could edit that external reference from within the drawing it's attached to? This wish was granted with AutoCAD 2000. The refedit command permits you to make the changes to the attached external reference and save them back to the original drawing.

How many CAD managers are cringing right now at this thought? I remember being accosted in Tulsa, Oklahoma, because a CAD Manager was mortified about this feature. It doesn't really let CAD users do anything they couldn't do before, but this way they can just do it a lot faster! Rest assured that if they don't have permission to access the referenced drawing, the new refedit command won't magically grant it to them. A system variable turns this feature off completely within a drawing if you really must. With the advent of AutoCAD 2002, I'm hearing nothing but good comments about this feature, so I'll take a good hard look at it.

This feature is also a great new way to update your block definitions. In fact, if you double-click on a block definition, AutoCAD launches Refedit. It grays out the parts of the drawing you're not interested in, focusing directly on the parts of the block. After you've made the modifications, it automatically updates all the blocks in your drawing.

To see how this works, open a drawing with an external reference attached, preferably one that could use a little editing. I'll use the drawing shown in Figure 16.5.

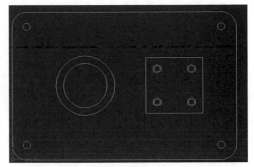

Figure 16.5 A drawing of a plate with an xref of four bolts.

Refedit

The refedit command is located in the Modify pull-down menu under In-Place xref and Block Edit. Here, you'll find the Edit Reference option and the Refedit toolbar (Figure 16.6).

So here's the scenario: the hole within the bolt is the wrong diameter. The two objects comprising the bolt are part of a block, and the block is inside the attached xref (the anklebone's connected to the shin bone …). Not only am I trying to change an attached external reference, but I'm trying to change a block nested within that reference. Yikes!

I start by executing the refedit command and selecting the bolt. The Reference Edit dialog (Figures 16.7 and 16.8) appears and tells me that I've selected a block nested within an external reference. Clicking on bolt_array|bolt or picking the Next button displays the image of the bolt. Notice the distinguishing icons for a block and an external reference. If you simply select

Figure 16.6 The Refedit toolbar.

the external reference, you do not automatically see the nested objects. Additionally, you can only edit one nested object at a time. If you want to edit five different nested blocks, you'll have to enter the refedit command five times. The preview images display the xref as it was last saved in the reference drawing, and any changes you make are not reflected in the preview during the current drawing session. You need to reenter the original drawing and execute a save to update the bitmap, which can get a tad confusing.

Note   Blocks inserted into a drawing using minsert cannot be edited.

Within the Refedit dialog, you'll find the path of the external reference. Underneath the path are two options.

Enable unique layer and symbol names   When you bind an external reference, AutoCAD assigns unique layer and block names, where applicable. For example, a layer called Furniture from a drawing called Mouse uses the drawing name $#$*layer/block name* format to display block and layer names while editing.

    Mouse0Furniture

If this option is not selected, layer and symbol names are the same as they are in the original referenced drawing.

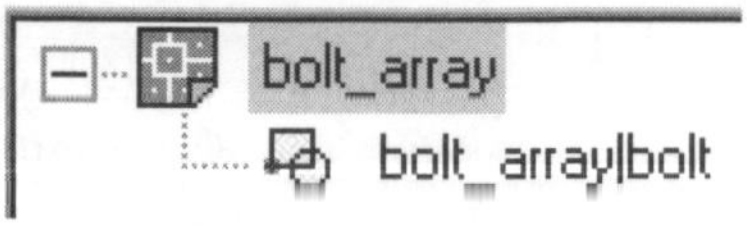

Display attribute definitions for editing   If   you decide to edit a block with attributes, you might want to edit the attribute definitions. I'll be the first to admit this isn't exactly intuitive. First, select this option so the attributes are visible for editing (even though the Help file indicates the opposite). I suggest using the new `properties` command to edit the attribute definitions. Next, save the changes (which I'll get to later). As it is with standard attribute definition editing, this will not affect any of the existing blocks — just those inserted after the changes have been made. You'll have to use `battman` or `attsync` to update the previously inserted block attribute information.

    After I've cycled through to the nested block Bolt, I dismiss the dialog by hitting the OK button. At the familiar Select Objects prompt, I select the circle in the middle of the bolt (because my goal is to edit its diameter). After selecting the circle and hitting an extra <Enter> to indicate I've finished selecting objects, all the other objects in the drawing are grayed out (very cool!). It's very clear I'm only dealing with the circle (Figure 16.9). All objects that are not grayed out are part of the working set. If you execute the command from the keyboard or pull-down menu, the Refedit toolbar pops onto the screen and lists the name of the selected reference.

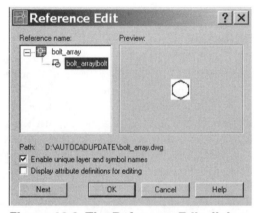

Figure 16.7 The distinguishing icons show the difference between a block and an external reference.

Figure 16.8 The Reference Edit dialog box indicates that I've selected a block nested within an external reference.

Note   If you change your mind and decide to exit the command, dismissing the Refedit toolbar isn't the route to take. Hitting <Esc> won't do it either; you'll feel like you're in Refedit limbo! You can, however, select the Discard Changes to Reference button on the toolbar or execute the `refclose` command.

Now I'm ready to edit my circle. I make it easy by entering <Ctrl-1> to summon the Properties dialog. I reselect the circle (I'm not sure why I have to pick the circle yet again) and change the value of the diameter to 10. When I've completed all my edits, I'm ready to save the changes back to the original drawing.

You can add an additional object to the working set (to be saved back to the original referenced drawing) one of two ways. Add the object while in Refedit mode, and the object is automatically added to the working set. You can select objects that existed before you executed the refedit

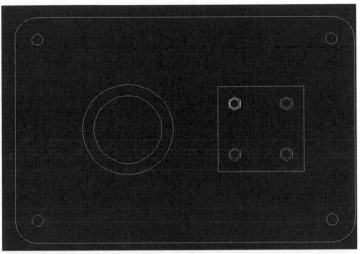

Figure 16.9 Selected objects are not grayed out, so I am only dealing with the circle.

command (and are currently grayed out) with the Add Objects to Working Set button. This brings the object to the forefront, and it becomes part of the working set. Objects added by an edit command such as fillet might not be added automatically to the working set. This means that you have to add these manually. For example, if you fillet two lines, the fillet arc needs to be added to the working set to be saved back to the final drawing.

If you want to remove an object from the working set (and delete it from the referenced drawing), you can do so by selecting Remove Objects from the Working Set. This allows you to keep the object in the current drawing and remove it from the referenced drawing (confused yet?). In most cases, I suspect you'd simply use the erase command to remove and object from the current drawing and the referenced drawing.

You can edit objects that reside on locked layers in the reference drawing. Of course you have to unlock the layer first (in the host drawing) before you can edit the object. The layer returns to its locked state in the original referenced drawing when Refedit completes.

After all the changes have been made and you're ready to save them to the referenced drawing, select the Save Back Changes to Reference button. This displays the friendly dialog shown in Figure 16.10, which is there to warn you that these changes are being saved to the original referenced drawing. It also gives you one last chance to back out. After hitting the OK button, all of my bolts now have holes with the proper diameter. Mission accomplished!

xedit **and** xfadectl

A couple of system variables enter into the equation while in Refedit. xedit controls whether the refedit command can be used on the current drawing. Setting xedit to 0 in a drawing blocks anyone from using the refedit command on it. Adamant CAD Managers might consider setting this variable to 0 in all drawings if they truly want to block xref editing.

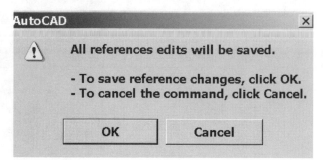

Figure 16.10 **This is the final dialog you see before changes are completed in your drawing.**

You also can control the fade factor on the objects not included in the working set. The higher you set the value of xfadectl, the more the objects fade. Fifty percent is the default, and you can't go higher than 90 percent.

> **Note**   If shademode is set to a value other than 2D wireframe during in-place reference editing, objects outside the working set do not fade.

Don't forget to try this command on your block references. The fading out of objects that don't belong to the block, along with the automatic updating of all the blocks in the drawing, makes it a viable alternative to the previous method.

So many drawings use multiple attached xrefs. Autodesk has provided another nice feature that makes it easier to make minor alterations without having to go out to the referenced drawing to do it.

CHAPTER 17

A New Dimension

For those of you faced with the arduous tasks of dimensioning your drawings, you'll be happy to know that AutoCAD 2002 has some awesome dimensioning features certain to eliminate much of the tedium. They've also granted a few more dimension variable wishes for those who still can't get dimensions to obey their every desire. In this chapter, I cover many of the changes made to the dimension world.

First and foremost, one of the absolutely best dimensioning features is the stunning qdim command (quick dimension). This former Express tool always receives oohs and ahs from audiences when I'm out preaching the AutoCAD gospel. Another Kurt Chase programming special, Qdim allows you to create a series of dimensions at one time, and although I think you'll find its strong point lies in baseline or continuous dimensioning, it also does a mean job at knocking out multiple dimensions on circles and arcs. I'll start with a simple example and then explain each option in more detail.

Figure 17.1 shows a simple drawing containing a few circles and arcs. After entering the qdim command, I'll start with some baseline dimensioning. Using a simple crossing window, as shown in Figure 17.2, I've selected the lines at the top of the drawing to dimension.

Command: QDIM

Select geometry to dimension: **Select objects to dimension**

Select geometry to dimension:

Specify dimension line position, or

[Continuous/Staggered/Baseline/Ordinate/Radius/Diameter/datumPoint/Edit]

<Continuous>: B

Specify dimension line position: **dynamically indicate where you want the dimensions to go.**

Voilà! The glorious end result is shown in Figure 17.3.

Do some experimenting by trying Continuous or perhaps Ordinate. You'll even find that if you change your mind down the road and want to change the dimensions from one type to another, you can reselect the objects (be sure to include the dimensions within the selection set), and the dimensions happily change to a different type. Next I'll look at dimensioning circles and arcs.

Command: QDIM

Select geometry to dimension: Specify crossing window

Select geometry to dimension: <Enter>

Specify dimension line position, or

[Continuous/Staggered/Baseline/Ordinate/Radius/Diameter/
    datumPoint/Edit]

<Baseline>: R

Specify dimension line position: Select a direction for the dimension lines

Second Voilà! The end result is shown in Figure 17.4.

It seems simple enough, so look at the other options within the command. (The Help file is less than enlightening when it comes to Qdim.)

Staggered   I must admit, the Qdim guru had to explain this one to me. Staggered was created for those instances when you need to dimension smaller distances within a larger dimension. Staggered dimensions are stacked on top of each other with their text staggered left and right as it ascends the stack (Figure 17.5). Apparently, most dimension standards (ANSI, ISO, JIS, and DIN) encounter this situation.

Baseline   Use this option to create multiple baseline dimensions (Figure 17.6). The dimdli system variable still controls the distance from one dimension line to the next.

Ordinate   This option creates multiple standard ordinates or datum dimensions based on the current UCS. Pulling the dimensions to the right or left typically display the Y datum dimension; pulling the dimensions up and down display the X datum dimension. I did notice that if the dimensions are too close together, they don't automatically jog; rather, they land on top of each other.

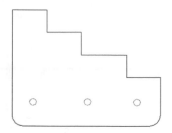

Figure 17.1 Apply dimensions to this simple image.

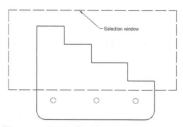

Figure 17.2 Select the top entities by using the crossing window (selection window).

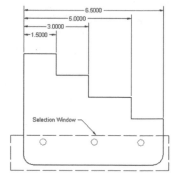

Figure 17.3 The result is a series of Baseline dimensions. Now, select the lower half of the drawing with another crossing window.

Diameter   Diameter works like radius dimensioning and dimensions according to the various dimension variable settings.

datumPoint   This is a handy option because it allows you to reassign a reference point on-the-fly for Baseline and Ordinate dimensioning. After selecting a new reference or datum point, AutoCAD returns to the previous point. This is much easier than reassigning the UCS.

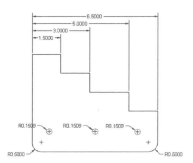

Edit   The Edit option is the absolute best! Here you can easily add or remove points you want AutoCAD to take into consideration when dimensioning. Figure 17.7 shows the points that show up when you select Edit mode. Simply select points you want to remove (or add) to the selection set. This allows you

Figure 17.4 It's easy to knock out multiple Radial dimensions in one shot.

even more control over the final dimensioning outcome. You can also use this option after the fact to correct existing dimensions.

So, there you have it. Rumor has it that lots of research went into Qdim, and it shows.

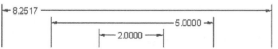

Figure 17.5 Staggered dimensioning works from the inside out.

The New Dimstyle

Next on the dimension agenda is the new Ddim (or now Dimstyle) dialog box. Either the `ddim` or `dimstyle` command sends you to the dialog shown in Figure 17.8. I'm going to assume you're somewhat literate in dimension style for the remainder of the chapter.

First, you'll notice the image on the right side of the dialog that provides a visual representation of the selected dimension style. It sure beats having to leave the dialog and create a dimension to view the resulting dimension style. Underneath the image is a list of the dimension variable settings that differ from the Current Dimstyle. If the information is too large for the box, you can click in the pane and use arrow keys to scroll up and down.

I did notice that the Dimension Style image fell short when displaying parent dimensions with child dimension styles. Although you can view the settings of the child dimensions (such as Angular and Radial, which are shown in Figure 17.8) by picking them, the parent dimension style image (Standard), doesn't seem to reflect the changes made to its children. For example, I altered the Angular child dimension line so that it included the color green. This doesn't manifest itself when I

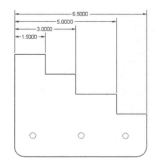

Figure 17.6 Baseline dimensioning stacks from left to right.

have the standard parent dimension style selected (back to Figure 17.8). This is not a huge deal, but it can be somewhat confusing.

Notice that there is no longer a Save button in the dialog. AutoCAD 2002 now saves the changes you make to the dimension style by default. You have to explicitly pick the Override button to create overrides AutoCAD Release 14 and before made it super-simple to accidentally create overrides, but this should no longer be a problem. It's basically the opposite of the way it was in Release 14. You used to need to pick the Save button to save any changes you made to the Ddim dialog in order to update the current dimension style; otherwise, it created overrides (and you found yourself with that nice little plus (+) sign next to the dimension style. Now it's the opposite, you must select the Override button or it will automatically save the new settings to the current dimension style. This new change should make many CAD Managers happy.

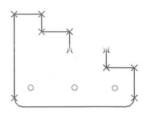

Figure 17.7 The Edit option Qdim makes it easy to select the objects to dimension.

The Process of creating new dimension styles has changed slightly as well. Picking the New button on the right side of the dialog sends you to the dialog shown in Figure 17.9. You can choose to work off a copy of any existing style. To create a child dimension style, simply make sure the parent dimension style is current, and drop the Use for list down. The child dimension will snap into the proper tree structure displayed in the main dialog.

To make changes to an existing dimension style, simply make sure it's selected and then select the Modify button off to the right of the dialog. You can set a dimension style to current by picking the Current button (double-clicking on the desired dimension style is just as simple), but keep in mind that only parent dimension styles can be current. I already addressed Override, so now I'll look at Compare.

The Compare Dimension Styles dialog (Figure 17.10) displays the different settings between two dimension styles. You can compare parent to child, child to child, parent to parent, and so forth. There's even a little mystery button (because it

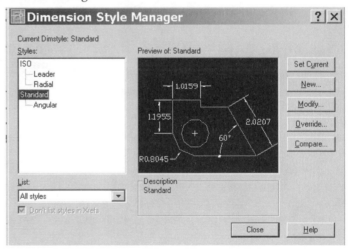

Figure 17.8 The new Ddim dialog box contains an image file that displays current settings.

has no tooltip) that copies the results of the comparison to the Windows clipboard for use in other programs. If you were putting together a Standards manual, this could prove to be a handy helper.

In the lower left-hand corner of the dialog, you can display all of the created dimension styles or just those referenced by dimensions within the current drawing. You can also suppress a listing of the dimension styles within any external references you have within your drawing.

AutoCAD 2002 also contains one more noticeable change to Dimension Style families. The original concept of the Dimstyle families was to permit you to make modifications to the parent dimension, and those changes would trickle down to the children (unless there were conflicting settings in the children). This theory hasn't worked since its conception. This is so hard to explain, so I'll illustrate with a simple example.

You have a dimension style called ProjectA. You create three child dimensions associated with ProjectA: Linear, Angular, and Radius. The text color for all of these dimension styles is green, except for Radius, which has a text color of cyan.

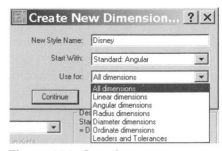

Figure 17.9 Creating a new dimension now starts in this dialog box.

You find out that you need to change the text to yellow. No problem; just jump into the parent dimension style of ProjectA and change it to yellow. Technically it should have trickled down to all the children, except for Radius because it already has its own setting. This has been the ideal, but it has never worked. Before AutoCAD 2000, it seemed as though the children became orphans — out on their own to fend for themselves — that were no longer directly linked to their parents. To change the text to yellow, you would set the settings in each of the children manually. What a drag!

I'm happy to tell you that no longer will your child dimensions be orphans; they now all work as originally planned.

If you're a dimension style maniac, do yourself a favor and put the dimension style dropdown list on your Object Properties toolbar. It's super-simple to do with a minimal amount of menu know-how, and it will save you lots of time (e-mail me if you need help doing this).

I would be remiss if I didn't mention the new true associative dimensioning that came out in AutoCAD 2002. This amazing new feature creates dimensions that are truly associated with the objects, so editing objects and dimensions are so much easier. Just make sure Associative dimensioning is on in the Options dialog box and you're good to go! For those of you who are command-line users, this means setting `dimassoc`

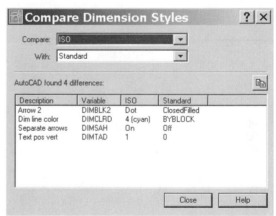

Figure 17.10 The Compare option compares one dimension style with another.

to 2. Should you want to take some of your pre-2002 dimensions and update them to the new True dimensions, try the dimreassociate command (what a mouthful!). And should you for some crazy reason want to break the associativity, use the dimdisassociate command. This returns it to the standard associative dimensions of 2000i and before.

CHAPTER 18

Demystifying Dimensioning Tabs

In the last chapter, I took a general look at the overhauled Dimension Style dialog box, as well as the awesome qdim command. Here, I unravel the mysteries of the dimension variable settings, starting with the tabs in the Dimension Style dialog box.

Gone are the days when you were forced to remember the convoluted dimension variables, although many users still find it simpler to key in dimvar directly. Now you can visually make changes within a dialog. Even so, there are so many tabs and options that it takes a real investment in time to set up your dimensioning to suit your individual needs.

To follow along, simply key in ddim. (The Dimension Style dialog box is also accessible via the dimstyle command. dimstyle is the preferred command, but I'm just used to ddim.) You can also find the Dimension Style dialog box located in the Dimension pull-down menu under Style. Now select Modify to view the different tabs for setting up your dimensions, and I'll step through the tabs one at a time.

Tab 1: Lines and Arrows

The Lines and Arrows tab is broken up into four different sections: Dimension Lines, Extension Lines, Arrowheads, and Center Marks for Circles (Figure 18.1). Any changes you make to the individual settings will appear in the image in the upper right-hand corner of the dialog. As you modify the dialog, the dimension variables connected to the dialog update as well. I will include the associated dimension variables because this information can prove very helpful to those of you who customize or write script files.

Dimension Lines

Within this quadrant, you can control the color of the dimension lines (dimclrd) as well as the line weight for the dimension lines (dimlwd). The latter came out with AutoCAD 2000. Note that the line weights don't display on the image tile.

If your arrowheads are any of the following — oblique, architectural, tick, integral, or none — you can choose extend the dimension line past the tick marks by specifying the distance. This vari-⟨⟨⟨⟨⟨⟩⟩ ⟨⟨ ⟨⟨⟨⟨⟨⟩⟩ ⟨⟨⟨ ⟨⟨⟨⟨ ⟨⟨⟨⟨⟨⟨⟨⟩ ⟨⟨⟨⟨⟨⟨⟩⟩⟩⟩

If you're creating Baseline dimensions, you can control the distance between the stacked dimension lines by selecting Baseline spacing. This setting is saved in the `dimdli` dimension variable.

Should you need to suppress one or both dimension lines, simply pick the checkbox by the dimension line you want to turn off. These settings are saved in `dimsd1` and `dimsd2`, respectively. When using either of these settings, how you select the objects to be dimensioned can make a big difference.

Extension Lines

The first two options are similar to those for Dimension Lines. You can control the color for the extension lines (`dimclre`), as well as the line weight (`dimlwe`).

You can control how far the extension line extends past the location of the dimension line (`dimexe`), as well as offset distance between the start of the extension line and the object you're dimensioning (`dimexo`). Figure 18.2 shows a simple drawing that displays these variable settings.

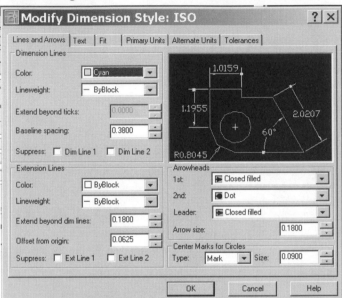

Figure 18.1 Use the Lines and Arrows tab to set up the format for Dimension Lines, Extension Lines, Arrowheads, and Center Marks for Circles.

You can also suppress the first, second, or both extension lines by selecting the checkboxes in the lower left-hand corner of the dialog. Note that the line weights for extension lines don't appear on the dimensioning image either.

Arrowheads

When you select an arrowhead for the first dimension line, AutoCAD automatically sets the second dimension line arrowhead identically. You also can specify your own custom arrowhead by picking the Other option from the drop-down list. The first dimension line arrowhead is saved under the `dimblk1` setting, and the second is saved under `dimblk2`.

You can also control the size of the arrowheads (`dimasz`) in this section.

Center Marks for Circles

Three dimensioning commands can use center marks: dimcenter, dimradius, and dimdiameter. The latter two only use center marks if the dimension line is placed outside of the circle. The three types of center marks are Center Mark, Centerline, or None at all. All of these are saved to the dimcen value. If dimcen is positive, you get center marks; if it's negative, you get center lines; if it's 0, well, I think you can figure that one out! A value of .9 indicates you've set the center mark to a size of .9. A value of -.9 indicates you've chosen center lines with a size of .9. In a

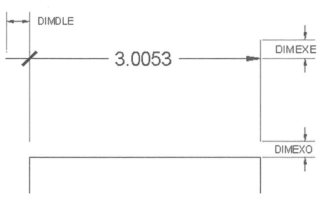

Figure 18.2 This diagram displays the settings for dimexe, dimexo, **and** dimdle.

nutshell, both size and type are saved in the same dimension variable.

Tab 2: Text

The Text tab is broken into three sections: Text Appearance, Text Placement, and Text Alignment (Figure 18.3).

Text Appearance

This section controls the dimension text format and size. Use the first option to set up text style for your dimension text from the existing text styles (saved to the dimtxsty system variable). Selecting the mystery button (no tooltip) with the ellipsis allows you to create or modify a text style on the fly.

You can assign a specific color for your dimension text (dimclrt), which is useful because you can't assign a line weight to it.

The next value is somewhat

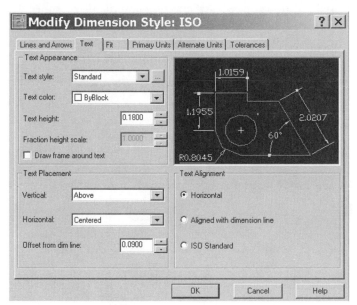

Figure 18.3 The Text tab controls the appearance, placement, and alignment of dimension text.

tricky. Here you can assign a desired text height to your dimension text (dimtxt). However, if the selected text style also has a text height setting, the text style height will win out over this setting (all the more reason to leave your text style height at 0). You'll also find that the dimension text height is always multiplied by the dimscale factor (as are the other numeric settings). So, if your desired text height is .18 and the scale factor for your drawing is $\frac{1}{4}$ inch, you need to set your overall Dimension Scale factor to 48 to get the proper result. This takes brings up an entirely different topic of scaling and dimensioning, which I'll cover later.

If your Units setting is set to Architectural or Fractional, you have control over the size of the fraction relative to the dimension text height. This is a scale factor. Hence, .5 would create fractions one half the size of the whole numbers. The value is saved in the dimtfac system variable.

Some applications require a frame to be drawn around the dimension text, so selecting the checkbox generates a box around the text and sets the dimgap variable to a negative value.

Text Placement

This part starts to get a tad sticky. You can control the vertical and horizontal justification of text along the dimension line. These settings don't necessarily affect all text; it depends on how they're individually laid out. Vertical justification (dimtad) controls the vertical position of text (primarily up and down movement) and has four options: Centered, Above, Outside, and JIS.

Centered places the dimension text within the dimension line (this is the default). This setting will affect just about all dimensions. Above places the dimension text above the dimension line. It primarily affects horizontal, radial, and diameter dimensions, leaving vertical and angular dimensions still centered. Outside pretty much affects all dimensions. This option places the dimension text on the side of the dimension line farthest from what you're dimensioning. JIS places the dimension text in accordance with the Japanese Industrial Standards (I won't even try to convince you I'm familiar with those settings.) The easiest way to clearly understand the different settings is to select each and watch the dimension image change.

Horizontal justification (dimjust) controls the horizontal position of the text (primarily left and right movement). Center centers the dimension text between the dimension lines. At Extension Line 1 moves the text closer to the first extension line; At Extension Line 2 moves the text closer to the second. The actual distance between the extension line and the dimension text is (are you ready?) two times the arrowhead size (dimasz) plus the text gap value (dimgap). But of course! It doesn't appear that either one of the last two options affects leaders or radial dimensions. They do affect angular dimensions, even though the image doesn't indicate this fact. You also can place the dimension text over the first or second dimension lines; this literally places the text at the end of the selected extension line (Figure 18.4).

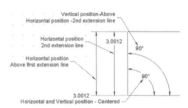

Figure 18.4 This diagram demonstrates the different placement options for dimension text.

Note that none of the horizontal justification settings apply unless the dimupt variable is set to 0 (or off). When dimupt is on, you manually control the horizontal placement when placing the dimensions on your drawing. This setting can also be found in the lower left-hand corner of the Fit tab under Place Text Manually When Dimensioning. If this setting is checked, AutoCAD ignores the horizontal justification settings.

The spacing between the dimension line and the dimension text is controlled by the dimgap variable (sound familiar?). You also can set this spacing in the Offset from Dim Line option in the lower left-hand corner of the dialog box. dimgap controls the distance between the dimension text and the dimension line, whether the text breaks up the dimension line or lies above the dimension line. Earlier I mentioned that it also controls whether or not a box is drawn around the text. If dimgap is -.09, AutoCAD draws a box around the text with a distance of .09 between the text and the dimension line. If dimgap is a positive number, no box is drawn.

Text Alignment

The last section in the Text tab has to do with the alignment of the dimension text (Figure 18.5). You can choose to always place the text horizontally, regardless of the angle of the dimension line, or you might prefer to place the text at the same angle as the dimension line. The third option, ISO Standard, is a combination of the two. It aligns the dimension text with the dimension line when the text fits within the extension lines, but places the text horizontally when it's placed outside of the extension lines. The two variables that come into play here are dimtih and dimtoh. dimtih (text inside horizontal) controls whether the dimension text that fits inside the extension lines is horizontal (dimtih set to 1). dimtoh (text outside horizontal) controls whether the dimen-

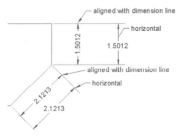

Figure 18.5 You can place the dimension text horizontally or align it with the dimension line.

sion text that is outside the extension lines is horizontal (dimtoh set to 1). The first option in the section, Horizontal, sets both dimtih and dimtoh to 1. The second option, Aligned with dimension line, sets both dimtih and dimtoh to 0. The last option, ISO Standard, sets dimtih to 0 and dimtoh to 1.

Tab 3: Fit

The Fit tab in the Dimension Style dialog focuses on the placement of dimension text, arrowheads, leader lines, and the dimension line (Figure 18.6). Basically I'm talking location, location, location. The upper left-hand corner of the dialog addresses what happens when there isn't enough room to place both the dimension text and arrows inside the extension lines. You are asked to select what you want moved outside the extension line first; either the text or the arrows, whichever fits best. Because the length of dimension text varies, this option basically will fit whatever it can within the extension lines. If there's enough room for text but not for the arrowheads, the text wins and the arrowheads are bounced out. If the text won't fit, then AutoCAD tries to place the arrowheads between the extension lines and bounce the text out. Should neither fit, they both are placed outside the extension lines (dimatfit set to 3).

Arrows   This option gives text the upper hand. When space is limited, text wins and the arrowheads are sent outside the extension lines. If the text doesn't fit, then both text and arrowheads are placed outside the extension lines. With this scenario, you would never see the arrowheads inside the extension lines without the dimension text (dimatfit set to 1).

Text   Here the arrowheads have top priority. When space is available for both text and arrowheads, they both remain inside the extension lines. If there is only enough room for one or the other, the arrowheads win and the text is placed outside. If there isn't enough room for the arrowheads, then both the text and arrowheads are placed outside. With this option, you would never see text inside the extension lines without arrowheads (dimatfit set to 2). Note that the Help file has switched the Text and Arrows information; hence, it is incorrect. Don't let this catch you off guard!

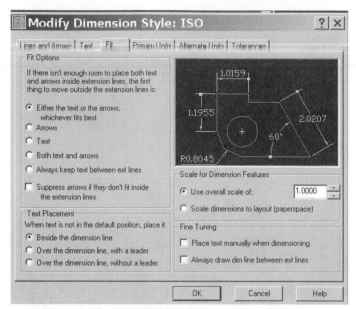

Figure 18.6 The Fit tab is primarily used to control the physical placement of text and arrows.

Both text and arrows   When space is limited, both the text and arrows are placed outside the extension lines. This means both the text and arrows are inside or outside; they will never be split up (dimatfit set to 0).

As a quick recap, the previous options are saved to the dimatfit (arrows text fit) variable.

- 0 places both text and arrowheads outside extension lines.
- 1 moves the arrowheads first, then the text.
- 2 moves the text first, then the arrowheads.
- 3 moves either text or arrowheads, whichever fits best.

Always keep text between ext lines   Text is placed between the extension lines even if there's no way it's going to fit. The text will be centered and written right over the extension lines. This sets the dimtix variable (text inside extension) to 1.

Suppress arrows if they don't fit inside the extension lines.   You also can select this option in conjunction with one of the above Fit options. If the arrows don't fit within the extension lines, the arrows are suppressed. This information is stored in the dimsoxd variable (suppress outside extension dimension).

Text Placement

This section deals with the placement of dimension text when it is moved from the default position.

Beside the dimension line   When moving the text, the dimension line follows (dimtmove set to 0).

Over the dimension line, with a leader   When   the text is moved away from the dimension line, the dimension line stays put and a leader is drawn that connects the text to the dimension line (Figure 18.7). If the text is too close to the dimension line, AutoCAD omits the leader line (dimtmove set to 1). I did notice that occasionally the leader line became fickle and would disappear, even though there was plenty of room.

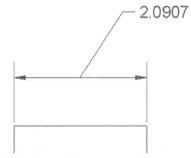

Over the dimension line, without a leader   The dimension text is free to move anywhere. When the text is moved away from the dimension line, no leader line is drawn (dimtmove set to 0).

Figure 18.7 When moving the dimension text, it's sometimes desirable to have a leader line connecting it to the dimension line.

I strongly recommend taking a look at the different options using the dimension image; it's helpful when determining the right combinations to use.

Scale for Dimension Features

Setting the scale factor is the key to proper dimensioning. In this section, I show you how to control the overall scale factor or set dimensioning for Paper Space scaling.

Use overall scale of   If you're sticking to Model Space, you'll want to set your scale factor to reflect your final drawing scale factor. This scale factor affects any of the dimension style settings that specify size, distance, and spacing. It doesn't affect the actual dimension text value. If your final scale factor is $\frac{1}{4}$ inch = 1 foot, your dimscale factor will likely be 48, and AutoCAD multiplies your dimension settings by 48. Then, when it is time to plot and you've specified your drawing scale factor ($\frac{1}{4}$ inch = 1 foot), AutoCAD scales your drawing back down by 48, and you get the desired size. This value is stored in the dimscale variable.

Scale dimensions to layout (paperspace)   If you plan on using Paper Space layouts for your drawings, you'll probably want to select this option. Selecting this option sets dimscale to 0. AutoCAD then uses the scale factor of the current viewport to determine the scale factor. If you're in a viewport that has been set to $\frac{1}{2}$ inch = 1 foot (or 24XP), AutoCAD multiplies all your settings by 24, thus ensuring you get the correct size, distance, and spacing for your dimensions. This allows you to set the dimscale factor once and let AutoCAD determine the proper value for you.

This is, of course, if you are in the Model Space viewport when you place the dimensions (my personal view of the way it should be done).

Many of you place your dimensions on your drawing while you're in Paper Space (`tilemode` set to 1). When you choose to take this route, AutoCAD uses the default scale factor of 1.0 for the `dimscale` system variable.

Fine Tuning

The last section in the Fit tab falls into the miscellaneous category.

Place text manually when dimensioning   When you place dimensions on your drawing, you can have the text automatically fall in the default position, or you can choose to manually position it. This option sets `dimupt` (user-positioned text) on and allows you to determine the text placement while you're creating the dimensions. All horizontal justification settings are ignored.

Always draw dim line between ext lines   This forces a dimension line to be drawn between the measured points even when the arrowheads are placed outside. This option turns `dimtofl` (text outside force line) on. With radial and diameter dimensions, this option draws a dimension line inside the arc or circle and places the text, arrowheads, and leader outside (when `dimtix` is off).

When working with Radius and Diameter dimensions and `dimtix` is set off, a dimension line is drawn inside the circle or arc and the text, arrowheads, and leader are placed outside.

Tab 4: Primary Units

This tab focuses on the format and precision for your primary dimension units (as opposed to your alternate units). It's broken into two major groups: Linear Dimensions and Angular Dimensions (Figure 18.8).

Linear Dimensions

Unit format   Just as you set your units for your drawing, you'll need to set your units for your dimensions. You have the same options available here as you do for your drawing units with the exception of an additional "Windows Desktop" option. Most users set the two the same, but there are some occasions when the units need to be set differently (`dimlunit` variable). If you choose an option with fractions, the relative size of the numbers in the stacked fractions is based on the `dimtfac` variable.

Precision   After selecting a system of units for your dimensions, you'll want to determine the degree of accuracy you want AutoCAD to display in your dimensions. This value is stored in the `dimdec` system variable.

Fraction format If you choose a format that uses fractions, you'll want to indicate how you want those fractions displayed. You can choose between Diagonal, Horizontal, and Not Stacked. Diagonal and Horizontal place the numerator and denominator above and below the separator line, whereas Not Stacked places the numerator and denominator side by side with a diagonal separator between them. This setting is stored in the `dimfrac` variable.

Decimal separator If you choose a format that uses decimals, you have three separator options: a period, a comma, or a simple space. This value is stored in the `dimdsep` variable.

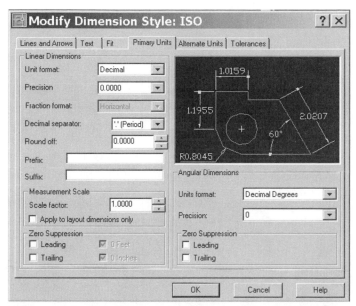

Figure 18.8 Use the Primary Units tab to specify the system of units for linear and angular dimensions.

Round off If you want AutoCAD to round off your dimension measurements, enter a Round off value. This affects all dimensions except Angular. A value of .5, rounds all distances to the nearest 0.5 unit. A value of 1, rounds all dimensions to the nearest whole number or integer. When fudging is legal in the office, this helps avoid the 1.9999 values by rounding to 2.0000 (if your precision is set to four places). This value is stored in the `dimrnd` variable.

Prefix If you want to add a prefix to the beginning of your dimension text, you can enter the prefix here. In addition to text, you also can use control codes to display certain characters. For example, `%%c` displays the Center diameter symbol.

You also can grab characters from Character Map by copying them to the clipboard and pasting them into the Prefix box (which is a pretty cool trick). If you add tolerances to your dimensions, the Prefix value is added to the tolerances and the main dimension. This value is stored in the `dimpost` variable.

Suffix This option adds text or special characters to the end of your dimension text. Suffix works much the same way as Prefix. If you are working in metric units, you'll probably set your units to decimal and add the appropriate suffix to your dimension text (mm, cm, m, and so forth); the suffix is added to tolerance values as well. The `dimpost` variable also stores the Suffix setting. To manually set Prefix and Suffix using `dimpost`, use the angle brackets (<>) to indicate the placement of the dimension text. For example, if you set a mm suffix, `dimpost` is as follows.

```
<>mm
```

If you want the Circle diameter symbol used as a prefix, set `dimpost` as follows.

`%%c<>`

If you need both a prefix and a suffix (using the above characters), it would look like this.

`%%c<>mm`

Measurement Scale

Scale factors can get confusing, especially when you wander into the world of dimensioning. The Fit tab has options for setting the `dimscale` factor. This factor affects the size of the dimensions, the arrowheads, the spaces, the dimension text, and so forth. However, `dimscale` does not change the dimension text in any way. The first option affects the dimension text value.

Scale factor   Setting this scale factor multiplies the dimension value by the factor entered here. Hence, if you key in 48 and the dimension measurement is 1, the dimension text reads 48. This setting came out early on, before anyone knew anything about the Paper Space world. Plus, so many AutoCAD users were fresh off the drafting table back then that they had a hard time adjusting to drawing 1:1 on a CAD system because they'd been scaling down for years. This option allowed them to draft as they always had, scaling down as they went so they could still plot at 1:1. Of course, they ran into serious problems when it came to dimensioning because the values came out wrong. For example, if you use a scale factor of $\frac{1}{2}$ inch = 1 foot, you can set `dimlfac` (the Linear Scale factor) to 24, and — abracadabra — the dimensions are correct. You can also use the `dimlfac` variable to convert metric drawings to imperial and vice versa. This setting only affects linear dimensions.

Apply to layout dimensions only   When this option is set, the linear scale factor affects only those dimensions created in Paper Space — it doesn't affect the Model Space dimensions at all — and `dimlfac` becomes negative. A value of `-2` means any dimensions drawn in a Paper Space layout is multiplied by two. The Help file is completely misleading here, so do yourself a favor and ignore it.

Zero Suppression

If you're using units that contain a decimal point, do you want trailing zeros (1.0000) or not (1)? Do you want leading zeros (0.5) or not (.5)? If you're using architectural units, do you want trailing inches (5'0") or not (5')? Do you want leading feet (0'6") or not (6")? The Zero Suppression options allow you to select the boxes that apply to your current dimensioning needs. This value is saved to the `dimzin` value. If you're an AutoLISPer, this setting also affects `rtos` (real to string).

Angular Dimensions

The previous settings affected linear dimensions only; the following options affect angular dimensions only.

Units format   Use this option to set the angular units for dimensioning (similar to the `units` command for setting the drawing units). This value is stored in the `dimaunit` variable.

Precision   Just as you can with the linear dimensions, you can control the precision for your angular dimensions. This value is stored in the dimadec variable.

Zero Suppression   Do you want 60.00 degrees or 60? Do you want 0.5 degrees or .5? Just as with the linear dimensions, select the setting that works for you. This value is stored in dimazin and also affects the AutoLISP function angtos (angle to string).

Tab 5: Alternate Units

Use Alternate Units whenever you need to display more than one numeric system of unit for your dimension values. The obvious scenario for this comes into play with global accounts, in which you might need to use imperial units for the United States and metric units for the rest of the world. Until the U.S. decides it's easier to divide by 10 than by 12, you're faced with the need to dimension in more than one format. (I admit it; my mathematics major is shining through here.) The settings in the Alternate Units tab are similar to those in the Units tab.

To turn on Alternate Units, simply select the Display Alternate Units option in the upper left-hand corner of the dialog (Figure 18.9). This also sets the dimalt dimension variable to 1. Alternate units do not affect angular dimensions.

The remainder of the Alternate Units tab is broken up into three sections: Alternate Units, Zero Suppression, and Placement. The Alternate Units section deals specifically with the units format. The Unit format drop-down list indicates the system of units in which you want the secondary units to display. This value is stored in the dimaltu dimension variable. (Should you choose a format that uses stacked fractions, the relative size of the numeric values are based on dimtfac, which is also used for tolerances).

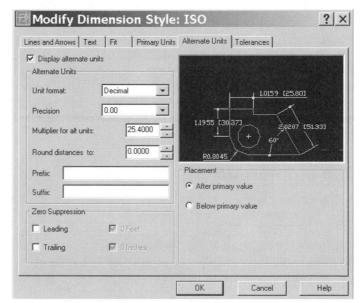

Figure 18.9 Choose between imperial and metric in the Alternate Units tab in the Modify Dimension Style dialog box.

The Precision option determines the displayed accuracy of the alternate units. This value is stored in the dimaltd dimension variable.

The Multiplier for alt units option is obviously the key to accurate alternate unit measure. The default for metric conversion, 25.4, is displayed. This is the value AutoCAD uses to multiply all nonangular dimension values. This value is not applied to rounding values or the plus/minus tolerance values. It is stored in the dimaltf dimension variable.

You can round off your alternate units value by setting the Round distances to option. If set to 1, all alternate values are rounded off to the nearest integer. If set to .25, they are rounded off to the nearest 0.25 value, and so on. Remember, however, that the precision setting still controls the number of digits displayed (although you might just end up with a bunch of trailing zeros). The alternate rounding value is stored in the dimaltrnd dimension variable.

The Prefix and Suffix settings work the same as those set in the Units tab. If your alternate units are in centimeters, select cm as your suffix; if millimeters, mm; and so forth. You can also use control codes here. Both values are stored in the dimapost dimension variable.

If you need to set dimapost manually back to a null value through a program or script file, you can do so by setting dimapost to a period ("."). This indicates to AutoCAD that you no longer want a suffix or prefix added to your alternate units.

The Zero Suppression options for alternate units follow the same rules as those set in the Units tab. Here, you have control over leading and trailing zero values (dimaltz dimension variable).

You can have alternate units placed after or underneath the Primary value, whichever works best for your office standards. This option is controlled in the Placement section of the dialog.

Keep in mind that the Help file indicates that placement of alternate units is controlled by the dimapost dimension variable. This is so not true (insert Southern California accent here)! It is controlled by the dimpost dimension variable. It took me a good 30 minutes to unravel this mystery, and I don't want you to fall prey to the same misinformation. You'll find that if you indicate that you want the alternate units placed beneath your primary units, the dimpost variable magically changes to /X. I couldn't find this information referenced anywhere in standard Help and it wasn't for lack of trying.

Tab 6: Tolerances

Many of you need tolerances or limits appended to your dimension text. The final tab in the dialog box, Tolerances (Figure 18.10), is dedicated to you. Four types of Tolerance settings are supported by AutoCAD: Symmetrical, Deviation, Limits, and Basic (Figure 18.11).

Symmetrical Tolerances (dimtol **set to 1)**   Simply add a single plus/minus value of variation to the dimension measurement in the Upper value section of the dialog. The plus and minus values are obviously the same.

Deviation tolerances (dimtol **also set to** 1**)**   This situation occurs when you have different upper and lower tolerance values. The values are set in the Upper and Lower value sections of this dialog.

Limits (dimlim **set to** 1**)**   When Limits is selected, the maximum and minimum values display as the dimension text. The maximum value is the dimension value plus the upper value; the minimum value is the dimension value minus the lower value.

Basic Basic dimensioning simply draws a box around the dimension text. The `dimgap` dimension variable stores the distance between the dimension text and the box. When you select Basic dimensioning, `dimgap` becomes a negative value.

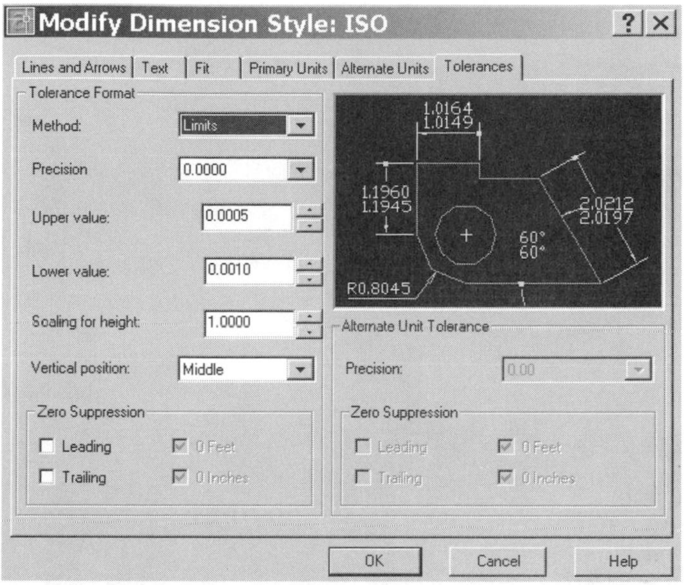

After indicating your choice of Tolerance method, you need to select the precision at which tolerances display (`dimtdec`), along with the upper and lower tolerance values (`dimtp`, `dimtm`). You'll also want to set the text height for the tolerance text. The Scaling for height value is a ratio of the tolerance height to the primary dimension text height (stored in the `dimtfac` dimension variable).

If you choose symmetrical or deviation tolerance methods, you also have the option of controlling the Vertical position of the tolerance text. You have three choices: Top, Middle, and Bottom. Top aligns the tolerance text to the top of the main dimension text (`dimtolj` set to 2). Middle centers the tolerance text and aligns it with the middle of the main dimension text (`dimtolj` set to 1). Bottom aligns the tolerance text to the bottom of the main dimension text (`dimtolj` set to 0).

Zero Suppression appears in this dialog as well. You need to define the leading and trailing zeros for your tolerances and limits (`dimtzin` dimension variable) just as you did for your various units settings.

You can further complicate matters by adding tolerance values to your alternate units. Setting the precision for alternate unit tolerances is saved to the `dimalttd` dimension variable. And, of course, Zero Suppression amazingly shows up in this section as well (`dimttz`).

That's it for dimensioning; I hope this clears up any of your questions about the Ddim dialog box!

Figure 18.10 The Tolerances tab in the Modify Dimension Style dialog box lets you apply limits to your dimension text.

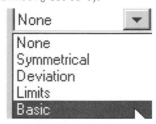

Figure 18.11 The four types of tolerance settings.

CHAPTER 19

Cool Tricks in AutoCAD

I've been using AutoCAD for more than 15 years (I started when I was 10), and over the course of upgrades and revisions, I've stumbled across many an obscure feature, shortcut, and so forth. I'm going to cover a few of these features, most of which you should be able to use in Release 14, AutoCAD 2000 through 2002, and even AutoCAD LT. Some of these functions you already know, but I'll be happy if you finish this chapter with one good nugget of information that makes your daily AutoCAD life just a little bit better. I'm going to dabble in a little bit of everything, with little or no rhyme or reason, so hold on!

Cool Trick #1: The Power of the Age-Old change Command

I'm sure most of you have thrown the antiquated change command by the wayside now that more powerful commands such as properties have come along. However, the plain old change command can do something no other command can do — and in very few steps. Have you ever needed to extend a series of parallel lines to a specific point on the screen? You can use the extend command if you have a boundary edge, and even then you have to select and extend each object one at a time. The change command allows you to extend without a boundary.

Draw four or more parallel lines on the screen, as shown in Figure 19.1. The goal is to extend those lines to a specific point in as few steps as possible.

```
Command: change
Select objects: Specify opposite corner: 5 found
Select objects: <Enter>
Specify change point or [Properties]:
then pick a point on the screen.
```

If Ortho mode is on, the lines will extend orthogonally (which is more than likely what you want, see Figure 19.2). If Ortho is off, all the lines will replace their endpoints with the new point, and they will all converge to the same point (Figure 19.3).

Cool Trick #2: A Hidden Option in the array **Command**

By default, to create a polar array you need to know three things: the center point of the array, the number of items in the array, and the angle to fill. Well, what if you don't know the total number of items in the array, but you do know the angle between the items? Hidden within the polar array command is an additional option that only pops up if you know the secret passageway! I'll use the command-line interface of the array command by putting a dash in front of the command name.

Command: -array

Select objects: Specify opposite corner: 1 found

Select objects: Enter the type of array
    [Rectangular/Polar] <R>: p

Specify center point of array:

Enter the number of items in the array:

OK, stop right here; this is where the trick lies. Do not answer this question. Instead, simply hit <Enter>, and AutoCAD will ask you an additional question down the line.

Specify the angle to fill (+=ccw, -=cw) <360>:

Angle between items:

Look! The extra question! The angle between items! Feel free to input any angle you want.

Rotate arrayed objects? [Yes/No] <Y>:

It's a very simple hidden trick, but a very cool one.

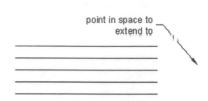

Figure 19.1 Draw parallel lines to illustrate the features of the change **command.**

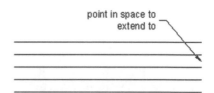

Figure 19.2 When Ortho is on, the lines extend orthogonally to the designated point.

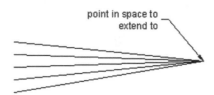

Figure 19.3 When Ortho is off, the lines converge on the selected point.

Cool Trick #3: Easily Select Objects That Are Too Close Together

If you spend time working on drawings in which all the objects are jam-packed together, you've certainly run into the problem of selecting the correct object when editing. A couple of releases ago, AutoCAD was given a cool, simple means of controlling which object is selected. The magical <Ctrl> key unlocks the door to this trick.

Draw several lines that cross, as in Figure 19.4. You want to erase one of the lines, and you're going to do so by selecting right at the point where they all intersect (crazy, huh?).

Enter the erase command, and hold down the <Ctrl> key as you pick the intersection point. This turns on Object cycling. Now, simply pick anywhere on the screen and watch as AutoCAD cycles through all of the objects that lay beneath the original pick point, as shown in the following syntax.

```
Command: ERASE
Select objects: <Cycle on>
<Cycle off>1 found
Select objects:
```

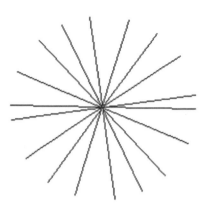

Cool Trick #4: Make Sure the Open Dialog Searches Your Drawings Directory

Figure 19.4 Draw a series of lines that cross at the center to illustrate object cycling.

I know that many of you have already sorted this out, but because I receive so many e-mails about it, I thought I'd throw it into the stack. To perform this operation you'll need to minimize everything so you can clearly see your desktop. (Hint: you can instantly minimize all windows by hitting the <Windows key–M>.)

Right-click on the AutoCAD shortcut, and a menu appears. Pick the Properties option (at the very bottom) of the menu, and you'll see the dialog box shown in Figure 19.5. Now go to the Shortcut tab and the box that says Start in. Enter the directory of your drawing files. Now whenever you use your shortcut to start AutoCAD, the Open dialog (and other file dialogs) will go straight to your drawings directory.

Note In AutoCAD 2002, to make sure AutoCAD uses the Start in section, you need to set rememberfolders to 0 (see Chapter 22, Cool System Variables (aka setvars), for more information).

Cool Trick #5: Controlling the Default Profile Setting (and Other Switches)

While you're setting up your shortcut, you also can add the instructions to load a specific profile setting (profiles store environment settings such as installed plotters, search paths, and object sorting methods). This trick is extremely useful for those of you who share AutoCAD workstations It starts in the Target section of the Shortcut tab (Figure 19.5) by adding a switch to the command line. The switch for Profile is /p.

The following syntax loads a Profile named after my infamous dog, Alex.

```
C:\Program files\\acad2002\acad.exe /p Alex
```

If you use spaces in a profile name, you must surround the name in quotation marks when you use the /p switch.

```
C:\Program files\acad2002\acad.exe /p "Alex the
   dog"
```

Other cool switches, such as /nologo, enable you to save a few moments of your precious time by not displaying the Autodesk logo while booting up AutoCAD; /b invokes a script file, /t loads a specific template file, /v displays a specific view, and there are others (look them up in the Help file under "Using Command Line Switches").

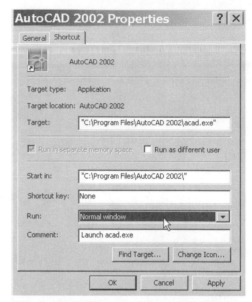

Figure 19.5 Be sure AutoCAD opens to your drawing directory by setting it in the Shortcut tab of the Properties dialog.

Cool Trick #6: Creating New Layers at Lightning Speed

Much time is spent negotiating through layers, and I want to make sure you know this nice little trick to create many layers, complete with their appropriate names, ever so quickly.

Enter the Layer dialog box and hit the New button. Key in the name of the layer you want to create, followed by a comma. As soon as you hit the comma key, AutoCAD automatically jumps down to the next line, ready for another new layer name. Veteran users of AutoCAD know this trick because they always used comma separators for layer names in the command-line interface of the layer command. It's not intuitively obvious for new users, but now you know!

Cool Trick #7: Seeing the Scale Factor or Rotation Angle of a Block Before You Pick the Insertion Point

How many times have you wanted to change your insertion parameters (rotation angle or scale factor) before you picked the insertion point? If you've ever had to move a block after the fact because you had a hard time negotiating the size or rotation, you can relate. Those of you in AutoCAD 2000+ will finally see those hidden options that only a few die-hard users knew about in Release 14 and before. Because many of you are still in Release 14, I'll show you these hidden options. First look at the insert command in AutoCAD 2002.

```
Command: Insert
Specify insertion point or [Scale/X/Y/Z/Rotate/PScale/PX/PY/PZ/ PRotate]:
```

All of these options exist in Releases 12 through 14 (and LT), but you just have to know when and where to key them in. Look at the `insert` command in Release 14.

```
Command: insert
Insertion point: S
Scale factor: .5
Insertion point: R
Rotation angle: 30
Insertion point:
```

When prompted for the Insertion point, key in the option you want. The following list explains many of the options available to you.

- Scale controls the X and Y scale factors.

- X controls just the X scale factor,

- Y controls just the Y scale factor, and

- Z controls just the Z scale factor for the block.

- Rotate controls the rotation angle for the block.

- PScale lets you enter a scale factor and then prompts for it again after selecting an insertion point (too much redundancy for me).

- PX does the same as PScale when you enter just the X scale factor (and prompts for it again).

I think you can figure out the rest of the options; I only use the first five.

Cool Trick #8: Groups

A rarely used method of object selection is the concept of groups. Similar to the block mind-set comes this ability to link objects together to form a group, which is a named group of objects that can be called on whenever needed. The members of these groups can be selected individually or as a team. You select unnamed groups of objects via windows, fences, and the like all the time. Now you have the added capability of applying a name to these objects. Group definitions are stored within the drawing and follow externally referenced drawings as well.

Although there is a command-line interface for the `group` command (`-group`), I'll create groups via a dialog box, as shown in Figure 19.6. The `group` command was designed with third-party developers in mind, but I'll find ways to use this feature to my advantage. Create a drawing with several circles and several rectangles. I'll use these objects to formulate my groups.

Enter the `group` command by keying it in (it's not to be found in any toolbars or pull-down menus). Begin by assigning a group name. Group names can be up to 31 characters in length and must follow all the assorted AutoCAD naming conventions. Do yourself a favor and keep the group names short. You can add an optional description of your group if you desire (for future reference). Under the Create Group options, pick New. The dialog box vanishes, and you can select the objects you want included within the group using the usual object selection techniques.

Try creating a group called Cir that includes all your circles and a group called Box that includes all your rectangles. Both these groups will display in the Group dialog box. Both groups are selectable.

Enter an edit command (move, copy, erase, and so on) and when prompted to select objects, key in g (for group). AutoCAD asks you for the group name — enter cir. All the members of the Cir group will highlight.

```
Command: ERASE
Select objects: G
Enter Group name: CIR
```

Also notice that if you pick one of the members of a group, all the group members are selected. If you want to individually select the members of a group, toggle Group mode off. <Shift-Ctrl-A>, which can be entered anywhere toggles Group mode on and off.

Under Group Identification, you'll see Find Name. This button removes the Group dialog box temporarily from the screen and lets you select an object.

Figure 19.6 The Object Grouping dialog box has several options for working with groups.

The Group Name display is convenient when you can't remember which group an object is a member of. Similar to this option is Highlight. When selected, AutoCAD highlights the members of the group selected in the Group Name list box.

Should you copy a group, the resulting copied objects also belong to a group. The new group has a randomly generated name that doesn't display in the Group Name list box. To display this new group's name, select the Include Unnamed toggle.

There are two toggles under the Create Group section of the Object Grouping dialog box: Selectable and Unnamed. As before, you can create a group with no name (actually it's a randomly generated name). This group doesn't display unless the Include Unnamed toggle is selected.

If a group is selectable, all of the objects within the group are treated as one group. When you select one member of the group, all are highlighted. An unselectable group doesn't have any group qualities at all. This option was generated with the third-party applications in mind. Through LISP and ADS, groups could be selectable one minute and unselectable the next, which would keep any groups made by these external programs from getting in your way. I am unaware of any reason you'd generate Unselectable groups.

After creating your groups, you may want to modify them. The Change Group section of the Object Grouping dialog box contains options to modify existing groups:

Remove   deletes one or more objects from the current group.

Add   adds one or more objects to the current group.

Rename   changes the name of an existing group.

Description   changes the group description.

Explode   deletes an entire group (an important one to know).

Selectable   changes the selectable status of an existing group.

Re-order   changes the order of objects within an existing group. In some applications, order is very important (e.g., tooling paths). This last option takes you to a subdialog box (Figure 19.7) that is only useful in very specific applications, so I won't spend much time on it. Essentially, you select the objects and assign those objects to a position.

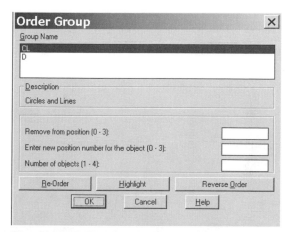

Figure 19.7 The Order Group dialog box is used rarely.

What happens when an object is a member of more than one group? Create a group called Boxcir with one rectangle and one circle (be sure your group toggle is off, or you'll never be able to select just one circle or rectangle).

Toggle Group mode back on <Ctrl-A> and enter an editing command. Select an object that is a member of two groups. Can you see how both groups are selected? If you would like to toggle between the two groups, use the object cycling I discussed previously. Select one of the members of the group while holding down <Ctrl>.

Cool Trick #9: lengthen

There's another nice editing command called lengthen. This command takes much of the guesswork out of simple length modifications. For example, you have a 4-$^3/_8$–inch line that you want to be five inches long. How do you scale or stretch it quickly to the correct length? The lengthen command changes the angle of arcs and the lengths of most open entities.

Command: LENGTHEN (Modify pull-down)

DElta/Percent/Total/DYnamic /<Select object>: pick an existing line

Current length: 5.4003

DElta/Percent/Total/DYnamic /<Select object>:T

Angle/<Enter total length (1.0000)>: 6

<Select object to change>/ Undo:

Select object   provides the current length/included angle of a selected object.

Delta   increases or decreases the selected objects by a specified increment. When dealing with arcs, you can suggest a delta angle. Positive values increase the length of selected objects; negative values decrease the length. The object is lengthened or shortened from the endpoint nearest the pick point on the object. If you specified a delta angle of 45 degrees, any arc selected would increase in size by an arc of 45 degrees.

Percent   uses a specified percentage of an object's total length to increase or decrease the selected objects. If you specified 50 percent, the length of the selected objects would be cut in half.

Total   is the total length you'd like an object to have, and AutoCAD calculates how much to trim or extend the object to get the desired results. Any modifications occur from the nearest endpoint.

Dynamic   visually changes the length of an object by moving the nearest endpoint.

The key to the lengthen command is to ensure that you pick the objects to lengthen toward the end you want to affect.

Cool Trick #10: Automatic Dimensioning

I am still amazed at the number of AutoCAD users who work much harder than necessary when it comes to dimensioning. Do you always manually select the two endpoints of extension lines? If so, you're working too hard. When dimensioning to the endpoints of lines, AutoCAD can do the job much faster than you can, so put it to work! I'll use the dimlinear command as an example.

```
Command: DIMLINEAR
First extension line origin or hit Enter to select: <Enter>
Select object to dimension:
```

After hitting <Enter>, a pickbox appears and you simply select the part you want to dimension. AutoCAD finds the two endpoints of the object you selected; no object snaps are required!

Cool Trick #11: The Displacement Option in the copy and move Commands

If you want to move an object in your drawing over three units to the right, how would you do it? Chances are good you'd use the move command, and chances are even better you'd take an extra step to do it. Have you ever taken advantage of the Displacement option in the copy and move commands? After all, Displacement is the default. Most of you would move an object over three units using the following method.

```
Command: MOVE
Select objects: 1 found
```

```
Select objects:
Base point or displacement: pick a base point
Second point of displacement:@3,0
```

You're taking an unnecessary step (plus that @ symbol is a pain). Try this option instead.

```
Command: MOVE
Select objects: 1 found
Select objects:
Base point or displacement: 3,0
Second point of displacement: <Enter>
```

Notice the prompt reads `Base point or displacement`. Displacement is the default, but most users seem to select a base point. Perhaps if the command read `Base point or <displacement>`, it would be more obvious. The trick is to hit an extra <Enter> when prompted for a second point, which tells AutoCAD to use the `3,0` (3 on the X-axis, 0 on the Y-axis) as a displacement value.

Cool Trick #12: Removing Objects from a Selection Set

What if you wanted to select all of the objects in a particular area except for one? Would you create a couple of windows and avoid that one object? Would you pick all of the objects individually? Or would you select all of the objects quickly and easily with a window and remove the one object you didn't want to include? I vote for the last method. Objects used to be removed by using the R notation to jump into the Remove Objects mode. Now, it's a piece of cake with the <Shift> key. Holding down the <Shift> key while selecting objects removes them from the selection set.

Cool Trick #13: Intersecting with `appint`

The Apparent Intersection (`appint`) object snap was sent from the 3D gods to help you grab visual intersections. Imagine you're looking at your drawing from a viewing angle where two entities look as though they cross, but in 3D reality, they don't. With the standard Intersection (`int`) osnap you could never grab the apparent intersection of the two entities. If those two entities didn't really cross, you were out of luck. If two entities appear to intersect in your current viewing plane, `appint` finds a way to grab this intersection.

Unlike the object snap modes of the past, `appint` also permits picking two entities rather than one. Say you want to draw a line from the intersection where two entities apparently intersect. The two entities beneath were drawn on two different UCSs, and you can see a visual intersection from your viewing angle, but they don't physically intersect in space. Proceed as follows when prompted for a startpoint of your line.

```
Command: LINE
From point: APPINT
of pick1 (pick the visual intersection)
```

You could also have AutoCAD find the apparent intersection by picking the entities one at a time.

Command: LINE

From point: APPINT

of pick1 (pick one of the entities)

pick2 (pick the other entity)

The final pick point is determined by the following very important rules.

1. The point returned lies on the apparent intersection of the first entity selected.

2. If more than one apparent intersection is possible, AutoCAD picks the intersection closest to the two selection points.

3. When picking two entities simultaneously, the point will lie on the last entity drawn. Selecting the entities individually permits you to have more control over the final pick point.

The intersection object snap is more intelligent than most realize, as well. Go back to 2D thinking. Have you ever wished AutoCAD was smart enough to mentally extend two entities until they meet and grab this imagined intersection? You don't want these two entities physically extended, but you do want the point of intended intersection. Welcome to the improved Intersection object snap. From now on, I'll refer to this as an extended intersection. Simply select the objects individually (not on an intersection) and AutoCAD finds the extended intersection for you.

Cool Trick #14: Did You Know ...?

* Did you know you can use the <Shift> key to get more than one hot grip?

* Did you know you can use the <Ctrl> key to prevent the docking of toolbars?

* Did you know that when you combine the <Ctrl> key with your mouse wheel you get the feeling you're cruising around in your drawing? (Try it, it's very odd!)

* Did you know you can hit <Ctrl-Tab> to page through all your open drawings and <Ctrl-Shift-Tab> to page backward through your open drawings?

* Did you know you can use the <Tab> key to toggle through the different object snap modes?

* Did you know that using the @ symbol, all by itself, will grab the last point?

These are just a few of the cool AutoCAD tricks I've collected over the years. I hope you were able to find something here you didn't already know.

CHAPTER 20

Excellent Changes to Everyday Commands in AutoCAD 2002

Show me a feature that removes one tedious click from my life, and I'll give you a round of applause! In this chapter, I'll focus on some of these little — but oh so cool — features in AutoCAD 2002.

Note Some of these tools might seem familiar because many originated as awesome Express Tools and morphed their way into core AutoCAD.

trim **and** extend **Commands Combined**

Do you find yourself flipping back and forth between the trim and extend commands while editing your drawings? That annoying nuisance is behind you now because you can extend while you're in the trim command (and vice versa). The <Shift> key is the magical secret to flipping from one command to the other. Take a look at the new extend command.

```
Command: EXTEND
Current settings: Projection=UCS, Edge=None
Select boundary edges ...
Select objects: 1 found
Select objects: <Enter>
Select object to extend or shift-select to trim or [Project/Edge/Undo]:
```

Do you see the reference to shift-select? Holding down the <Shift> key switches to Trim mode, and while in the `trim` command, holding down the <Shift> key switches to Extend mode. For you Express Tools fans, this is similar to the tron function.

Smarter `fillet` and `chamfer` Commands

When you wander into the `fillet` command and set your radius —poof! — AutoCAD returns you to the command prompt, as if the only thing you had in mind was setting your radius. I'm guessing your ultimate goal was to `fillet` something. Right? In one of the new (but tiny) improvements to the `fillet` command, AutoCAD leaves you to proceed as planned (the same applies to the `chamfer` command). Have you ever tried to `fillet` between two polylines? It sounds simple enough, but AutoCAD refuses to do the dirty deed. You end up exploding one of the polylines (an icky extra step in your drawing life) to satisfy the strict `fillet` criteria. Release 2002 is more than up to the task and has no problem `filleting` (or `chamfering`) between the two polylines. One feature I really liked in the Express Tools `exfillet` command was the ability to do multiple `fillet`s. The new command still restricts you to one `fillet` before returning you to the command prompt.

Enhancements to the `pedit` Command

You have five polylines in your drawing that need a larger width factor, and you find yourself entering the `pedit` command five times to complete that task. Or perhaps you'd like to join two or more polylines together, but they don't meet perfectly at the endpoints (they're not contiguous). Forget it, right? Instead, you end up filleting them together with a zero radius (or something creative like that) to ensure they play according to the `pedit` rules.

The new, updated `pedit` command in AutoCAD 2002 is much more easygoing. If you want to edit multiple polylines at once, no problem. Those polylines don't quite meet perfectly at the endpoints? The new `pedit` lets it slide if so desired.

```
Command: PEDIT
Select polyline or [Multiple]: m
Select objects: Specify
opposite corner: 12 found
Select objects:
Convert Lines and Arcs to
polylines [Yes/No]? <Y>
```

Is this last question really necessary? I'm in the polyline editing command; hence, you would expect I need to be working with polylines. Right? The amusing thing is that if I say "No," I'm not allowed to proceed with the command.

Let me set up a joining scenario. Say you have a badly drawn polyline that obviously doesn't meet at the corners (Figure 20.1). I can join them using the new `pedit` command, but I need to specify two pieces of information: Fuzz Distance and Jointype.

Fuzz distance is the maximum distance you'll permit AutoCAD to accept when connecting endpoints. You don't want AutoCAD joining endpoints that aren't even in the same general vicinity. You can key in a Fuzz distance or you can manually show it (I prefer the latter).

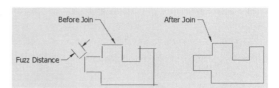

Figure 20.1 The pedit **command now lets you join polylines that are not contiguous.**

There are three possible Jointype values: Extend, Add, or Both. The default Extend option joins the selected polylines by extending or trimming the segments to the nearest endpoints, whichever is appropriate. The Add option adds a straight segment between the nearest endpoints before joining. The Both option extends where it's possible and adds as a backup. For example, if you have two plines that are nearly parallel, the Extend option might extend out to some point in space, yielding undesirable results. The Add option simply adds a segment to join them.

```
Enter an option
[Close/Open/Join/Width/Fit/Spline/Decurve/Ltype gen/Undo]: j
Join Type = Extend
Enter fuzz distance or [Jointype] <0.0000>: Specify second point:
11 segments added to polyline
```

After selecting the Fuzz distance and Jointype, AutoCAD works its magic and joins the polylines together into one polyline. The very powerful Express Tools pljoin and mpedit were the prototypes for these two additions.

closeall

When you first started using AutoCAD 2000, did you find yourself faced with countless open drawings at the end of the day? Pre-MDI life taught me that AutoCAD would close one drawing before opening another. It took a while to remember that MDI permits you to open multiple drawings at one time (which, incidentally, was the number-one wish list request going into AutoCAD 2000). The new closeall command carefully closes all your drawings at once, prompting you to save when needed.

One <Esc> to Clear Grips

Do you always find yourself hitting the <Esc> key multiple times to get rid of those blue boxes? Now it only takes a single escape to rid yourself of grips. (Now what will you do for exercise?)

properties **Command Updated**

The properties command was a pleasant new addition to AutoCAD 2000, but it was missing one key element: the ability to use the traditional Select Objects prompt. Now you can use your favorite selection set options such as Fence, Previous, Last, Crossing Polygon, Window Polygon, and so on. AutoCAD 2002 also added an interesting feature that uses the old pickadd variable, which was added for quick and effective object editing. When pickadd is on (1), you can edit one group of objects within the Properties dialog, and when you select a second group of objects, the first group is automatically deselected for you, thus eliminating one tedious step. A word of caution, however; be sure to turn pickadd back off (0) before leaving the dialog, or you'll find this same functionality following you through all editing commands. For example, if pickadd is set to 1 and you individually select three objects to delete in the erase command, guess what happens? Only the last object selected is erased.

The last improvement in the Properties dialog is that Quick Select is finally Quick! Quick Select is a great, low-stress filtering tool, but on large drawings it could take a lifetime to pull up on the screen. You won't run into this problem anymore; it has been tightened up nicely! Figure 20.2 shows the three icons in the properties command just mentioned.

Figure 20.2 The upper right-hand corner of the Properties dialog contains two new options.

Double-Click to Edit Objects

It takes one command to edit text, a different one to edit dimension text, and a completely different one to edit attribute text. Who can possibly remember all the different editing commands for all the different types of objects? I personally made a plea to the Express Tools gang to create a low-stress function that lets me double-click on an object and AutoCAD automatically uses the proper editing command. It started as an Express Tool and worked its way up to a real, live AutoCAD feature (I'll avoid any reference to Pinnochio at this juncture). It's simple. You just double-click on the object you need to edit, and AutoCAD displays the editing command that corresponds to it. Double-click on text, you get ddedit; on an attribute, ddatte; on a block, refedit (great for editing block definitions); and so on. Now you can spend those brain cells remembering other important things (like your anniversary).

Drawing File Access

Now more than four previous drawing files can be displayed in the File pull-down menu (Figure 20.3). This option is controlled in the Options dialog box under the Open and Save tabs. You can set the value as high as nine. (Does anyone else think nine is an unusual limit?) You also can tell AutoCAD you want to view the full path name in the title at the top of the screen, which is especially useful if you use duplicate drawing names but keep them in different directories. This option also is in the Open and Save tabs in the Options dialog.

Speed, Speed, Speed

On any AutoCAD release, speed is of the utmost importance. New features are great, but not if they come at the expense of a slower overall program. It seems as though AutoCAD can never go quite fast enough to make my dreams come true, but I'm happy to report that AutoCAD 2002 is definitely faster than 2000. If you have vast amounts of text using TrueType fonts in your drawings, you'll be delighted to know that the algorithm behind them has been improved dramatically. Those of you who model with 3D solids will find yourself moving faster as well. Are you tired of regenerating between layout tabs? Have you ever gone to the Status Bar but accidentally hit a layout tab instead and chastised yourself while you waited for the drawing to regenerate? Well, you won't be regenerating anymore. After an initial regeneration to cache the display, you'll notice that tab switching is virtually painless! Of course, if you get paid by the hour, you might not want to upgrade.

New...	Ctrl+N
Open...	Ctrl+O
Close	
Partial Load	
Save	Ctrl+S
Save As...	
eTransmit...	
Publish to Web...	
Export...	
Page Setup...	
Plotter Manager...	
Plot Style Manager...	
Plot Preview	
Plot...	Ctrl+P
Drawing Utilities	▶
Send...	
Drawing Properties...	
1 pljoin.dwg	
2 1st floor architectural.dwg	
3 1st floor furniture.dwg	
4 1st floor electrical.dwg	
5 1st floor lighting.dwg	
6 3Dorbit.dwg	
7 Plate.dwg	
8 layout2000i.dwg	

Figure 20.3 You can list more than four previous drawing files in the File pull-down menu.

CHAPTER 21

Splines and Ellipses

The nurbs-based curves introduced several releases ago were a welcome addition. No more make-shift ellipses or splines — now you can have the real thing. The ellipses and splines of previous AutoCAD versions were merely approximations, comprised of polyline and polyarc segments. Manipulating the segments or grabbing key geometric points was difficult. Now AutoCAD incorporates nurbs mathematics and algorithms into its functionality to generate true ellipses and splines. These ellipses and splines also use less disk space and memory than the polylines of previous releases.

Nurbs stands for nonuniform rational basis splines (simply called B-splines). The nonuniform nature of the splines permits the uneven spacing of knots, should you need to create a sharp curve. The rational basis permits regular geometry, such as arcs and ellipses, to be combined with the irregular free-form curves. B-spline refers to the precise curve-fitting ability generated from data points (thanks to Bezier).

Ellipses

The following command creates an ellipsis.

```
Command: ELLIPSE
Arc/Center/<Axis endpoint 1>: pick one axis endpoint
Axis endpoint 2: pick the second
<Other axis distance>/Rotation: select the other axis distance
```

The new `ellipse` command still has the Center, Axis, and Rotation option from the old `ellipse` command. When creating an elliptical arc, first define an entire ellipse, then indicate the starting and ending points of the desired arc.

```
Command: ellipse
Arc/Center/<Axis endpoint 1>: a
<Axis endpoint 1>/Center: pick one axis endpoint
Axis endpoint 2: pick the other axis endpoint
```

```
<Other axis distance>/Rotation:
```
Parameter/<start angle>: pick the starting point of the arc

Parameter/Included/<end angle>: pick the endpoint of the arc

You can also select an included angle after specifying the starting point of the elliptical arc. The Parameter option, shown in Figure 21.1, is difficult to interpret and even more difficult to explain. This option was derived from basic drafting practices for creating an ellipse or elliptical arc.

```
Command: ellipse
Arc/Center/<Axis endpoint 1>: a
<Axis endpoint 1>/Center:
Axis endpoint 2:
<Other axis distance>/Rotation:
Parameter/<start angle>: p
Angle/<start parameter>:
Angle/Included/<end parameter>:
```

As before, first define an ellipse and then define the part of the ellipse you want to keep (the arc). Imagine a circle drawn with the same diameter as the major axis of the ellipse (Figure 21.1). Select the two points on this imaginary circle, as previously indicated, to define two parameters. AutoCAD drops two perpendicular projections into the ellipse to determine the length of the final elliptical arc. You will rarely need to create this type of ellipse, but because it's not defined in the User Reference Manual, I thought it would be helpful to define it here. Those of you who started on drafting boards should find this procedure familiar, whereas those who began with CAD will no doubt find this option of little use.

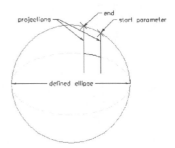

Figure 21.1 The Parameter option can be confusing.

The Isocircle option from previous releases remains in the `ellipse` command. When set to isometric drawing mode (`snap` command, Style option), the command sequence for `ellipse` is modified to include the Isocircle option. When selected, AutoCAD will draw isocircles with a desired location and radius parallel to the current isometric plane. This procedure is 2D only and simply gives the appearance of 3D.

```
Command: ellipse
Arc/Center/Isocircle/<Axis endpoint 1>:
Axis endpoint 2:
<Other axis distance>/Rotation:
```

After constructing an ellipse or two, notice how easy it is to edit with grips. The ellipses accept object snaps (Center and Quadrant) as well.

Words of warning   An offset ellipse yields a spline, which is mathematically accurate.

Splines

Nurbs curves can be confusing and somewhat intimidating at first, but with practice and some basic information, you'll be splining in no time. The nurb spline is a fourth-order curve but can be elevated using the `splinedit` command.

As you create a spline (with the `spline` command), you define data points. AutoCAD fits the spline to the data points. The final step is defining the spline's tangency constraints (optional). I'll review the basic prompt sequence for creating a nurb spline.

```
Command: spline
Object/<Enter first point>:
Enter point:
Close/Fit Tolerance/<Enter point>:
Close/Fit Tolerance/<Enter point>:
Close/Fit Tolerance/<Enter point>: <Enter>
Enter start tangent:
Enter end tangent:
```

Select a series of points to create an M-shaped figure. Notice how the spline travels through each of the data points you select. When you're finished selecting points, hit <Enter>. You will be asked to select a new starting tangent constraint and an ending tangent, defined by a vector located at your cursor connecting to the starting or ending points of the curve. As you spin this tangent vector, notice the changes that take place on your spline.

If you want to leave the curve as it originally was defined, hit <Enter>. Accepting the defaults creates a smooth curve with "C2 continuity." A curve such as this has no sudden changes in the curvature of the spline.

The `spline` command has a few defaults that need addressing: Object, Close, and Fit tolerance.

Perhaps you want to take an existing old spline comprised of polyarcs and convert it into a nurb spline. Select the Object option of the `spline` command (even though you might have expected to find this capability in the `splinedit` command). The order of the spline is preserved. If you recall, two types of splines were available previous to the nurbs-based spline — cubic and quadratic. The cubic splines were fourth order and the quadratic third. If you convert a quadratic spline to the nurbs-based spline, it will maintain an order of three (major yawn!).

The Close option creates a closed spline. You are still asked for a tangency constraint. If you list a closed spline, you'll find that closed splines are periodic, whereas open splines are considered nonperiodic.

The Fit tolerance option controls how closely the spline fits the data points. A tolerance value of zero (the default setting) draws the spline directly through each of the data points. As you increase the value of the tolerance, you'll notice the curve pull away from the data points. Figure 21.2 is an illustration of the dramatic difference a tolerance value can create.

The options might lead you to think you can have different tolerance values for different parts of the spline, which is not true. It doesn't matter at what point you change the tolerance value because the setting affects the entire spline.

Editing Splines

Using entity grips is the easiest method of editing a spline. Through grips, you can stretch a spline through the data points to make minor modifications. Major and more detailed modifications to a spline must be done through the `splinedit` command.

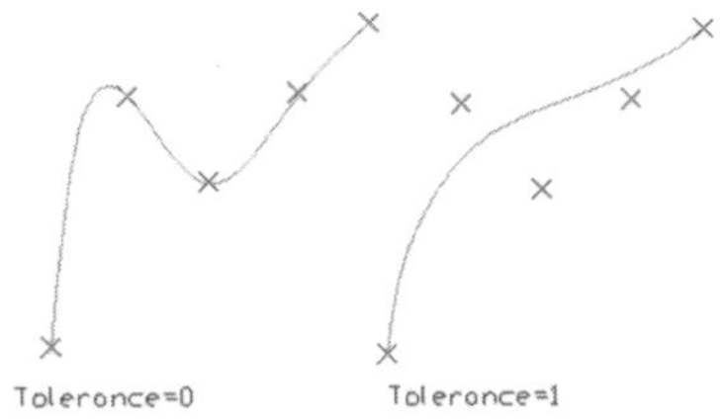

The `splinedit` command allows you to edit the actual spline (using the previously defined data points) or the control frame. A Bezier control frame is associated with every spline. To see this frame, you need to turn the `splframe` system variable on (1) and regenerate the drawing (Figure 21.3). As soon as you enter the `splinedit` command, the grips appear on the control frame, not on the spline, as you might expect.

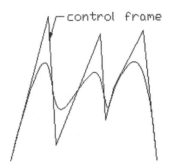

Figure 21.2 Using the Fit Tolerance option, you can establish the degree to which the spline follows the data points.

```
Command: splinedit

Select spline:

Fit Data/Close/Move Vertex/Refine/rEverse/Undo/eXit <X>:
```

To edit the spline directly, choose Fit Data (for data points). The grips appear on the spline, and you encounter an entirely new list of options.

Add/Close/Open/Delete/Move

Add   This option adds more data points to the spline. You select the existing data point (now a grip) that you want to add a data point after. The grip selected and the next grip turn red. You can now select the position of the new data point. You can continue adding data points between the two highlighted grips or select another data point to work from. Adding data points could change the existing spline.

Figure 21.3 A Bezier control frame is associated with every spline.

Close   The Close option closes an open spline (it doesn't appear as an option if the spline is already closed). The tangent becomes continuous (smooth) at its endpoints.

Open This option opens a closed spline (it doesn't appear as an option if the spline is already open). If the spline was previously closed in the `splinedit` command, it returns the spline to its original state.

Delete The Delete option removes data fit points and recalculates the spline.

Move The Move option is similar to the `pedit` command in that it moves existing data points. You can't pick the desired grip; rather, you must step through all of them to get to the data point you want to move. Additional options appear to assist you in this process.

Purge/Tangents/Tolerance/Exit

Purge The Purge option removes all fit data points, leaving you only the control frame to work with. You are returned to the main `splinedit` prompts, and the Fit Data option is removed from the command sequence. Although you can Undo immediately to bring the Fit Data information back, there isn't a command option to restore these data points, so choose this option carefully.

Tangents This option permits you to modify the start and end tangents of the spline. If the spline is closed, you are only prompted for one tangent. You can use the Tangent or Perpendicular object snaps to snap to other objects, if necessary.

Tolerance The tolerance option permits you to change the existing tolerance value for the spline.

Exit The Exit option returns you to the main `splinedit` options.

All of these options are a subset of the Fit Data option. As you can see, the `splinedit` command can become overwhelming because of the number of options. I'll return to the main `splinedit` options in an effort to clear up the confusion.

Fit Data/Close/Move Vertex/Refine

Close This Close option is the same as the Close option in the Fit Data options. It closes an open spline.

Open The Open option opens a closed spline. I've noticed that Open works somewhat differently from the Open in the Fit Data options. When I opened a spline I closed in `splinedit`, it removed the starting segment rather than the closing segment. I expected my spline to be returned to its original state.

Move Vertex This option relocates the selected control points. You have to step through the vertices to get the desired grip. Additional prompts are provided to facilitate this function.

Refine   The Refine option provides an additional tool to fine-tune your spline. I'll review the sub-options.

Add Control Point/Elevate Order/Weight

- **Add Control Point**   This option increases the number of control points on the control frame and is easier than the Add option under Fit Data. Simply select a point on the screen, and the spline recalculates accordingly.

- **Elevate Order**   With this option, splines are created as fourth-order equations (lines are second order, circles and arcs are third). You can elevate the order and increase the number of control points accordingly. The highest order permitted is 26. As you elevate the order, you cannot go backwards (mathematically impossible). If you change the equation to eighth order, you cannot reduce it to sixth. Elevating the order permits more localized control of the spline.

- **Weight**   The Weight option allows you to weight the various control points. Weight references the distance between the control point and the actual spline. The larger the value (integer only), the more the spline is pulled toward the selected control point. Once you weight the spline, AutoCAD makes it rational. The default is 1.

The `splinedit` command is filled with more options than you'll ever need. Experimenting with the command will help you feel more comfortable modifying your splines. Despite the number of options available with the `splinedit` command, it is not too complicated to work with.

Now you're a nurbs expert. Enjoy the ellipses and splines as you incorporate them into your AutoCAD drawings.

CHAPTER 22

Cool System Variables (aka setvars)

To be a true AutoCAD wizard, you have to know a few incredibly cool system variables (setvars). Veteran AutoCAD users throw out system variable names right and left just to impress the socks off a new kid on the block. Sometimes it sounds as though they're speaking a foreign CAD language! I'm going to expose you to some of the extra cool system variables so you, too, can cavort with the CAD elders.

Why do the CAD elders hold on to their setvar knowledge? Because they know the importance of unlocking the system variable doors to enhanced productivity. Most of the system variables can be accessed through dialog boxes or alternate commands, but some of them cannot, which means if you don't know what it is or does, you won't be able to take advantage of its power. System variables are also great assets to menu macros (or toolbars). You can't tell a menu macro to pick a checkbox on a dialog box — you have to know the name of the system variable.

I won't cover all the system variables, just a few of the more powerful (and popular) setvars that you might use in your everyday CAD life.

Setvars have ugly technical names. Because of this, many users have run from them thinking they're too advanced to understand or use. However, setvars are not difficult, they just look that way. So hold on!

System variables can be saved in a variety of places, and where they're saved can be important. If a system variable is saved in the configuration file, it affects all of your drawings. If the system variable is saved in the drawing file, it will affect only future revisions of the same drawing. If you would like these system variables to affect all new drawings, you need to change the setting within your various template files. Some system variables are not saved at all — they are valid only for the current drawing session and resort to their default value the next time you open the drawing.

Here is a selection of system variables in alphabetical order.

attdia

Advantage   Attributes become more user friendly

Function   When set to 1, an attribute dialog box displays, not the command prompt interface.

Default   0 (Off, no dialog box)

Saved in   Drawing file

attreq

Advantage   Speeds up the process of inserting blocks with attributes

Function   When set to 0, AutoCAD assigns the default attribute value to all attributes and suppresses the attribute prompts. If you're in a hurry and don't have time to enter attribute information, you can set attreq to 0, turn the attribute display off (attdisp command), and enter the attribute values at a later time.

Default   1 (On)

Saved in   Drawing file

clayer   **Advantage**   A fast, transparent method of setting a new current layer

Function   If you want to change to a new current layer from within a command quickly, you can execute the clayer command and key in the desired layer command. If you're a dialog box junkie, you won't care for this function. If you create layers with incredibly long names, you won't care for it either. If, however, you like to key in commands, this method is a speedy way of changing layers. Better yet, you can include this command in your menu and toolbar macros to ensure you're on the correct layer before executing certain commands. The Layer drop-down list is a great method of changing current layers, but it can't be executed transparently.

Default   Current layer name

Saved in   Drawing file

dispsilh

Advantage   Improves 3D viewing with little decrease in speed

Function   When set to 1, AutoCAD displays the silhouette curves of 3D objects (in wire frame mode, Figure 22.1). Combining this setting with a low value for isolines permits quick viewing with reasonable drawing detail. Imagine facing a wall, holding an object, and shining a flashlight on the object. The silhouette (the outline of the shadow) would shine on the wall. This silhouette is similar to the one dispsilh controls.

Default   0 (Off)

Saved in   Drawing file

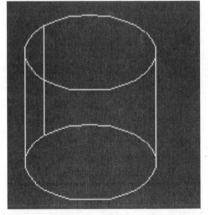

Figure 22.1 The dispsilh **is setvar is set to** 1.

expert

Advantage   Turns off those annoying extra prompts; not recommended for beginners (hence, the name, expert)

Function   Controls the issuance of certain prompts provided to ensure that the user doesn't make a mistake. If you're a well-versed AutoCAD user, you probably don't need to see these same prompts over and over. Several values of expert control several types of prompts.

1   Suppresses two all-familiar prompts: "About to regen, proceed?" (caused when regenauto is turned off) and "Really want to turn the current layer off?"

2   Suppresses "Block already defined. Redefine it?" (block command). expert set to 2 is also supposed to suppress the prompt "A drawing with this name already exists. Overwrite it?" (save, saveas, or wblock command).

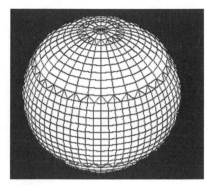

Figure 22.2 The facetres **setvar is set to** 2.

3   In addition to 1 and 2, a value of 3 suppresses prompts issued by the linetype command should you try to load previously loaded linetypes or create duplicate linetype names within the same file.

4   In addition to all of the previous values, a 4 suppresses those warning prompts when you try to save a UCS or viewport with a previously defined name.

5   In addition to all of the previous values, this one suppresses warning prompts that appear when you try to save a dimension style with a previously defined name.

Suppressing any or all of these prompts simply means that AutoCAD assumes you know what you're doing and accepts a value of Yes, which means "Yes, I want to turn off my current layer," "Yes, I want to reload this linetype," and so on. The Super AutoCAD user could choose to live dangerously by selecting an expert value of 5.

Default   0 (Off). Does this mean AutoCAD infers that not everyone's an expert?

Saved in   Not saved (valid for drawing sessions only)

facetres

Advantage   Useful in improving the display of 3D shading and hidden line removal; can also affect rendering

Function   Controls the resolution of the various facets that appear while hiding, shading, and rendering. Acceptable values range from .01 to 10. Even a value of 2 can produce a nicely faceted object (Figure 22.2). Any value less than 0.5 starts to dramatically decrease the smoothness of any solid objects (Figure 22.3). The higher the value of facetres, the slower the hiding, shading, and rendering; obviously, the opposite is true as well. When speed is important, set facetres to a low value. When the display is important, increase the facetres setting.

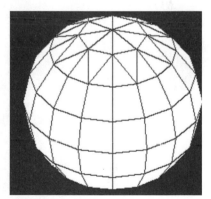

Figure 22.3 The facetres **setvar is set to** .5.

The user reference manual doesn't mention that facetres affects rendering, but it does.

Default   0.5

Saved in   Drawing file

hideprecision

Advantage   Useful if you want to do a quick hide

Function   When set to 0, it uses single-precision (fast) calculations; when set to 1, it uses double-precision (slow) calculations.

Default   0

Saved in   Not saved

hidetext

Advantage   Hide objects behind text as well as text strings

Function   When set off, text acts as it always has and doesn't hide anything behind it unless the text has a thickness assigned to it. The text won't hide either. When set on, text can hide objects behind it, and text, dtext, and mtext can also be hidden.

Default   On

Saved in   Drawing file

isavebak

Advantage   Gets rid of those pesky backup files and helps speed up saves

Function   When set to 0, AutoCAD does not create BAK files. Copying file data to backup files can dramatically increase the time it takes to save (especially in Windows). BAK files also take up valuable storage space on your disk.

Default   1 (backup files created)

Saved in   Configuration file

isavepercent

Advantage   Speeds up saves

Function   Convinces AutoCAD that it doesn't need to do a complete save every time you use a function that saves your drawing. isavepercent controls the amount of wasted space within your drawing. Say isavepercent is set to 50 (which conveniently happens to be the default). This setting means that AutoCAD performs quick-and-dirty saves until 50 percent of your drawing is filled with wasted space. A quick-and-dirty save consists of tacking on new information and marking old information for designated changes. After reaching that 50 percent wasted space limit, AutoCAD performs a full save. A clean (full) save takes extra time because AutoCAD does a total save — repacking and removing any extra wasted space. You'll notice that a full save compresses your drawing file, making the file smaller than those quick-and-dirty saves. Setting the isavepercent variable to 0 turns this feature off altogether, yielding only full saves.

Default   50

Saved in   Configuration file

isolines

Advantage   Improves the speed of regenerating 3D solids

Function   The isolines setvar controls the number of tessellation lines that display on 3D solids (Figure 22.4) to help you visualize a curved surface (cone, sphere, cylinder, and so on). You can't snap to isolines, they are for display only. The more tessellation lines, the slower the regeneration and vice versa. Setting isolines to 1 and turning dispsilh to 1 (On) can produce a simple display that regenerates quickly. When displaying splines, AutoCAD subtracts four from the value of isolines to determine the number of tessellation lines to display. For example, an isolines setting of 8 yields a total of four tessellation lines on the splined surface. This system variable also is intended to speed regeneration.

Default   4

Saved in   Drawing file

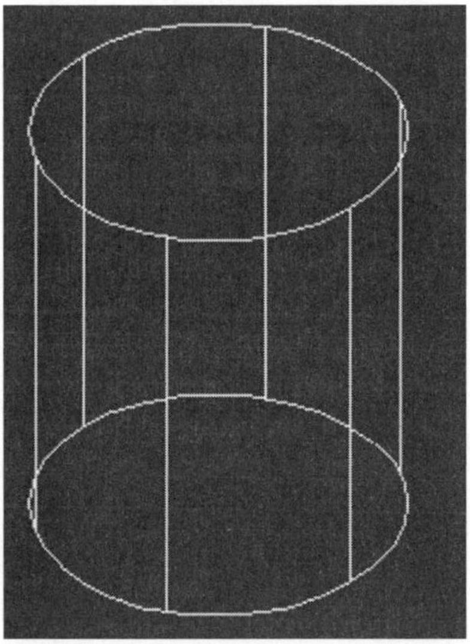

Figure 22.4 The isolines **setvar is set to** 6.

maxactvp

Advantage   Can speed up regenerations in Paper Space

Function   Controls the number of active viewports in Paper Space (when tilemode is set to 0). The lower the number, the faster the regenerations. An inactive viewport does not display its contents but will still be plotted.

Default   16

Saved in   Not saved

maxsort

Advantage   Tells AutoCAD to stop alphabetizing named objects, such as layers

Function   Controls the number of named objects AutoCAD will sort alphabetically. If you prefer your layers to be listed within the layer dialog box in the order they were created, this system variable can help. Perhaps you'd like to list layers by priority, order of use, frequency, or some other criteria. Setting maxsort to 0 tells AutoCAD not to alphabetize any of your layers; they'll display in the order in which they were placed into the drawing.

Caution   This variable controls all named objects including blocks, views, UCSs, and so on. You might have to weigh the advantages and disadvantages to your daily drawing routine.

Default   200

Saved in   Configuration file

mbuttonpan

Advantage   Tells the third button on your input device to reference the menu (for those of you who don't have wheels on your mice)

Function   When set to 0, it supports the action defined in the menu file; when set to 1, it supports panning and zooming (best with a wheel).

Default   1

Saved in   Configuration file

mirrtext

Advantage   Can keep your text from mirroring when you use the `mirror` command

Function   When selecting a group of objects to mirror, you might want any included text to be copied to the designated coordinate, but probably not mirrored. When `mirrtext` is set to 0, AutoCAD copies rather than mirrors text when using the `mirror` command.

Default   1 (too bad)

Saved in   Drawing file. (Change your prototype drawing to 0, and you won't have to modify it for each individual drawing.)

nomutt

Advantage   Turns off "mutterings" while you run script files and LISP routines

Function   When set to 1, AutoCAD dismisses message displays that might mess up your script files or LISP routines. This is only in effect during script files, LISP routines, and so on. When set to 0, it's business as usual (mutterings galore).

Default   0

Saved in   Not saved

pellipse

Advantage   Allows you to create the polyline ellipses used for years rather than the Nurbs-based splines

Function   With the Nurbs-based curves, you finally have true geometric ellipses. To my surprise, several users still need a way to create the old polyline ellipses. When `pellipse` is set to 1, AutoCAD draws the age-old ellipse made of many polyarc segments.

Default   0 (creates the new ellipses)

Saved in   Drawing file

plinegen

Advantage Tells AutoCAD to consider an entire polyline when placing linetypes (Figure 22.5, right), not each individual vertex (Figure 22.5, left)

Function When plinegen is set to 1, AutoCAD generates a linetype in a continuous pattern across all the vertices of a polyline. When set to 0, AutoCAD tries to squeeze the linetype between the vertices

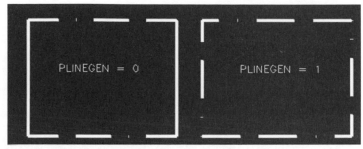

Figure 22.5 When plinegen **is set to** 1, **AutoCAD generates a linetype in a continuous pattern across all the vertices of a polyline.**

— if there's enough room to do so. If you haven't been happy with the way your linetypes display on your polylines, this system variable should cheer you up.

Default 0
Saved in Drawing file

plquiet

Advantage Suppresses the display of dialog boxes and error messages while plotting

Function When set to 1, you can run your batch plots and script files without interruption; when set to 0, it's business as usual.

Default 0
Save in Registry

rasterpreview

Advantage Speeds up saves

Function rasterpreview controls the type of preview file saved with the drawing. Every time AutoCAD executes the save command, the preview file is recreated. As you plug along all day on the same drawing, the preview file isn't necessary. It's not really necessary until you exit the drawing. The CAD elders know that by setting rasterpreview to 3, the save includes no preview image. Before you leave the drawing, you can set it back to 0 to save a nice final bitmap of your drawing on your way out. The settings for rasterpreview are as follows.

0   BMP file only
1   BMP and WMF files
2   WMF file only
3   No preview image created

This variable is a must in a toolbar or menu. It's too long and too painful to key in every time you want to modify its value. It is great combined with a high setting of isavepercent when you start a drawing (rasterpreview set to 3). Then, before you finish your drawing, set isavepercent to 0 (to do a complete cleaning) and set rasterpreview back to 0.

Default 0
Saved in Drawing file

rememberfolders

Advantage   Tells the File dialog boxes to remember the last directory you accessed

Function   When set to 0, AutoCAD uses the Start-in path from the AutoCAD icon (legacy behavior); when set to 1, the last path is remembered in each particular standard file selection dialog (it ignores the Start-in path).

Default   1

Saved in   Registry

splframe

Advantage   Makes it easier to edit splines (Figure 22.6).

Function   When set to 1, splframe displays the control frame on splines. It also works on polyline splines. When editing the new Nurbs-based splines, it's quite useful to see the control frame while you're in the splinedit command. splframe also displays the invisible edges of 3Dfaces.

Default   0

Saved in   Drawing file

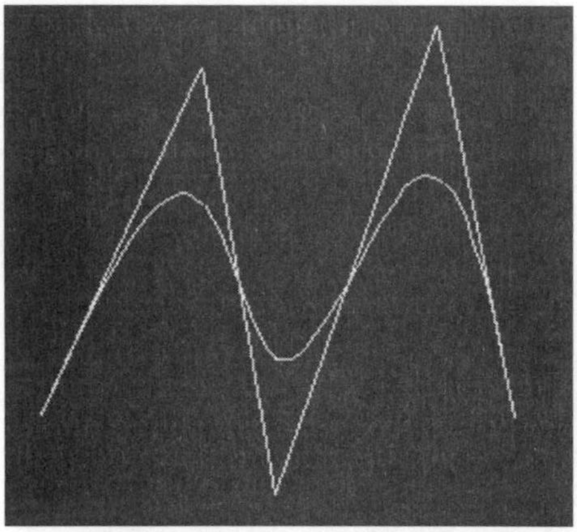

Figure 22.6 The splframe setvar is set to 1, which makes it easier to edit splines.

surftab1

Advantage   Permits greater control over the end results of the surface commands: rulesurf, tabsurf, revsurf, and edgesurf

Function   If you're a 3D Surfaces user, you might find these next two system variables particularly useful. Surftab1 controls the number of tabulations generated in rulesurf and tabsurf. If you want a smoother surface mesh, escalate the default value until you get the desired result. Surftab1 also controls the number of 3Dfaces generated in the M direction for revsurf and edgesurf. The higher the value, the smoother the mesh.

Default   6

Saved in   Drawing file

surftab2

Advantage   Permits greater control over the end results of revsurf and edgesurf

Function   revsurf and edgesurf have an M and N direction (3Dfaces going both ways). The surftab2 system variable controls the number of 3Dfaces appearing in the N direction. The higher the value, the smoother the mesh.

Default   6

Saved in   Drawing file

textfill

Advantage   Improves the look of TrueType fonts

Function   When set to 1, textfill displays text as filled characters. It takes effect after the first regeneration. It will slow you down, but it looks great!

Default   0

Saved in   Drawing file

textqlty

Advantage   Can speed up regenerations and text plotting

Function   textqlty sets the resolution of TrueType and ranges from 0 to 100. The default setting of 50 is equivalent to a text resolution of 300 dots per inch. The highest value, 100, sets the text resolution to 600 dpi and requires more time to regenerate and plot. With a low setting, such as 25, the text appears more jagged, but regeneration and plotting speeds up. If you're looking for speed, set textqlty far below the default value.

Default   50 (300 dpi)

Saved in   Drawing file

ucsfollow

Advantage   Eliminates having to use the plan command whenever you change your UCS

Function   When ucsfollow is set to 1, AutoCAD automatically generates a plan view whenever you change from one UCS to another. If you prefer to work on the plan view of your current construction plane, this system variable proves invaluable. ucsfollow is viewport dependent, so you aren't forced to use this setting in all viewports. ucsfollow is saved separately for Paper Space and Model Space. Also, it is ignored when tilemode is set to 0 and you are working in Paper Space.

Default   0 (Off)

Saved in   Drawing file

visretain

Advantage   Eliminates the tedious restructuring of layer settings each time you enter a drawing with external references

Function   visretain controls whether AutoCAD saves the modifications you've made to an external reference file's layers. When set to 0, the default, AutoCAD discards any changes made to the visibility, color, or linetype of dependent layers. It can be frustrating when you pull up the drawing at a future time to find your hard work has not been saved. Setting visretain to 1 forces AutoCAD to remember whether a dependent layer is on or off, frozen or thawed, or a particular color or linetype.

Default   0 (Change this value in your prototype file to 1 if you're an xref user.)

Saved in   Drawing file

wmfbkgrnd

Advantage   Turns the AutoCAD background transparent in WMFs for use in other programs (that would include dragging and dropping)

Function   When set to 1, WMFs have the current AutoCAD background color; when set to 0, WMFs have a transparent background.

Default   1

Saved in   Not saved

zoomfactor

Advantage   Allows more control over the zooming movements of the mouse wheel

Function   Any value between 3 and 100 is valid; the higher the number, the more the incremental change.

Default   40

Saved in   Registry

Do you feel worthy of associating with the CAD elders now? These are just a few of the powerful system variables hidden within AutoCAD. Try these and others to fine-tune your AutoCAD skills. It's doubtful you'll want to key in these laborious command names, so it's to your advantage to automate these variables as much as possible by assigning them to a toolbar or menu item. I hope you've found at least one system variable that will increase your productivity in AutoCAD.

CHAPTER 23

Finding Your Way In Paper Space

So who needs Paper Space? Anyone who creates drawings containing multiple scale factors; anyone who creates 3D drawings and wants to plot multiple views; anyone who wants to draw one-to-one and plot one-to-one; anyone who is tired of multiplying text and dimensions to outrageous sizes so they're scaled correctly for models; anyone who wants to remain a cool AutoCAD operator. Get the picture? To succeed as an AutoCAD guru, you really need to have a good grasp of Paper Space. I'll start with a quick overview and then dig deeper.

Down in the lower left-hand corner of the drawing editor are the Model Space and Layout tabs (Figure 23.1). If the Model tab is selected, you're in Model Space; the Layout tabs indicate you're in Paper Space. By default, the Paper Space tabs are called Layout1 and Layout2, but

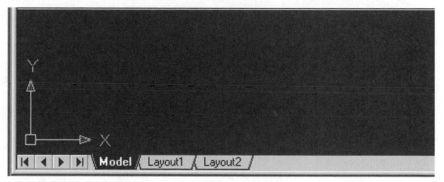

Figure 23.1 The tabs in the lower left-hand corner of the drawing editor control whether you're in Paper Space.

you can rename them anything you'd like by simply right-clicking on them. You can also add and delete layouts. Clicking on a layout puts you into a different view, as shown in Figure 23.2. The Ucsicon turns into a triangle (indicating you're no longer in Kansas — or Model Space), and the drawing area now resembles a piece of paper. Your background color is now white, and the dashed rectangle indicates the printable area of the drawing. Drawing outside of the dashed rectangle will create objects that do not display on the final plot.

The first time you enter a Layout tab you'll probably get the Page Setup dialog box (Figure 23.3). This provides instructions to AutoCAD related to your plotting needs. Page setups are really just plot settings saved with each layout. Rather than launch into a completely different topic (plotting), I'm going to focus primarily on the Paper Space world. I'm going to postpone any in-depth discussion on the Page Setup dialog for now. Although I don't necessarily recommend it, you can turn off this dialog in the Options dialog or by unchecking the Display When Creating a New

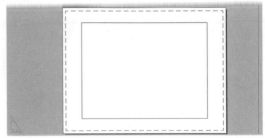

Figure 23.2 Selecting a Layout tab puts you in Paper Space.

Layout option in the lower left-hand corner of the Page Setup dialog. Most of your drawing time will be spent in Model Space. Here, you'll create the geometry for your model (one-to-one). If you're drawing a floor plan 50 feet by 40 feet, you'll draw it exactly that size. If you're drawing a sensor 4 mm by 2 mm, then you'll draw it exactly that size as well. You'll set up your limits, grid, and snap to accommodate your model, focusing on creating the actual model and saving the title block, dimensioning, and annotations until later.

Viewports

There are two distinctly different types of viewports in AutoCAD: the viewports you create in Model Space and the viewports you create in Paper Space. They're very different animals that view your model in different ways. The viewports you create in Model Space must be tiled. Like the tiles on a floor, they lie side-by-side and must fill up the entire display area. When in Model Space, you can only plot one viewport at a time. The viewports you create in Paper Space don't follow the same rules. Instead, they can lie on top of each other, within each other, overlap each other, and so forth. Viewports can be copied, moved, stretched, erased, and so on. In Paper Space you can plot as many viewports as you like. In Paper Space, a viewport is considered an object.

To create viewports in Model Space, use the vports or viewports command (View pull-down menu–Viewports, Figure 23.4). Here you can pick a viewport configuration to suit your needs. For 3D users, there's a great 3D viewport option that automatically displays three different viewpoints of your model — just change the Setup option from 2D to 3D. Several view options (Figure 23.4) allow you to choose to display the views from Northeast, Southeast, and so on. Within this same dialog, you can save a specific viewport configuration for use later (note the Named Viewports tab).

You've drawn your model one-to-one, and now you're ready to move to the final stages of AutoCAD drafting — annotation, dimensioning, and plotting.

Select the Layout1 tab to go to Paper Space. You should be looking at a blank piece of paper. If the Create Viewport in New Layouts option is checked in the Options dialog, you will see a default viewport appear with your model showing through. I'll assume those of you who have a viewport already appearing on the screen can simply erase it if you choose to follow along.

For you pre-AutoCAD 2000 users (with no model or Layout tabs), pick the Tile tab on the Status Bar to go back and

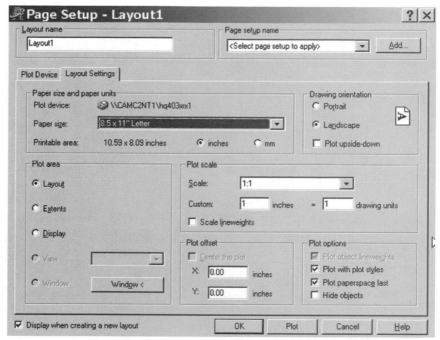

Figure 23.3 The Page Setup dialog should be used when creating a new layout.

forth from Model Space to Paper Space. When `tilemode` is on, you can only have tiled viewports; hence, you're in Model Space. When `tilemode` is off, you aren't restricted to tiled viewports anymore; hence, you're in Paper Space.

The first thing you want to do is make sure the piece of paper you're looking at is your ultimately plot size. The easiest way to do this is to select a paper size in the Page Setup Layout under the Layout Settings tab (make sure you have the correct printer or plotter selected). If not, simply go into the `limits` command and set up the piece of paper manually (this would primarily apply to Release 14 users). Setting the limits in AutoCAD 2002 is not as easy as it looks. Notice that AutoCAD now allots for the unprintable area in the drawing, which requires some math, so you're much better off setting limits in the Page Setup dialog. If you ran past the Page Setup dialog and would like to make some changes, you can always call it back with the `pagesetup` command. After setting up your page size, you might want to set up an appropriate grid and snap setting as well.

Your paper is set up, and you're ready to insert a full-sized border, along with your title block. This is done easily by inserting it within the dashed rectangular area (I'm assuming you have already created a border with a title block). Now all you need is your model!

Before I go any further, I want to make sure you understand the fundamental concepts of Paper Space and Model Space that cause confusion for many. First, understand that there are two worlds in AutoCAD — the Model World (where you create your model) and the Paper (or Layout) World. If `tilemode` is set to 1, you're in the Model World; if it's set to 0, you're in the Paper World. While you are in the Model World, you can't see any Paper Space objects, you can only see the objects you created in the Model World.

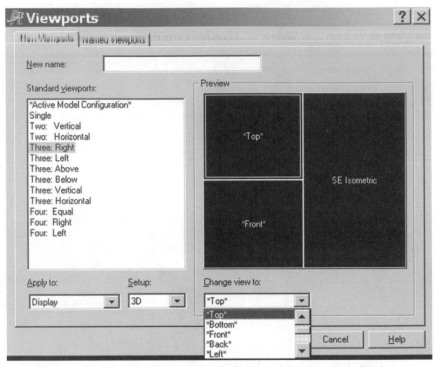

Figure 23.4 The Viewports dialog box is used to create tiled viewports in Model Space.

You can move easily between these two worlds by hitting the Model and Layout tabs located in the lower left-hand corner of the drawing.

Setting `tilemode` to 0 (or hitting a Layout tab) sends you to the Paper (Layout) World. You can tell you've arrived because the UCS icon looks the same as it does in two spaces that can coexist within your layout, Model Space and Paper Space. If the icon displays as a triangle (Figure 23.5), any objects you create land in Paper Space. If you double-click inside a viewport or hit the Status Bar button to go to Model Space and create an object, you're actually adding it to Model Space. Consequently, when you hit the Model tab to return to the Model World, you'll see your newly created objects appearing there as well. While in a layout, you have access to some commands you can't use in the Model World (such as `mview` and `vplayer`).

Now you have a confusing collection of tabs and buttons that say Model or Paper (or Layout). Which is which? The Model and Layout tabs located in the lower left-hand corner of your drawing move you between the Model and Paper (Layout) World. The Model/Paper button that resides on the Status Bar (along the lower edge of the drawing editor) toggles you between Model Space and Paper Space within the Layout, as shown in Figure 23.6. You can't select this button if you're in the Model World.

Paper Space Viewports

Phew! I hope you were able to follow along that cryptic path. So where's the model? Back in Model Space where it belongs. Now, take a look at creating Paper Space viewports so you can see your model while in the Paper Space world. Viewports are actual objects in Paper Space. They can be stretched, copied, moved, and so forth (just like other objects). In most cases, you won't want your viewport boundary edge to display on the final plot, so you should typically create a layer just for viewports so you can turn them off before plotting. Interestingly enough, when you freeze or turn off the viewport layer, the model continues to display as the boundary disappears. I'll start this off right by creating a layer called Vports and making it current.

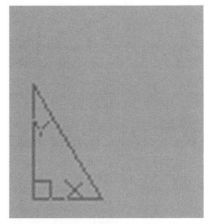

Figure 23.5 The triangle indicates that you are in Paper Space.

Go into the mview command to create your viewports. These viewports are your windows to the Model World. There are several different theories out there as to what the M in mview stands for. I've always known it to stand for Make View, but I've heard others say it stands for Model View or even Meta View (my least favorite). The mview command was greatly enhanced in AutoCAD 2000 with the addition of nonrectangular viewports. that, you had to piece viewports together to get the desired results, and it wasn't pretty!

The default option in the mview command is to pick two opposite corners to form a rectangular viewport. You can put these viewports anywhere on your piece of paper, even one within the other. Each time you create a new viewport to the Model World, AutoCAD fills the viewport with the model (as though it was a Zoom Extents). Notice that you can select these viewports by their boundaries and stretch them, move them, copy them, and so forth. As you modify the viewport boundary, notice that the zoom scale factor remains the same. Now, create several viewports, and then I'll look at moving from one viewport to another.

AutoCAD 2000 added the ability to double-click within a viewport to go to Model Space. Double-clicking outside of a viewport puts you back into Paper Space. The Model/Paper Space button on the Status Bar can also be used to switch between Model Space and Paper Space. AutoCAD will jump to the last current viewport (or the last one you created if you haven't entered a viewport yet). If you prefer, you can also type in PS or MS to get the same result.

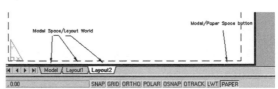

Figure 23.6 You can move around from the Model World to Layout World with tabs.

Double-clicking was a great time-saving feature that eliminated the constant PS, MS, and occasionally a PMS input (just seeing if you're paying attention). I find that setting your crosshairs to a value of 100 makes it much easier for you to identify whether you're in Paper Space or Model Space. (Hoorah to all of you who refuse to grow up and still have your crosshairs set at 100!). If you have problems getting into a specific viewport (perhaps it's a viewport within a viewport), you can use the magical <Ctrl-R> to toggle from one viewport to another.

Note   Toggling from viewport to viewport used to be done using <Ctrl-V> before Windows stepped in, reserving <Ctrl-V> for Paste. AutoCAD now uses <Ctrl-R> in its place.

The `mview` **Command**

Go back to the `mview` command, and I'll tour its options one at a time.

On/Off   Turning a viewport off makes the contents invisible (although the boundary remains). If you're freezing and thawing many layers of a large drawing and you have many viewports, you could find yourself losing patience as it regenerates each viewport. Hence, it is common procedure to turn off viewports you aren't using in order to increase performance. You can't make a viewport current if it's turned off (which makes sense). The `maxactvp` system variable controls the maximum number of viewports you can have on at any given time. The default number is 64 (it's doubtful you'll ever exceed this value). This value has no effect on the number of viewports plotted. However, if a viewport is turned off, the contents within the viewport are not plotted.

Fit   This option creates one viewport that fills the layout to the edge of the paper margins. Consequently, you're looking at one large layout, and it's nearly impossible to accommodate a border and title block as well.

Hideplot   This option is essential if you're using Paper Space to display 3D objects. Hideplot instructs AutoCAD to perform a hidden-line removal within the selected viewports. I've received many e-mails over the years from readers who can't figure out why their viewports won't hide, even though they've selected Hide Objects within the `plot` command. So don't forget where this important option hides.

```
Hidden line removal for plotting [On/Off]: on
Select objects: (select all the viewports you want to perform a hide while plotting)
```
It's a little ironic that you select `on` to turn the hidden lines off while plotting.

Lock   One of my favorite additions in AutoCAD 2000 is the ability to lock in the scale factor of viewports. You go to all the trouble to set the scale factor in a viewport, and then you mess it up by accidentally `zooming` within the viewport. This new option will save you from yourself by locking the display and preventing Model Space zooming. You can also lock a viewport by picking on the boundary edge of a viewport to highlight it, right-clicking to bring up the shortcut menu, and selecting the Display Locked option from the menu.

Object   Also new is the ability to create a viewport out of a closed object. This paves the way to creating circular and curved viewports. The closed objects you can use to create a viewport are polylines, ellipses, splines, regions, and circles.

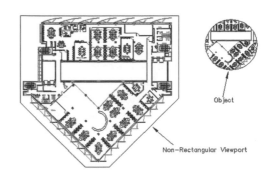

Polygonal   I use this option all the time to create odd-shaped viewports, as shown in Figure 23.7. Simply pretend you're in the pline command and draw away. You'll find you can even switch over to arcs to add some curves to your viewport.

Figure 23.7 AutoCAD 2002 makes creating nonrectangular and circular layouts easy.

```
Specify start point: Specify a point
Specify next point or [Arc/Close/Length/Undo]: Specify a point or enter an option
```

Arc   This launches into the same types of options you'll find in the pline command. The arc segment insists on being tangent to the previously drawn segment unless you change the direction.

```
[Angle/CEnter/CLose/Direction/Line/Radius/Second pt/Undo/
   Endpoint of arc] <Endpoint>:
```

Close   This closes your new viewport boundary. If you hit <Enter> after specifying at least three points, AutoCAD automatically closes the boundary for you.

Length   This is one of the most underused options in the pline command and will probably not be used much in the mview command either. If you need to extend the previously drawn segment a specific amount in the same direction, you can use this option (or you can Undo the previously drawn segment and just do it properly). If you want to extend a straight-line segment tangent to the last arc drawn, perhaps I can see using this option.

Undo   Do you really this one explained? This removes the last segment or arc drawn.

Restore   If you have saved a tiled viewport configuration in Model Space (vports command) and want to bring that same configuration into Paper Space, you can do so by entering the name. You can also bring your current tiled viewport configuration into Paper Space using this option. You'll be asked to select the area in which you want the configuration placed by picking two corners or using the Fit option.

2/3/4   These options permit you to set up multiple viewports at one time. The viewports will display tiled, and you'll be asked to select various parameters, such as horizontal and vertical (for 2,

3, and 4) and above, below, left, and right (for 3) to indicate where the large viewport should be placed.

What scale factors are your viewports using? Good question! AutoCAD simply fits the model into the viewport, and it's up to you to scale it properly. You might feel the need to use the standard `scale` and `move` commands to display your model correctly, but that would be a big no-no; it will change the integrity of the model you've worked so hard to create. It would also affect any other viewports you've created. All your scaling in the Paper World will be done via the standard `zoom` and `pan` commands: `zoom` to control the scale factor and `pan` to move the model into its appropriate position within the viewport. This part gets a tad tricky, so be sure to hold on! I'll discuss the age-old official means of controlling the viewport scale factor, and then I'll take a look at a few of the new features that came out in AutoCAD 2000.

The XP Option

The XP option in the `zoom` command will become your best friend when setting your viewport scale factors. XP stands for Times Paper Space. Essentially, you are indicating to AutoCAD the ratio between Model Space units and Paper Space units. This is much easier to explain with some solid examples.

Say you want your scale factor within the viewport to be $\frac{1}{4}$ inch = 1 foot. If you were doing standard drafting, you would be dividing everything by 48 to get it to fit on your paper, whereas 1 inch = 1 foot means you'd divide by 12, $\frac{1}{2}$ inch = 1 foot means you divide by 24, and so forth. Perhaps you're going the other direction and need to enlarge your model to get it to fit on your paper. Your scale factor might be 2X or 4X, and if you use the much more sensible units to the base 10 (metric) and not base 12 (imperial), you might have scale factors such as 1 centimeter = 20 meters or 1 centimeter = 50 meters.

Figure 23.8 The Properties dialog makes it easy to set viewport scale factors.

After you've determined the scale factor you want to apply to your viewport, simply make the viewport active (double-click inside) and enter the `zoom` command. I'll assume your model needs to have a final scale factor of $\frac{1}{4}$ inch = 1 foot.

zoom **Command**

```
Specify corner of window, enter a scale factor (nX or nXP), or [All/Center/Dynamic/
  Extents/Previous/Scale/Window] <real time>: 1/48XP
Regenerating model.
```

In case you're curious, a simple X (vs. XP) will scale times the current view, so 4X zooms you in four times the current display scale factor toward the display center. It's not uncommon to need to pull back your zoom just a tad, and many veteran users know to use .7X to take a giant step backwards.

Table 23.1 shows a sampling of some standard scale factors and their final XP value.

You can also enter the scale factor values in decimal; for example, the list in Table 23.1 would appear as the factors shown in Table 23.2. You get the idea. Simply jump into each viewport and set your scale factor using the zoom command.

AutoCAD 2000 introduced two new ways of setting the scale factors for your viewport. Although both of these methods are easier to use because you simply select the scale factor from a list, you might still find you have to enter some custom scale factor values.

The first method uses Properties. While in Paper Space, highlight the intended viewport by picking on its frame and then right-click and pick Properties from the shortcut menu. This is even easier in AutoCAD 2000i or 2002: simply double-click on the viewport frame and that will pull up the Properties dialog automatically.

Figure 23.8 shows the Properties dialog as it relates to viewports. The key section to check out is the Misc section, which contains many great options to help you set up your viewport to your specifications. The Standard scale section contains a great drop-down list to select your scale factor (no thought process required here!). You can also key in a custom scale factor if the one you need is not included in the drop-down list. This can be done in the Custom scale section. You can enter the scale factor in fractional format, just as you did with the XP value, or use the decimal equivalent.

Table 23.1 Standard scale factors and their XP value.

Scale Factor	XP Value
$^{1}/_{2}$ inch = 1 foot	1/24XP
$^{3}/_{8}$ inch = 1 foot	1/32XP
$^{1}/_{4}$ inch = 1 foot	1/48XP
$^{1}/_{8}$ inch = 1 foot	1/96XP
2 =1	2XP
4 =1	4XP

Table 23.2 Standard scale factors and their XP values in decimals.

Scale Factor	XP Value
$^{1}/_{8}$ inch = 1 foot	.01XP
$^{1}/_{4}$ inch = 1 foot	.02XP
$^{1}/_{2}$ inch = 1 foot	.04XP
1 inch = 1 foot	.08XP
1 = 2	.5XP
1 = 4	.25XP
2 = 1	2XP
10 = 1	10XP
50 = 1	50XP

If you've created a nonrectangular viewport, it will be frustrating for you when you select the viewport and it highlights the boundary object along with the viewport (more than likely a polyline). Notice that the Properties dialog indicates that you have two objects selected even though you only picked one. Simply drop down the list, as shown in Figure 23.9, and select Viewport. Then you'll be able to select a scale factor using the above method.

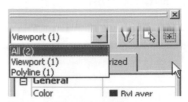

Figure 23.9 Use the Properties dialog drop-down list to isolate a nonrectangular viewport.

I'd like to point out the other cool options you can find in the Misc section of the Properties dialog.

On   This option easily lets you turn a viewport on or off.

Clipped   If you create a nonrectangular viewport (user defined), clipping is on. This option is read-only.

Display Locked   This is extremely cool! After you've set up your scale factors, it's soooooooo easy to undo your hard work with a misplaced zoom or a touch on the wheel of an IntelliMouse. With AutoCAD 2002, you can lock the display so this won't happen. This also can be done from the right-click shortcut menu (Figure 23.10). If you try zooming within a viewport, AutoCAD will only allow you to zoom in relative to Paper Space. This means you can still zoom in on the model for a better view, but your assigned scale factor remains intact.

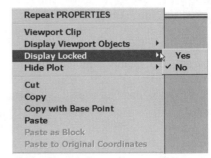

Figure 23.10 The right-click shortcut menu also locks viewport displays.

UCS Per Viewport   You can choose to have one UCS setting that affects all viewports or individual UCS settings per viewport. This is another nice, new addition to AutoCAD 2002 and comes in handy if you do a lot of 3D work.

Hide Plot   If you use 3D drawings, you probably want to remove the hidden lines during plotting. This needs to be turned on for each viewport you want to hide and can be set here in the Properties dialog or within the mview command. You'll still have to turn on hidden-line removal in the plot command as well.

The Viewports Toolbar

Last but not least, if you're into toolbars, the Viewports toolbar is one of my favorites. I leave this docked up by my Standard toolbar when working in Paper Space. Figure 23.11 shows the new Viewports toolbar that contains a drop-down list for assigning viewport scale factors.

Note that scaling or stretching the layout viewport border does not change the scale factor of the viewport. It's really the zoom command that could potentially modify the scale factor unexpectedly.

After you've set up the appropriate scale factor for your viewports, you might need to pan around within the viewport to get the desired final view.

Now that you have a grasp on the basics, play around a little in Paper Space. Try out the Tabs and customize some viewports. Once you feel at home in this new world, move on to Chapter 24 and put your knowledge to the test.

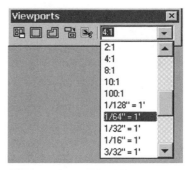

Figure 23.11 The Viewport toolbar contains a drop-down list of viewport scale factors.

Dimensioning in Paper Space

Now it's time to tackle the most complex aspect of Paper Space — Dimensioning! There are two schools of thought on dimensions as they relate to Paper Space layouts: one school believes the dimensions should be placed in Model Space; the other believes the dimensions belong in Paper Space. (One year at Autodesk University, I had two Paper Space instructors: Shane Bartley of Disney, who was adamant that dimensions belonged in Paper Space, and Dave Espinosa-Aguilar of Toxic Frog Multimedia, who absolutely believed they belonged in Model Space.) Both choices have their pros and cons.

So who is right? I'm not about to tell you that one way rules supreme over the other, but I am prepared to share with you the pros and cons of both so you can decide what works best for you.

I'll look at the basics from the 10,000-foot level. If you use AutoCAD 2000i or before and you place your dimensions in Paper Space, it's very easy to ensure you're getting the proper text height, arrow size, and so on. Simply set the dimension variables to reflect the actual output value. However, when you dimension the Model Space objects from Paper Space, you immediately see that you don't get the proper dimension text value. You have two options here — override the dimension text and key in the proper value (lots of work and bad CAD manners) or change the `dimlfac` (linear scale factor) to reflect the scale factor of the viewport. Hence, you're back to the lovely world of figuring out the proper scale factor settings. If your scale factor is 1:2, set `dimlfac` to 2; if your scale factor is $^1/_4$" = 1', you're looking at a scale factor of 1 = 48, which means you set `dimlfac` to 48, and so on. All this scaling gives me a serious headache (which makes me *really* love AutoCAD 2002).

Note You can also set the `dimlfac` value in the Dimension Style dialog box by entering a Scale factor in the Measurement Scale section of the Primary Units tab (Figure 24.1).

If you place your dimensions in Paper Space you move the model (accidentally or otherwise), you'll see that your dimensions couldn't care less. They stay right where you put them (well-trained dimensions). I refer to these type of dimensions as stupid dimensions. They have no idea that they're referencing an object on the screen. You can change the size of the object, and the dimension ignores you. The Paper Space dimension looks exactly the same regardless of what you do to the model, which makes for happy dimensions, but a very low IQ.

That's one school of thought; now look at the second and more popular school: placing your dimensions in Model Space.

To place your dimensions in Model Space, you need to set one

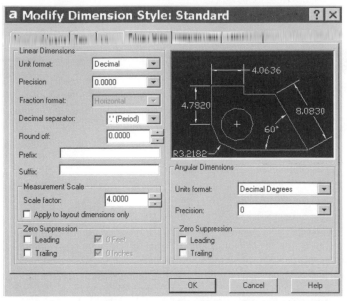

Figure 24.1 The Primary Units tab lets you modify linear dimensions, angular dimensions, and more.

key dimension variable to ensure proper results. First and foremost, the dimscale factor absolutely must be set to 0. This can also be set easily in the Dimension Style dialog box (ddim or dimstyle) by checking the Scale dimensions to layout (paperspace)value under the Fit tab (Figure 24.2). Setting dimscale to 0 tells AutoCAD to look at the scale factor of the viewport then scale the dimensions accordingly. This ensures that dimension text, arrowheads, and so forth display at the proper value. Do not (and I repeat, do NOT) attempt to manually set the dimension text, arrowheads, and the like to the reciprocal of the scale factor or you will get a terrible headache. Let AutoCAD do the work for you.

What happens if you change the scale factor of the viewport? You'll see that although these dimensions are smarter, in that they follow the model, they don't automatically rescale to the proper physical values. Consequently, your arrowheads and text might appear too large or too small. However, a simple update (Dimension pull-down menu–Update) corrects this. Each time you change the scale factor you need to update the dimension.

Note   You can also use the -dimstyle command (don't forget the dash) and the Apply option to yield the same results, as well as the dim command followed by upd to get to the old Update command.

If you recall from the last chapter, one of the appealing features within Paper Space is the ability to individually control the display of layers within viewports. If you choose to place your dimensions in Model Space, you'll also want to make sure you create a separate dimension layer for each viewport. When creating multiple viewports, you will undoubtedly want to control the visibility of the dimensions per viewport. For example, you can decide whether or not the DIM1 layer appears in any or all viewports.

One of the coolest new features in AutoCAD 2002 is trans-spatial dimensioning. Yes, of course this is another new AutoCAD buzzword (as though there aren't enough). This new feature permits you to

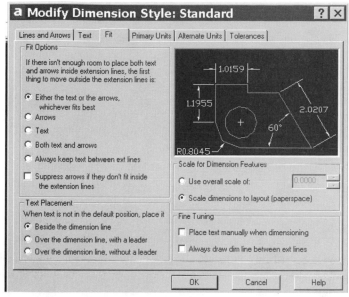

Figure 24.2 The Fit tab lets you display dimension text at the correct value.

enjoy the simplicity of dimensioning in Paper Space while maintaining the intelligence of dimensioning in Model Space. Trans-spatial dimensions are smart: as you change the model, the dimensions update.

First you want to make sure you turn on the new Associative dimensioning, as shown in the lower right-hand corner of Figure 24.3. Simply go to the User Preferences tab in the Options dialog box (or set dimassoc to 2) and select the Make new dimensions associative option. Now dimension your model from Paper Space by reaching into the viewport to select those parts that need to be dimensioned. It's embarrassingly easy and doesn't require any fancy scaling mumbo jumbo.

Note   The wonderful Quick Dimensions (Qdim), which came out in AutoCAD 2000, are not associative; consequently, they cannot create the smart trans-spatial dimensions. It just about broke my heart when I found this out because I'm such a huge Qdim fan.

Layers in Layouts!

Because layers are so important when dimensioning in Paper Space, this is probably a good time to mention a couple of key ingredients to Paper Space success. It's not uncommon to want some objects to show up in one viewport and not in others. You control this by placing those objects on specific layers and then controlling the visibility of the layers in the Layer dialog. While in a Layout, notice two additional columns in the Layer dialog box: Current VP Freeze and New VP Freeze. You might have to widen the dialog box to see these columns

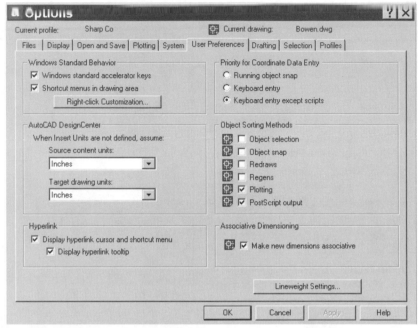

Figure 24.3 Turn on Associative Dimensioning in the User Preferences tab.

because they land to the far right. Current VP Freeze freezes the selected layer in the current viewport and New VP Freeze freezes the selected layer in any future viewports you create. You can freeze a specific layer in many viewports by highlighting multiple layers with the <Shift> or <Ctrl> key and selecting the icon in the Current VP Freeze column of one of the layers.

You also can freeze and thaw layers per viewport in the Layer drop-down list on the Object Properties toolbar (as long as you aren't in AutoCAD 2000). For some reason, the Toolbar Gods decided to remove this option in AutoCAD 2000 and replace it with the new no-plot feature. Realizing the error of their ways, this very valuable option was returned in AutoCAD 2000i.

You might find that you need to use various crosshatch scale factors to get the desired results in various viewports. It's not uncommon for users to have several different hatch layers to achieve the proper results.

You can also control your layers with the `vplayer` command. You might find the many options in the `vplayer` command to be more appealing when doing extensive layer control in viewports. Because you can use wildcards in `vplayer`, it's sometimes more efficient to use than manually selecting the viewports in the standard `layer` command. Besides, the `vplayer` command contains one of the most intimidating default options in AutoCAD: `vpvisdflt` (Viewport Visibility Default). It only sounds scary, and it works much like the New VP Freeze option does in the Layer dialog.

You'll also probably want to set your viewport layer to no-plot so you don't see the viewport boundaries on your final plot.

Another important variable is `psltscale`. To ensure your linetypes display correctly in your viewports, set `psltscale` to 1 (On), which makes AutoCAD look at your current viewport scale factor and scale your linetypes according to the `ltscale` and `celtscale` settings.

One Final Tip

Have you ever tried to create aligned viewports using the `mview` command? Good luck! The easiest method of lining up your viewports is by copying them to the desired location and stretching a viewport (preferably using grips) to the desired size.

The following steps will let you live happily ever after in Paper Space.

1. Create your model.

2. Select the Layout tab and set up the proper paper size (along with other assorted print settings) in the Page Setup dialog.

3. Insert your boundary and title blocks.

4. Create layers for your viewports and dimensions. Make the viewport layer current.

5. Use the `mview` command to create your viewports.

6. Set the proper viewport scale factor in each viewport and pan around if necessary to get the proper view of your model.

7. Make the appropriate dimension layer current and create your dimensions in the space of your choice (AutoCAD 2002 users will use Paper Space; pre-AutoCAD 2002 users will probably use Model Space). Be sure to set the various dimension variables appropriately, as mentioned earlier in this chapter.

8. Annotate your drawing (in Paper Space).

9. Freeze the viewport layer (or set to no-plot) and plot your drawing.

10. Plot at a scale of 1:1 (and I recommend using the Layout option for plotting).

11. Pat yourself on the back for becoming a Paper Space guru!

CHAPTER 25

Taking a Tour Through Options

The correct system variable settings can make your AutoCAD life wonderful. Unfortunately, incorrect settings can do just the opposite. Trying to find the exact system variable that seems to be plaguing your drawing can be like finding a needle in a haystack. Many key settings reside in the Options dialog box. Those of you familiar with Release 14 will note that the dialog had a name change (and a major overhaul) from the preferences command.

Do yourself a favor. Whenever a new release of AutoCAD comes out, check out the Options dialog for the latest and greatest. In doing so, I have found some awesome settings nestled within that have really made a difference in my AutoCAD world. If you're a CAD manager, you will live a longer, happier life once you've explored the depths of the Options dialog box because you will be able to ensure your users have the proper settings for optimal productivity.

You have several ways of getting to the Options dialog. You can right-click on the command line or the drawing editor and select Options from the right-click shortcut menu (if no command is active). If you've terminated the life of your right-click menus, you will find Options hiding in the Tools pull-down menu, and you can always do it the old fashioned way by keying in options.

The Files Tab

The first tab is Files (Figure 25.1). Here, you designate all the various directories you want AutoCAD to search for the various support files in your drawing life. I'll peruse the various folders.

Support File Search Path This is perhaps one of the most important settings in the Options dialog. Here, you indicate all the directories you want AutoCAD to search to find a variety of important files such as font files, menu files, linetypes, and hatch patterns. AutoCAD also searches the support directories when looking for drawing files. Add search directories by hitting the Add button on the right and Browsing until you find them.

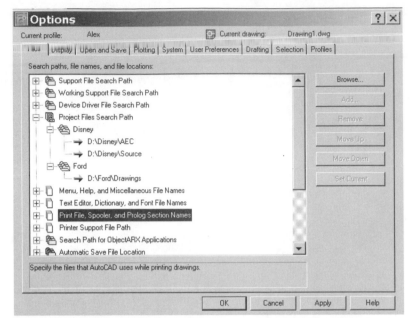

Figure 25.1 You use the Files tab in the Options dialog box to set up your various file search paths.

Working Support File Search Path You've set up the search path for your support files. What if, for some reason, AutoCAD can't find those directories? Maybe a server goes down and AutoCAD can no longer see it. The Working Support File Search Path shows you the active directories — those AutoCAD can actually see at any given moment. This section is read-only.

Device Driver File Search Path Indicate the directories AutoCAD should search for device drivers for your input device, printer, plotter, and video display.

Project Files Search Path Do you find yourself working on several projects that require drawings from completely different directories? If so, you might consider setting up a project file that tells AutoCAD which project you're working on and exactly which directories to be working from. Figure 25.1 shows two projects: Disney and Ford. Each project searches different directories. It's a simple process of adding a named project and then adding the directories you want AutoCAD to use. The project name is saved to the `projectname` system variable.

Menu, Help, and Miscellaneous File Names Indicate the location and filename to be used for the menu file (you can also use the `menu` command), the AutoCAD Help file, and your default Internet location, should you select the Launch Browser button on the Standard Toolbar or the Connect to the Internet option on the Help pull-down menu in AutoCAD 2000. As far as I can tell, this option is no longer valid in AutoCAD 2002 because those two options have been replaced with a variety of additional Internet features, none of which I could tell talked to this setting. You can also set the `inetlocation` system variable manually. The good old configuration filename (`acad2002.cfg`) and location is also shown here, although rumor has it you can't change the setting here (it's read-only). To change this setting, you need to use the `/c` command-line switch in the AutoCAD Properties settings.

The License Server option indicates the network server running the Autodesk License Manager, from which you receive a usage license. This setting is also read-only and needs to be set via the `acadserver` environment variable (which is done through the Windows Control Panel under System). Your best bet is to follow the AutoCAD Help function information regarding environment variables should the need arise to modify this setting. This value is read only at the beginning of each AutoCAD session. If the value is changed, it won't be displayed until AutoCAD is closed and reopened.

Text Editor, Dictionary, and Font File Names   You can control the text editor used for editing Mtext objects. Earlier versions of Mtext made this only slightly attractive. By default, AutoCAD uses the internal editor, which does the trick just fine. This value is also stored in the `mtexted` system variable. The Main Dictionary specifies which dictionary you plan to use for spell checking. You'll find options for American English, two for British English, and two for French. I need the California English version (which apparently isn't included). You also can use the `dctmain` system variable.

If you have a custom dictionary you'd like to use, indicate the name and location here or by using the `dctcust` system variable. On those occasions when AutoCAD can't find a specific font file (usually when someone else gives you a drawing file), you can specify the alternate font you'd like to take the missing font's place. This value can also be set via the `fontalt` system variable.

I know many CAD gurus who set fontmaps for their slowwwwwwwwww fonts (undoubtedly TrueType fonts). This permits you to map a slow font to a speedy one. Then when you're ready to plot, just map the fonts back. The Font Mapping file indicates the location and name of the font map file. This file is stored in the Registry (which means it affects all files). You can also set this using the `fontmap` system variable.

Print File, Spooler, and Prolog Section Names   This section displays a variety of settings related to the wonderful world of plotting. If you have some legacy plotting script files you're still using, you can indicate the default name for the temporary plot files created with earlier versions of AutoCAD. The default name is the name of the drawing followed by .plt (e.g., `columbia.plt`). If you're using AutoCAD 2002 drawings, the default name is the drawing name layout followed by the PLT extension (e.g., `columbia-layout1.plt`). This particular option only affects the default plot filename used for plotting scripts created with earlier versions of AutoCAD. If you have a Print Spooling program, you need to specify the application to use. You can also include command-line arguments in the value. If you use `psout`, you can indicate the prolog section to be read from the `acad.psf` file. This value is also saved in the Registry file and can be set via the `psprolog` filename.

Printer Support File Path   This section specifies some additional path settings for printer support files. You select the location you want AutoCAD to write the plot files to and indicate where your PC3 files are located in the Printer Configuration search path. You also indicate here the location for your PMP (printer description) files. Your plot style table files (STB and CTB) will land in the path indicated here as well.

Search Path for ObjectARX Applications   There's conflicting information on this option, and I couldn't sort it out myself. The Help files indicate that if you're using ObjectARX apps, you'll want to enter a number of URL addresses (separated by semicolons) for AutoCAD to search when an associated ObjectARX application can't be found. The tooltip indicates that this is the path AutoCAD searches to find ARX routines that custom objects detected when a drawing file is read. I'm not sure on this one guys, so flip a coin.

The Automatic Save File Location   Indicate exactly where you want to store automatically saved files. The default is buried in several subdirectories; you might want to place it in a more obvious location. This value can also be set with the savefilepath system variable.

Data Sources Location   Define the path for your database source files. Any changes made won't take effect until you close and restart AutoCAD.

Drawing Template File Location   This setting indicates where you store your template files for the AutoCAD Setup Wizards.

Log File Location   If you choose to maintain a log file (the Open and Save tab), this is the path used. This option is controlled by the logfilepath system variable.

Temporary Drawing File Location   Where do you want your temporary files stored? These are files that AutoCAD creates while you're drawing and deletes when you exit (as long as you exit gracefully). If you don't specify a directory, the Windows Temp directory is used as the default.

Temporary External Reference File Location   If you select Enabled with Copy (Open and Save tab) in the Demand Load Xrefs section, you need a temporary directory in which to place the copy of the xref files. This value is also stored in the xloadpath variable.

Texture Maps Search Path   Last, but not least, is the Texture Map Search Path (I can't believe there are so many different file settings). This is the directory AutoCAD searches for rendered texture maps.

The Display Tab

The Display tab (Figure 25.2) customizes the AutoCAD Display (no revelations here). I hope you've set your display up to match your AutoCAD lifestyle. Do you want the screen menu displayed? Scroll bars? What background colors do you want? All this is controlled here. I'll work my way through it so you don't miss out on anything.

The primary sections of the Display tab are Window elements, Layout elements, Display resolution, and Display performance. It also has two slider bars at the bottom of the dialog box that control the Crosshair size and Reference Edit fading intensity.

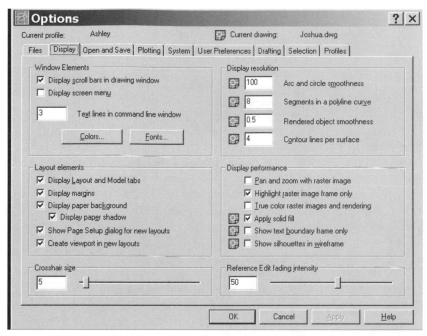

Figure 25.2 The Display tab in the Options dialog customizes the AutoCAD display.

Window Elements

Display scroll bars in drawing window Do you use the scroll bars along the right side and bottom of the display screen (Figure 25.3)? These scroll bars can be used to pan around in your drawing and seem to be popular with new users. If you're an Intellimouse user, then you're no doubt addicted to the more powerful mouse wheel and wouldn't dream of using the scroll bars. If you're not using them, get rid of them. Free up that valuable real estate!

Display screen menu If you're a veteran AutoCAD user, you remember when the only menu option you had was the screen menu that displays along the right side of the screen. Now you have pull-down menus, right-click menus, toolbars, and so forth to help you get the job done. Still, many of you love the screen menus and prefer them to any of the other options.

If you key in AutoCAD commands, the AutoCAD screen menu is handy because it tends to follow the commands you're in. No need to right-click to get to a shortcut menu; the options you need appear right there on the screen. Fewer clicks means more productivity. Unfortunately, the screen menus aren't as developed as they used to be. I remember when every single AutoCAD command resided in the screen menu. It's unfortunate they no longer get the attention needed to make them the valuable resource they could be. For example, when at a Select objects prompt, it would be great if the various object selection options appeared.

At the top of every AutoCAD screen menu screen you'll see two lines.

ıₗₗₗ|ₗₗₗ'ₗₗₗ

* * * *

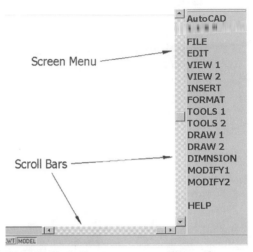

For the record, picking on the word AutoCAD sends you back to the primary main menu. Picking on the four asterisks sends you to the Object Snap submenu.

Text lines in command-line window   You   can control the number of lines that display in the command prompt area in this section of the Display tab (you also can resize the command prompt area manually). The default is 3, but I tend to set it to 4. Because most of my AutoCAD life is spent speaking on the road, I put my command prompt at the top of the screen for easier viewing by an audience.

Figure 25.3 Some users still prefer using the Screen menu to the pull-down menus.

Colors   The Colors button takes you to the Color Options dialog (Figure 25.4), where you set up the various colors assigned to the different sections of the AutoCAD display. For example, I prefer to work with light vectors on a dark background while in Model Space. But when I submit screen shots for my column, I've been asked to submit them with dark colors on a light background (so you can read them easily in print). Therefore, I need to change the background colors around to make my extremely kind, sweet, and charming editor happy. If you find yourself taking AutoCAD drawings into Word, you've probably been faced with the same issue.

If you've totally messed up the color scheme and want to go back to ground zero, simply select the Default All button. The Default one element button only puts the selected setting back to its original value.

You can mess with your friends by setting up the display so the text, crosshairs and background colors are all the same. That should keep them busy!

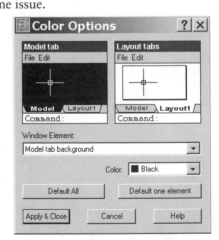

Fonts   The Fonts button lets you change the display font value and size for the command line. If you have a high-resolution graphics card, you might want to increase the font size and maybe even make it bold.

Layout Elements

The Release of AutoCAD 2000 introduced you to the world of multiple Layout tabs. This was intended to replace the tedious task of setting `tilemode` to 0 to get to Paper Space,

Figure 25.4 Customize the AutoCAD display by assigning colors to the different areas.

which was far from an obvious road to take! In this section are a variety of options that enable you to set up your layouts to suit your needs.

Display Layout and Model tabs   A great improvement to the user interface in AutoCAD, merely select these tabs to go from Model Space to Paper Space (or vice versa). It would seem a shame to turn these off unless your company doesn't use Paper Space at all.

Display margins   The paper margins display as dashed lines in Paper Space layouts. Should you choose to draw outside of this area, you will likely find part of your drawing clipped or omitted. If these margins bug you, turn them off.

Display paper background   Do you want a representation of the paper size in your Paper Space layout? How about a shadow?

Show Page Setup dialog for new layouts   I personally don't like being prompted for the page setup (for plotting) when I initially go to a new layout, so I've turned this feature off. If selected, the Page Setup dialog box displays and expects input needed to plot your drawing.

Create viewport in new layouts   By default, AutoCAD creates a Paper Space viewport in all new layouts. If you're new to Paper Space, this is a great way to figure out what Paper Space is all about. If you're a veteran user, the last thing you want is AutoCAD determining where and what size your viewports are, so you'll probably opt to deselect this option.

Display Resolution

This section controls the quality of the display of objects. Setting high values for display can sometimes impair the performance, so keep that in mind.

Arc and circle smoothness   I'm sure AutoCAD veterans remember the old `viewres` command that allowed you to control the smoothness of circles, arcs and ellipses. This option controls `viewres` — the higher the value, the smoother the results when zooming in on curved objects. The values range from 1 to 20,000. It's my belief that if you have a decent computer, you really won't notice much degradation in speed even when set at the highest value on an average-sized drawing. So if those choppy circles bug you, by all means try cranking up this value. Because this setting is saved in the drawing file, you might consider setting this in your template drawing files to maintain it. You can still set this value in the good old `viewres` command.

   I also came across the `whiparc` system variable that supposedly controls whether the display of arcs and circles is smooth. I can't get it to work. Can any of you?

Segments in a polyline curve   When creating a spline curve within the `pedit` command, AutoCAD approximates the curve using smaller, straight polyline segments. This value (also controlled by the `splinesegs` variable) controls the number of polyline segments between each vertex. The higher the number, the smoother the curve and, possibly, the slower you go. This setting does not affect splines created using the `spline` command.

Rendered object smoothness   If you create 3D objects, this option is invaluable in controlling the smoothness of shaded and/or rendered curved solids. Believe it or not, this value (assigned to the facetres system variable) is multiplied by the viewres setting to determine how to display solid objects. A higher `facetres` number improves the display but could potentially decrease display performance. The valid range is from 0.01 to 10.

Contour lines per surface   The `isolines` variable enters here. This setting controls the number of contour lines per surface on 3D objects. The valid range is 0 to 2,047 with a default setting of 4.

Note   Many options in the Options dialog have a red drawing icon in front of the setting. This indicates that the setting is saved within the current drawing only! If you want to save these settings for all drawings, consider setting them in your template drawings or create a simple script file to set them.

Display Performance

This section controls the display settings that affect your performance.

Pan and zoom with raster image   If you often put raster images in your AutoCAD drawings, you quickly realize performance is a real issue. When this option is selected, a copy of the image moves with the cursor as you use real-time pan and zoom, which can slow your display tremendously. If you turn this feature off, an outline of the object is displayed instead (hence, you'll pan and zoom much faster). This affects the `rtdisplay` system variable (and not the `dragmode` value as cited in the Help file).

Highlight raster image frame only   This option turns your raster image to a frame during object selection. This definitely will speed up your selection process. It's controlled by the `imagehlt` system variable.

True color raster images and rendering   True Color is awesome; but can you say SLOW? Selecting this option displays your images in True Color or at the highest display quality available for your system; you may need to pack a lunch between regens.

Apply Solid Fill   Turning off your filled objects can speed you up a tad, but I'm not sure it's really worth it. These might be solids, polylines with width attached, filled hatching, and so on. You won't notice any change until a regeneration occurs. This is linked to the `fillmode` system variable as well as the old `fill` command.

Show text boundary frame only   You can convert your text objects to rectangular frames to speed up your display as well. You won't notice a change until a regeneration occurs. This controls the `qtext` command and `qtextmode` system variable.

Show silhouettes in wireframe   Here's another 3D option you'll probably want to keep on. It controls whether silhouette curves display and whether a mesh is drawn during a `hide`. This is set to the `dispsilh` system variable.

Crosshair Size

Of the two slider bars across the bottom of the Display tab, Crosshair size is self-explanatory. I must confess, I still leave mine set to 100. If you're a Paper Space user, you can't beat a setting of 100 for making it easy to tell whether you're in viewport. This value is saved to the `cursorsize` variable.

Reference Edit Fading Intensity

This option controls the intensity value of objects during the refedit command. It definitely is not one of the more vital commands to AutoCAD, but hey, if it matters to you, by all means change it. It has a default setting of 50, and I've never been motivated to fuss with it. This value is set to the `xfadectl` system variable.

The Open and Save Tab

Clicking on the third tab displays the Open and Save tab in the Options dialog box (Figure 25.5). I'll begin the tour in the upper left-hand corner of the dialog and work my way down and across.

File Save

The File Save section deals with options related to saving a file in AutoCAD. The first option allows you to specify a persistent save file format to the current or previous format. If you're on AutoCAD 2002 and you're work-

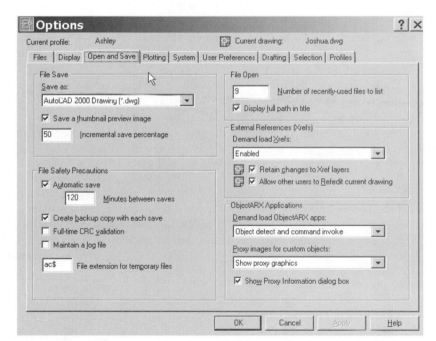

Figure 25.5 The Open and Save tab in the Options dialog box provides many options.

ing with a customer on AutoCAD Release 14 but don't want to worry about saving to the right format, this allows you to automate it. The following are valid formats.

```
AutoCAD Release 14/13 (DWG);

AutoCAD LT 98/97/95 (DWG);

a drawing template file (DWT);

a drawing interchange file (DXF) for AutoCAD 2002, 2000, R14, R13, R12, LT98, LT97,
    LT95 and LT2.
```

However, I must warn you that saving to a DXF format will slow you down.

Save a thumbnail preview image   This setting controls whether or not a bitmap image is saved and displayed in any of the File dialogs. It also controls the `rasterpreview` system variable. If you're working on a large drawing (and I mean very large) and want to speed up your saves, you might consider turning this feature off until you're finished for the day. Every little bit helps and saving an image along with the drawing on every save can slow you down a small amount.

Incremental save percentage   This setting has caused great controversy since it was added to AutoCAD a couple of releases ago. I'm going to share with you the `isavepercent` gospel according to Lynn, but I'll be the first to admit you'll find others who will disagree with me.

For years, AutoCAD did a full, clean save whenever you saved your drawing. These saves ended up with a nice, neatly condensed file. They also took their toll on the impatient CAD user because they could take a long time to process. Enter the incremental save. Saves take less time, but the resulting files aren't as neat, clean, or compact (think of your sock drawer).

The value set here indicates the maximum amount of wasted space your drawing is allowed to contain before AutoCAD does a full save. An entry of 50 means 50 percent of your total drawing could be not-so-nice-and-neat space. The lower the number, the less wasted space there is and the slower your saves are. The higher the setting, the more wasted space is allowed and the faster your saves are. The higher the setting, the larger your file size (all that wasted space added onto your drawing file). A value of 0 always forces a full save.

Tip   Create two toolbar buttons: one that sets the incremental save percentage (aka the isavepercent system variable) to 80 and one that sets it to 0. Hit the 80 button when you first enter large drawings; hit the 0 button when you leave the drawing. This way, the last save you execute before leaving the drawing yields a nice, neat drawing file.

File Safety Precautions

Automatic save   I can't help but chuckle every time I see a default of 120 minutes (or two long hours) for the Automatic save value. It still amazes me how many of you live on the edge. You're obviously much luckier and much more confident of yourself than I am to leave this setting so high. I set mine to 20 minutes, but you should set yours to whatever makes you feel the most comfortable. These automatic saves work like the real save; hence, they can take a few seconds out of your drawing life, so setting it too low could lead to frustration. I know some users who don't like the automatic save feature at all and turn it off (set it to 0). I don't fall under that category, however. This setting sets the `savetime` system variable. The location of the saved file can be controlled in the Files tab of the Options dialog. Also note that the automatic save file has a unique name that doesn't have a DWG extension. By default, the name of the automatic save file is named after your drawing file with an SV$ extension.

Say you're working in a drawing called `alex.dwg` (named after my Cocker Spaniel). First I'd ask you why you're naming your drawings after my dog. Your automatic save is set to 15 minutes. You work for two hours without any type of save and then the power goes out — Doh! Your `alex.dwg` file is now behind by two hours. No problem, you can go get the automatic save file called `alex.sv$` and use it. In the worst-case scenario, this file will only be 14 minutes and 59 seconds behind (much better than two hours). However, you can't open a file with an SV$ extension; you must rename it. Just for safety's sake, call it `alex2.dwg`. Now you can open this drawing, hope it has only been a few minutes since the automatic save kicked in, and smile because you didn't lose all that work after all.

Create backup copy with each save   Whenever you save your drawings, AutoCAD automatically creates a backup file with a BAK extension. The Backup file is always one save behind. If these miscellaneous BAK files bug you, by all means turn them off. If you run into problems with your drawing file and try to revive it from your backup file, you'll need to change the BAK extension to DWG. This setting affects the `isavebak` system variable.

Full-time CRC validation   This gives you the option of making a cyclic redundancy check. I haven't concerned myself with this setting for many years and would be fine if it mysteriously disappeared. Are any of you out there avid users of this? CRC validation used to be quite important when faced with a corrupt file in need of observation. With CRC turned on, each object added to your drawing is given a complete checkup to ensure it's a healthy object. If your drawing is acting suspiciously, you can turn this option on for added insurance. Do you think turning the CRC validation on will slow down your drawing? You betcha!

Maintain a log file   In this section, you can specify that you want the text from your command line to page out to a Log file. Instructors find this option handy to check up on the practices of their students. You can set up the name and location for the Log file in the Files tab of the Options dialog.

File extension for temporary files   The last option in this section allows you to control the extension of the various temporary files AutoCAD creates while in use. If you're in a networking environment, it might be necessary to change the extension of each individual's temporary files so they don't accidentally step on each other, depending on how you have your work environment set up.

File Open

Two nice additions to AutoCAD 2002 appear in this section. You now can control the maximum number of recently used files listed in the Files pull-down menu (it used to be 4 but now can be set as high as 9). Apparently 9 is the magic maximum because a value of 10 would conflict with the #1 filename when running AutoCAD via the keyboard. Well, that's the rumor anyway. I'm okay with it just above the Menu entries Maximum number.

Also notice that the entire full path of your drawing files now appears at the top of the AutoCAD screen — very kewl.

External References (Xrefs)

Demand loading really sped up the use of external reference files. Now you need only load in the part of the xref that's needed to regenerate the drawing. For example, if you have a map that contains a clipped external reference file and you're only using a small part of the attached drawing and only a few layers as well, regenerating the entire drawing and all the layers simply isn't necessary! Demand loading saves the day. Demand load looks at what you need and forgets the rest ... hoorah!

You probably want to work with Demand load Xrefs enabled, and if others need to access your drawing while it's in use, you can set this to Demand load enabled with a copy. This selection would let users access the original drawing file you have attached to your current drawing, and you'll just work with a copy of that attached file.

Remember the visretain system variable? This setting proved valuable for xref users and is set by the Retain changes to Xref layers setting. It's easiest to explain this using an example.

Say you have a drawing called Jake (yes, another dog) that contains an attached xref. You change the layer settings of the xref (some are turned off, some are on). You leave AutoCAD and go home to a nice hot dinner (but I digress). The next morning, you come in and open the Jake drawing only to see that the layer settings were not saved; they've regressed back to their original settings, and you feel like you're in the twilight zone. If visretain had been set to 1, this wouldn't have been a problem. In most cases, you're going to want to have Retain changes to Xref layers checked.

The Allow other users to Refedit current drawing setting is the last in this section. Leaving this setting as is allows the refedit command to work on drawings that have the current drawing file attached. This also affects the xedit system variable. If you turn this selection off and users try to use refedit on this drawing (when it's attached as an external reference), they'll be kindly told their access is denied.

ObjectARX Applications

Demand load ObjectARX apps If you work with applications that contain custom objects, these settings could be important to you. Disable load on demand just turns off the loading of any custom objects, period. Custom object detect demand-loads the source application when you open a drawing containing custom objects. It does not, however, attempt to demand-load the application when you invoke one of the application's commands. Command Invoke works the opposite of Custom Object Detect. It loads the source application as soon as you try to invoke one of the application's commands, but not just because you have custom objects in the drawing file. Last but not least, Object Detect and Command Invoke demand-load the source application when you open a drawing file with custom objects or you invoke the commands from the application (a combination of the two previous options).

Proxy images for custom objects   When you insert a drawing with custom objects and you don't have the application that goes with it, you can control their display. By default, AutoCAD creates proxy graphics to display these custom objects. You can turn the display of these objects off altogether by selecting Do not show proxy graphics. You can also see the custom objects by selecting Show proxy graphics. If you prefer a bounding box to the proxy graphic, simply select the last option, Show proxy bounding box.

Show Proxy Information dialog box   You can suppress that annoying dialog that pops up in AutoCAD warning that you are opening a drawing containing custom objects. Even though it can be important to know whether the drawing contains proxy objects, I do find the constant reminder a tad annoying. But then I always hated it when my mother asked me to clean my room.

I've skipped the Plotting tab on purpose. Someone — not me — could write an entire book on the Plotting tab and still not cover everything. I hope you're not too disappointed.

The System Tab

I'll continue with the System tab (Figure 25.6), but I'm going to go quickly through the rest of the tabs, so hold on. Here you'll find an option new to AutoCAD 2002: Layout Regen Options.

Layout Regen Options

The concept of layouts was added to AutoCAD 2000 to replace tedious changes with `tilemode`. Layouts also brought along the capability of multiple Paper Spaces, and, consequently, the unfortunate addition of regenerations whenever

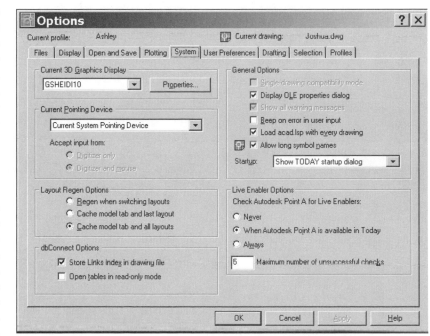

Figure 25.6 The System tab of the Options dialog Box.

you hit one of the Layout tabs. Along with the good came the costly bad, which was remedied in 2000i. Now AutoCAD can cache the display list to memory; hence, it remembers its contents as you move from one layout to the next. There are three options here; I personally opt for the last one. This setting is assigned to the `layoutregenctl` system variable (what a mouthful).

Regen when switching layouts   This option returns regens to the AutoCAD 2000 standard (use this setting if you get paid by the hour).

Cache model tab and last layout   This option caches the last layout you were in to memory, along with the model tab. Regens take place when you switch between any other layout.

Cache model tab and all layouts   This option caches all display lists to memory. Regenerations occur the first time you visit a layout but not thereafter.

Note that this isn't a foolproof guarantee against regens. If you redefine a block in Model Space, you'll probably see another set of regens as you change layout tabs (for obvious reasons).

Note   If you have many layouts in a large drawing, caching the display list might take too much of your precious memory and inevitably slow you down. This could also happen if you're low on memory. In either of the above cases, you might choose to go back to the standard regen when switching layouts.

General Options

I think the General Options section of the dialog is also dabble-worthy. I'll go through these check-boxes in detail.

Single-drawing compatibility mode   The ability to open more than one drawing at a time (MDI) was introduced in AutoCAD 2000. It was a big shock at the end of my first AutoCAD 2000 drawing day when I discovered I had 10 open drawings (you too?). But now I couldn't live without this feature, and I suspect many of you feel the same. If you don't, however, you can check this option, SDI (single document interface) is turned on, and you'll be back to the days of AutoCAD Release 14 and before.

Display OLE properties dialog   This one is pretty simple; it controls whether or not the OLE Properties dialog appears when inserting OLE objects into your drawing.

Show all warning messages   You've all seen the famous "Don't display this warning again" option in a variety of different dialogs. If you select this option, you can overrule any previous settings specific to each dialog.

Beep on error in user input   Personally, this is my favorite way to drive coworkers crazy. A little beep goes off whenever you provide invalid input.

Load acad.lsp **with every drawing**   When the ability to open more than one drawing at a time was delivered with AutoCAD 2000, the option of loading acad.lsp into each drawing file also came into discussion. If you choose not to load acad.lsp into each drawing, then any functions that reside in acad.lsp are only available in the first drawing file. I'm guessing that 99.9 percent of you will want this option selected.

You can avoid dealing with this option altogether by putting your LISP routines into a new file called acaddoc.lsp. This file loads up in every drawing file, period. I cried when they changed acad.lsp and created yet another file to worry about (am I alone here?), but this lovely checkbox option made the change bearable. The behind-the-scenes system variable that controls this is acadlspasdoc.

Allow long symbol names   This option was a great addition to AutoCAD 2000, especially for those who'd run into the 31-character limit of named objects. Although 31 characters seem like plenty, they're not if you use a lot of external references in your drawings. The extnames system variable that controls this option.

Startup   This drop-down list controls what you're faced with when you first enter AutoCAD 2002 and when you start new drawings. As I tour around speaking to users, I've found that AutoCAD TODAY comes with mixed reviews. I've also found that many of you have turned it off without even looking at it (what's up with that?). I recommend you give it a good look before terminating it. It does have some nice extras in it, including a window to Point A, but if you still choose to sentence

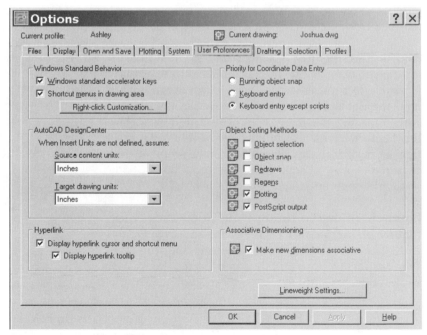

Figure 25.7 The various options in the User Preferences tab.

AutoCAD TODAY to death, here's the place to do so. You can opt for the traditional startup dialog box or no dialog box at all when starting AutoCAD or new drawings.

The User Preferences Tab

The User Preferences tab (Figure 25.7) controls units, standard behavior, and input priority, among other things.

Windows Standard Behavior

These options are key to ensuring you're using the keyboard and mouse setups that make you the most comfortable.

Windows standard accelerator keys   Veteran users of AutoCAD remember when the <Ctrl-C> combination canceled AutoCAD commands. These were the pre-Windows days of DOS. Windows introduced the CopyClip <Ctrl-C> combination and a conflict arose. Autodesk had the foresight to go the way of the Windows world and reassign <Ctrl-C> to CopyClip and replacing Cancel with the <Esc> key. Change is always such a drag, but somehow I managed to get used to it. Face it, the <Esc> key is easier to get to and makes so much more sense, but old habits die hard. For those who just couldn't adjust, AutoCAD provided a way to put the settings back. <Ctrl-V> was another casualty of Windows, having been used by AutoCAD to switch from one viewport to another. Now <Ctrl-V> Pastes and AutoCAD uses <Ctrl-R> to toggle between viewports.

Shortcut menus in drawing area   A multitude of right-click menus were introduced in AutoCAD 2000. It was perfect for new users, but a thorn to those who used the right-click button on the mouse as <Enter>. After realizing the many cool options hiding within these shortcut menus, the adjustment to the new right-click world was complete. This is another key example of how change inevitably turns out to be a good, although initially a tad annoying, thing.

Right-click Customization   The Right-click Customization button displays the dialog shown in Figure 25.8. This allows you to control where and when the shortcut menus appear. You can even tell AutoCAD you'd prefer a right-click to yield an <Enter> when a command is in progress. These settings are saved to the shortcutmenu system variable.

Figure 25.8 Hit the Right-click Customization button to get this dialog box.

AutoCAD DesignCenter

This next section has had little publicity, yet it is extremely powerful. If you ever need to convert a drawing from metric to inches or to insert a block that was created in inches but needs to be in millimeters, then read on.

AutoCAD 2000 introduced DesignCenter — the ability to drag and drop important data from one drawing to another. The DesignCenter section in the User Preferences tab of the Options dialog allows you to indicate the source and target units. I'm sure there's an easier way to do this, but here's one of the many solutions.

Say Drawing A is in inches, and I want to convert it to millimeters. Set the Source content units to inches and the Target drawing units to millimeters. While in Drawing A, create a block of all the objects in the drawing, leaving the base point at 0,0. Start a new drawing, Drawing B. Drag and drop Drawing A into the new drawing using DesignCenter, explode it, and voilà! You might have to monkey around with the dimensions (actually you will have to monkey around with the dimensions).

For the record, you also can set the source unit and target unit settings with the insunitsdefsource and insunitsdeftarget variables, respectively. For your amusement, here's a list of the various settings you can choose from: Unspecified-Unitless, Inches, Feet, Miles, Millimeters, Centimeters, Meters, Kilometers, Microinches, Mils, Yards, Angstroms, Nanometers, Microns, Decimeters, Decameters, Hectometers, Gigameters, Astronomical Units, Light Years, and Parsecs. Light Years is my personal favorite.

Priority to Coordinate Data Entry

In the upper right-hand corner of the User Preferences tab is the Priority for Coordinate Data Entry section. This option can be key to whether your osnaps win out over keyboard coordinate entry. If you've ever keyed in a specific coordinate only to find that an object snap kicked in and yielded an incorrect final coordinate, then you'll love this. I use the Keyboard entry except scripts setting; my keyboard entry wins all the time, except during script file operations. The osnapcoord system variable is set here.

Associative Dimensioning

The last section of the User Preferences tab that I'm going to discuss is found in the lower right-hand corner. It contains the new checkbox for turning on Associative Dimensioning. Make sure it's checked for maximum productivity.

The Drafting Tab

The Drafting tab, as shown in Figure 25.9, controls a variety of general editing options (all of which start with the letter A). Once you set this tab to your preferred settings, it's doubtful you'll visit it often.

AutoSnap Settings

I tend to leave the AutoSnap settings as they lie. By default, the AutoSnap markers appear with magnetic force fields that snag you, along with a tooltip that indicates which force field got you. These settings are also controlled by the autosnap system variable. If you prefer the age-old aperture box to the new AutoSnap symbols, toggle that option on in the Drafting tab (or by setting the apbox system variable).

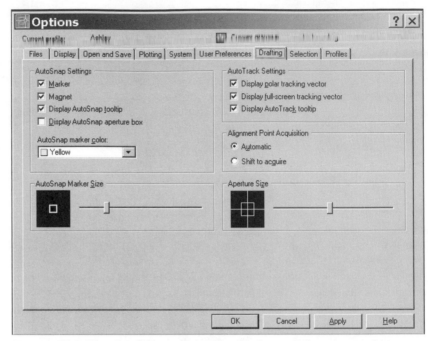

Figure 25.9 The Drafting tab in the Options dialog controls a number of general editing options.

AutoTrack Settings

Object snap tracking surfaced in AutoCAD 2000 and is one of the most underused, least understood, and yet powerful features in AutoCAD. Once you figure out how to use it, you'll wonder how you did without it. The upper right-hand corner of the Drafting tab tackles the AutoTrack settings — a combination of object snap and Polar tracking options. I'll take a quick peek at each of these values.

Display polar tracking vector   Ortho mode makes it easy to snap to the angles 0, 90, 180, and 270. Polar tracking makes it equally easy to snap to auxiliary angles. Select the angle(s) in the Settings dialog box and make sure that Polar snapping is on (easily done from the Status Bar). The tracking vector that appears is controlled here, and I see absolutely no reason why you would ever choose to turn this feature off. It's a great means of quickly constructing objects at alternative angles. This setting is controlled by the trackpath system variable.

Display full-screen tracking vector   When you have turned object snap tracking on (also easily controlled from the Status Bar), you'll definitely want the tracking vector displayed so you can see the proposed extended point. If you're trying to figure out the world of object snap tracking, do yourself a huge favor and make sure the Extension object snap is selected in the Settings dialog along with your favorite object snaps. Perpendicular is another osnap that comes in handy with object snap tracking (notice how I'm providing all these hints without actually explaining how to use object snap tracking). Tracking vectors are essentially construction lines that display to help you draw objects at specific angles or in specific relationships to other objects. The trackpath system variable also controls this setting.

Display AutoTrack tooltip   You'll probably also want to select the Display AutoTrack tooltip, which indicates which angles and object snaps AutoTracking uses to determine the final point. Figure 25.10 shows a picture of tracking vectors and a tooltip.

Alignment Point Acquistion

When using object snap tracking, you can acquire points by hovering over an object snap (Automatic) or by holding down the <Shift> key to grab the point. I prefer hovering (I'm too lazy to hit an additional key), but the choice is up to you, and it's controlled in this section of the Drafting tab.

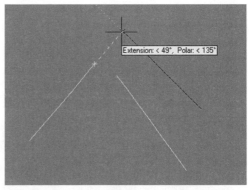

Figure 25.10 Object snap tracking is a powerful tool for constructing objects.

The Selection Tab

The Selection tab (Figure 25.11), controls the settings related to object selection. Over the course of many years, object selection has changed quite a bit. Most users are fine with the current settings, but it's nice to know all your options because object selection is such a critical part of the drawing procedure. I find most people wander into this tab when something has gone awry; namely, someone has been playing around and changing the settings. I hope to provide you with the information and ammunition to put everything back just exactly the way you like it.

Selection Modes

I'll wander through the various selection modes one at a time.

Noun/verb selection   Have you noticed that when you have objects selected and you execute a command that would normally prompt you to select objects, the selection set is passed directly to the command? The pickfirst variable controls this feature. If objects are already selected, those objects are used. If no objects are selected, AutoCAD prompts you for some. I strongly recommend leaving this features as is because without it you won't be able to use the extremely powerful Grips feature, and you know that using AutoCAD without grips just isn't worth the effort!

Use Shift to add to selection   The pickadd system variable definitely plays a larger role in AutoCAD 2002. The Properties dialog box has a button specifically dedicated to turning pickadd on and off. So what exactly does pickadd do? It allows only one active selection set at a time. For example, you use a crossing window to select five objects. You have one active selection set. If pickadd is on (or if Use Shift to add to selection is on) and you try to select additional objects, a new selection set will replace the original selection set of five objects. Why would you want this?

Autodesk had many requests from users who wanted the option to edit objects individually in the Properties dialog. They wanted to pick a text string and then edit the text string, pick a circle and then edit the circle, pick some arcs and then edit those arcs, and so on. They didn't want to have to clear the selection set each time by hitting <Esc> 10 times between operations. If pickadd is on, there's no need to clear the selection set between editing operations. If you still can't follow this explanation, try it yourself. Turn pickadd on, go into the erase command, and individually pick three objects. How many objects are you really erasing? Only one! And it's the last one that you picked.

So, you ask, how do you add to the active selection set if pickadd is on? Hold down the <Shift> key, and AutoCAD allows you to add objects to the current selection set (hence the setting Use Shift to add to selection).

Press and drag   This option was originally thrown in to appease the Mac users of the world who are used to holding down the mouse button to create a window. If you have no Mac hang-ups, you simply don't need it. This setting is also controlled by the pickdrag system variable.

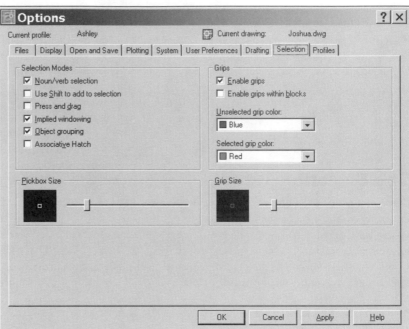

Figure 25.11 The Selection tab in the Options dialog controls the settings that relate to general object selection.

Implied windowing   This crucial setting allows you to perform automatic windowing. You know by now that if you pick a point on your drawing that doesn't land on an object, AutoCAD launches into an automatic window. Drawing the window from right to left executes a standard window and selects only those objects that fall completely within the windowed area. Drawing the window from left to right executes a crossing window and selects any and all objects that fall within or across the windowed area. It's doubtful you would ever turn this feature off, but you can by setting the pickauto system variable.

Object grouping   Groups are another creature I addressed in Chapter 19, — Cool Tricks in AutoCAD. The group command allows you to create a set of objects for selection purposes. If you pick one member of the group, the entire group highlights. If you turn off grouping so you can individually select the objects, you can do so here in the Options dialog. Easier yet, simply press <Ctrl-A> to turn groups on and off. If you've never dabbled in the world of groups, take a look at them because you could find them valuable. The `pickstyle` system variable controls object grouping.

Associative Hatch   When you pick a hatch pattern, do you want the boundary objects selected as well? The `pickstyle` system variable controls this setting.

You also can control the size of the pickbox in the Selection tab. Have fun with coworkers who are really bad shots and set it to 50 pixels — the highest number possible. Those of you on Release 14 can set it as high as 32,767, which opens up all kinds of possibilities!

Grips

I hope you haven't chosen to suppress those beautiful blue grip boxes that allow you to edit faster than a speeding bullet! If you have, I strongly encourage you to give them a chance. (See Chapter 4, — Grip Me Baby!). This section has the Enable grips and Enable grips within blocks options. Enabling grips within blocks tells AutoCAD to display all the grips for each object within a block (which can be overwhelming). It doesn't allow you to individually edit those objects, which logically might be your first thought, but you can use those grips as alternative base points, for example. When grips within blocks are not enabled, AutoCAD uses the insertion point of the block as the grip point. The `gripblock` system variable controls the latter option, whereas the `grips` system variable controls the former.

You also can control your grip colors in this tab. I have mine set to yellow because they're easier to see, and I need them to be visible to my audiences while I'm speaking. Blue is more subdued and less intrusive, but the colors you use are completely up to you. You also can control the size of your grips within this tab.

The Profiles Tab

Here you are — the end of your Options journey. Amazingly, the Profiles tab is the key to all option settings and probably the most important part of the Options dialog. It is here you create and save your favorite profiles, making sure to lock in the various settings that make your drawing life comfortable.

Figure 25.12 displays the profiles I have on my system. I have a profile for presentations, one for working, and a couple for various projects. I'll run down the list of profile settings, although most are self-explanatory.

Double-clicking or hitting the Set Current button sets the current profile. All the settings assigned to that profile are now used by the system. You can change settings by going to the appropriate tab, making a change, and hitting the Apply button at the bottom of the Options dialog. You can make new profiles by selecting the Add to List option, which essentially saves the selected profile under a different name. You can Rename or Delete a profile; you can't delete the current profile. You can Export or Import profiles from other drawings. Profiles have an ARG extension.

This is a great way to share profiles with other users (and the CAD manager's dream come true). Profiles are saved in the system Registry of your computer.

The Reset option is used when you want to reset the values in a profile to the system default settings, which is especially helpful when you make a real mess of things.

What is saved with a profile? — The settings found in the Options dialog along with your current desktop configuration, including partial menus. This is important, and in many cases key, to keeping users of the same machine from hurting each other. Now all users can set up their own environment, save it under a profile, and call it up when necessary.

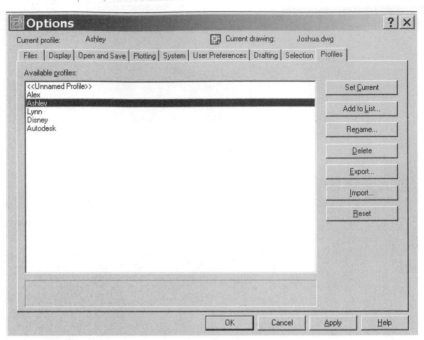

Figure 25.12 The Profiles tab makes it easy to store your user preferences for future use.

BRING ON THE ASPIRIN

You've made it to my favorite section! Hidden within are the keys that unlock the door to AutoCAD Gurudom. The ever-popular columns on attributes and those focusing on conquering customization are contained within this final section. So go get your aspirin bottle, set it next to the computer, brace yourself, and have a look at the most advanced chapters in this book. Remember — no pain no gain!

CHAPTER 26

Are Your Blocks Smart?

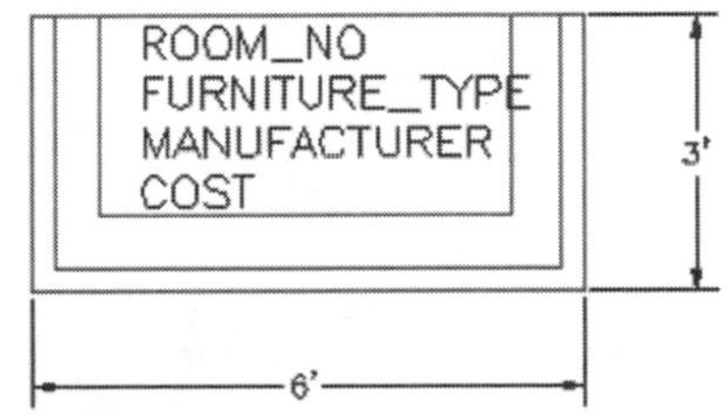

Just about everyone uses blocks in their day-to-day drawing life. Why not make them smart? When you insert a title block, do you tediously go through the process of entering line after line of text to fill in the boxes, or do you have it setup so the block automatically prompts you for the answers while you sit back and watch AutoCAD fill in the boxes for you? When you insert a part, would you like to store the model number, cost, or anything else along with it? Perhaps later you'd like to extract the information into a bill of materials and insert the information into the drawing. All of this is possible with attributes.

Figure 26.1 The four attributes of the sofa block are Room_No, Furniture_Type, Manufacturer, and Cost.

I'm going to use a simple example of a sofa with four attributes: Room No., Furniture Type, Manufacturer, and Cost. The sofa looks similar to Figure 26.1 after adding the attributes.

Follow along by drawing a simple sofa. The rectangular dimensions for mine are 6' by 3' (or 72" by 36"). The basic rectangular shape is really all you need to complete this exercise. Before you make a block out of the sofa, add the desired attributes with the `attdef` (attribute definition) dialog box. In AutoCAD 2000+, keying in `attdef` executes the dialog box automatically. In Release 14 or before, you'll need to execute the `ddattdef` command to get the dialog box. You can also find the Attribute Definition dialog box in the Draw–Block–Define Attributes pull-down menu.

Figure 26.2 shows the Attdef dialog with the first attribute. Get familiar with the dialog box before you jump in and create your attribute definitions.

Mode

You can apply four different modes to your attributes: Invisible, Constant, Verify, and Preset. An Invisible attribute contains data, but that data doesn't display on the drawing. An example of this might be the cost of an object. The information is stored with the drawing; you can extract the information, but you don't want it to display on the final plotted drawing. You can override an attributes Visibility mode by setting `attdisp` on. Make Cost an Invisible attribute.

I find that Constant attributes are seldom used. A Constant attribute can never change. It's practically the same thing as assigning Text to a block, except you can export this text to an external file. When inserting a block with a Constant attribute, you are not asked to input any information; the data stored when the block is created always remain the same. Set your Furniture Type attribute to a constant of Sofa. This object will always be a sofa. Later you might choose to extract the furniture types into an external file.

Verify attributes are a rare breed as well. If you have a complicated model number or a key piece of information that absolutely must be accurate, you might choose to use the Verify mode when creating your attributes. When inserting a block with a Verify attribute, you are prompted twice to verify that the information you provide is correct. If `attdia` is set to 1, this attribute mode

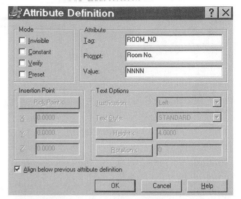

Figure 26.2 Use the Attdef dialog to define block attributes. I added Room_No to the definition and set no modes.

has no effect. Just for the heck of it, set your Manufacturer attribute to Verify.

If you have an attribute that defaults to a specific value 90 percent of the time, you might consider making it a Preset attribute. This mode is similar to Constant in that you won't be prompted for the attribute value, but it's changeable after the fact. If `attdia` is set to 1, you won't notice the effect of setting the Preset mode on for an attribute. (I address the `attdia` function later.)

Attribute

The attribute definition comprises three main parts: Tag, Prompt, and Value. The attribute tag is the name you use to refer to the attribute. Specify what information you want extracted using this tag, which can have up to 256 characters but no spaces or exclamation marks. AutoCAD automatically converts the tag to uppercase. I found, however, that I could use the Object Properties dialog to override that (but heaven only knows what problems this might cause).

When inserting a block with attributes, you will see a prompt asking what you want the attribute value to be. You have complete control over this prompt. If you are asking for a revision number, that prompt could look like either of the following.

```
Enter revision number:
```

```
Revision number:
```

If you leave the attribute prompt empty, AutoCAD substitutes the attribute tag for the prompt. Unlike the tag, you can use spaces in the attribute prompt. There are no prompts for Constant attributes because they are unchangeable.

Just as you do with all good commands, you'll want to include a default value. In most cases, this value should be the most common value assigned to the attribute. This eliminates extra work when inserting the block because you can accept the default and go on. In some cases, for example, you can use the default to denote the type of input.

```
Date <dd/mm/yy>:
```

dd/mm/yy is the default, indicating you want the date to be input by day, month, and year.

After you've selected the modes and set up the description, you need to position the attribute definition on the block. Do you want it centered? What height and text style do you want the attribute to use? All of this information is determined by the lower half of the Attdef dialog box. I think this information is self explanatory, so I'll proceed. For the record, the height I used on my sofa was 4 units.

The first attribute I'm including is the room number attribute. Figure 26.2 shows that I've set no modes for this attribute, that the Tag is called Room_No, the prompt is Room No., and the default denotes I'd like four digit input (NNNN).

Figure 26.3 shows the settings you'll use for the second attribute. Because it's a Constant attribute, the Verify and Preset modes are grayed out (you can never change the value). Also notice that the Prompt is grayed out because the user is not asked to input any information on Constant attributes.

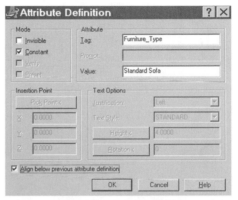

Figure 26.3 Because Furniture_ Type is a Constant attribute, its Verify, Preset, and Prompt options are grayed out.

I wanted the second attribute to go directly beneath the first attribute. In the lower left-hand corner of the dialog, notice the Align below previous attribute definition option. When selected, you won't be prompted for height, rotation, or placement because it is all controlled for you.

Figure 26.4 shows the third in the line of attribute definitions. This attribute is Preset and also is placed beneath the previous attribute.

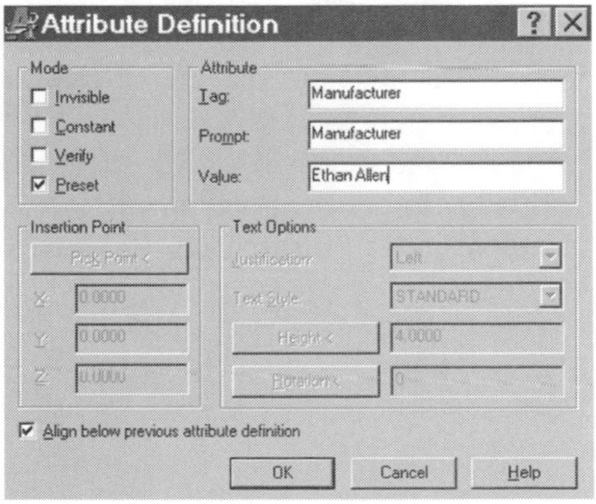

Figure 26.5 shows the fourth (and last) attribute, Verify. Because the Prompt and the Tag are the same, I left Prompt blank.

Notice the $ in the value? If you ever choose to extract the data, you'll probably want to leave the dollar sign out of the attribute definition. I suspect you'd want a numeric field, and that pesky dollar sign will definitely cause problems.

I've heard of users making one attribute, copying it several times on a block, then editing the default values to save time. This is fine as long as you have no intention of extracting the data. If your blocks have multiple attribute tags with the same values, scary things will occur in the extraction process!

Figure 26.4 For the Manufacturer attribute, use a Preset value of Ethan Allen.

After you've added your attributes, you are ready to make a block (or wblock) out of your new sofa. Go ahead and make your block as you usually do with the ~~arrangement of time cmd~~. ~~the order in which you select the attributes~~ will be the same order in which AutoCAD prompts you for them when inserting. If you want AutoCAD to prompt you starting from the top down, then you should individually select them in that order. If you use a window to select the objects, there's no telling in what order the attributes will prompt . It's much easier to get the prompts in the proper sequence now than to change the prompt order after the fact.

Now you're ready to `insert` your new block with its attributes. The command-line sequence below should mirror your results.

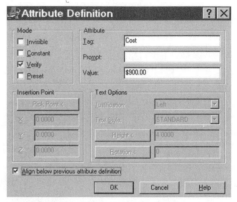

Command: INSERT

Specify insertion point or [Scale/X/Y/Z/Rotate/
    PScale/PX/PY/PZ/PRotate]:

Enter attribute values

Cost <$900.00>: $795.00

Room Number <NNNN>: 1043

Because the Manufacturer attribute has a Preset mode, you were not prompted to change it, and the default value was set to Ethan Allen. The Constant attribute, Furniture_Type, will never change, so no input was required. Also notice that because you made the Cost attribute tag invisible, it doesn't show up on the inserted blocks.

Figure 26.5 The fourth (and last) attribute, Cost, sets the Mode at Verify.

Many users prefer to see the dialog box for their attributes rather than the command-line interface. By setting `attdia` to 1, AutoCAD displays a dialog box in its place (Figure 26.6). Also notice that the Preset attribute displays in the dialog box and is available for modification.

Go ahead and insert a few desks. Should you decide you want to see the invisible attributes, the attdisp command displays all the attributes, invisible or not, when set on.

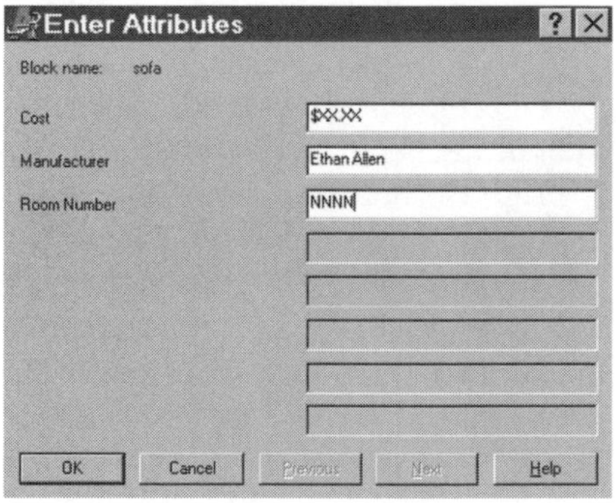

Figure 26.6 Setting `attdia` **to 1 causes AutoCAD to display a dialog box for attributes, if you prefer not to use the command-line interface.**

Editing Your Attributes

You've inserted a variety of blocks with attributes, and you want to edit the attribute values. ddatte to the rescue! You can key in ddatte at the command prompt or grab it from the pull-down menus using Modify–Object–Attribute–Single.

ddatte prompts you to select a block, after which a dialog similar to that shown in Figure 27.1 appears. Notice that I'm still using the Sofa block definition I created in Chapter 26. ddatte is simple enough to figure out. Simply key in any attribute values that need to be changed. If you have more than eight attributes in a block, you'll need to page through them. Also, you cannot edit attribute values that reside on locked layers. Note that Constant attributes can never be changed — they're pretty much cast in concrete!

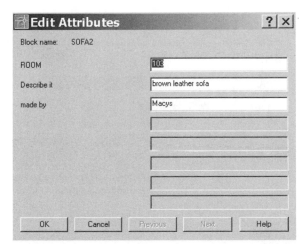

Figure 27.1 Use the ddatte **command to Edit attribute values**.

Global Editing

So what if you need to change all of the Ethan Allen sofas from $375 to $475? It would take a great deal of time to comb all of the sofa blocks and change them all using ddatte. And what if you need to change an attributes height, layer, color, or placement? Then you'd need to use a more stellar (but somewhat archaic) command called attedit.

The attedit command hasn't changed much over the years, so it has unfortunately been left behind somewhat technically. However, it does the job and that's all that matters. If you're in AutoCAD Release 14 or earlier, just key in the command at the command prompt or use the pull-down menus (Modify–Object–Attribute–Global). AutoCAD 2000 users can grab it from the pull-down menus as well (Modify–Attribute–Global) or key in -attedit. Unfortunately attedit was mapped to the Ddatte dialog in AutoCAD 2000, so you need to key in the extra dash to use the command.

```
Command: -attedit
Edit attributes one at a time?
[Yes/ No] <Y>:
```

This is the first fork in the attedit road. If you choose No, you can edit your attribute values globally. You can replace one text string with another text string in as many blocks as you like. If you needed to change all of your manufacturer attributes from "Ethan Allen" to "Levitz," this would be the perfect means for doing so.

```
Edit only attributes visible on screen? [Yes/No] <Y>:
```

Do you want to be prompted to manually select the attributes you want to edit (Y), or do you want AutoCAD to take a look at all of the attributes, visible or not (N)?

The next three questions help you narrow down the field of attributes to edit using a variety of filters.

```
Enter block name specification <*>:
```

Would you like to narrow down the blocks you're interested in? The asterisk default indicates that all blocks are possible candidates.

```
Enter attribute tag specification <*>:
```

Would you like to narrow down the attribute tags you're interested in editing?

```
Enter attribute value specification <*>:
```

Would you like to further narrow down the candidates by keying in attribute values you're interested in editing?

```
Select Attributes: Specify opposite corner: 8 found
Select Attributes: 8 attributes selected.
Enter string to change: Ethan Allen
Enter new string: Levitz
```

The end result is that all of the attribute text that read "Ethan Allen" has been replaced with "Levitz." Keep in mind that attribute values are case sensitive, so you must enter the identical text case found in the attribute text in order to edit it. If you have any null attributes [no value assigned], you cannot select them for editing. To select a null attribute value, simply enter a back-slash (\).

Edit One at a Time

Route number two is editing the attributes one at a time. The first three prompts are familiar; you saw them when you chose to go the global route.

```
Enter block name specification <*>:
Enter attribute tag specification <*>:
```

```
Enter attribute value specification <*>:
Select Attributes: 8 found
```

(Manually select the attributes you're interested in editing using the usual object selection techniques. The selected attributes must be on a UCS parallel to the current UCS.)

```
Select Attributes:
8 attributes selected.
Enter an option [Value/Position/Height/Angle/Style/Layer/Color/Next] <N>:
```

Look at what's hidden in the `attedit` command: the ability to edit the attribute value, position, height, rotation angle, text style, layer, and color.

After selecting the attributes you want to edit, AutoCAD steps through the attributes one at a time. An X appears on the current attribute. Select the option you need, make the necessary edit, and the change appears instantly. When you're finished making edits to the current attribute, `next` takes you to the next attribute for editing.

`attedit` lets you step your way through each selected attribute, making the necessary modifications along the way.

What if you need to add a couple more attributes to a block? Can you just explode the block, add the attributes, and redefine as usual? You would think so, but you'd be very wrong. Unfortunately, redefining blocks with attributes has always been a thorn in AutoCAD's side.

Updating Block Definitions Before AutoCAD 2002

The `attredef` (attribute redefine) command was added as a bonus routine many releases ago and has now made its way into the core product. This, along with several of the fantastic Express Tools, has made redefining a block with attributes somewhat easier. Here's how it works.

Say you want to remove the Cost attribute and add a Model Number attribute. Insert an exploded Sofa block, delete the Cost attribute, and enter the `attdef` command to add a new attribute for Model Number. Next enter the `block` command, reselect all the attributes, and redefine the block. What happens? You'll notice that all of the existing blocks remain just as they were and that new block insertions reflect the changes you just made to your Sofa block. This is bad news because now you have two different types of the same block residing in you drawing. Fortunately, `attredef` can come to the rescue. Be sure you have the exploded Sofa block before you enter the command. You need to key it in because it's Top Secret and doesn't reside in any of the menus.

```
Command: ATTREDEF
Enter name of the block you want to redefine: SOFA
Select objects for new Block...
Select objects: Specify opposite corner: 14 found
Select objects:
Specify insertion base point of new Block: end of
```

All of your existing Sofa blocks are updated, as well as any new insertions you chose to add. In fact, there is no need to use the `block` command at all to redefine blocks with ~~attributes all it could~~ ~~will do it all for you.~~

What happens if you need to explode a block with attributes? The attribute values return to their original tag values — probably not what you had in mind. However, an Express Tool called Burst explodes the block but keeps the attribute values.

Awesome Attribute Editing in 2002

Face it, Autodesk hasn't upgraded the attribute editing capabilities in AutoCAD for nearly a decade! Day after day, attribute after attribute you've been using some fairly painful ancient functionality! Well happy days are here at last because AutoCAD 2002 has delivered an awesome set of new attribute commands that range from editing to extraction. The remainder of this chapter covers these new Attribute editing commands.

The first command I'm going to discuss started out as the Express Tools `battman` (block attribute manager). The genius behind this tool is one of my favorite Autodesk Programmers, Tom Stoeckel, who as an AutoCAD user in a former life knew how to get the job done right! You'll see this for yourself as you make your way through this dialog. My only regret is that the original `battman` had a darling little icon of a bat in the upper left-hand corner, and when it graduated to the full-fledged AutoCAD command, apparently the powers-that-be changed the bat to the new AutoCAD icon (I'm guessing there were some trademark issues). Figure 27.1 shows the new AutoCAD 2002 `battman` command.

It's important to understand that this is a global attribute editor. Because this physically changes the block definition, `battman` affects all instances of an attribute in a block. You can physically select the block you want to edit by picking the Select block icon or by picking the desired block off the drop-down list (Figure 27.2). If you manually select a block with no attributes, AutoCAD is more than happy to tell you that. Either way you select the block, `battman` displays the associated attributes in the dialog. Beneath the attribute list, you'll see the total number of the selected blocks

Figure 27.2 Select blocks manually by picking or by choosing from the drop-down list.

inserted in the drawing as well as the number found in the current space. For example, you might have a total of nine doors inserted into the drawing, but only eight of them in your current space (Model Space or Layout).

You can control which aspects of the attribute display in the attribute list by selecting the Settings button, which takes you to the dialog shown in Figure 27.3. By default, Tag, Prompt, Default, and Mode properties of the attributes are displayed. The Settings dialog provides many different options for complete control over your attribute display list (Figure 27.4). Notice the Tag option is always selected and unchangeable (if you can't change it, why is it even listed?)

I hope by now you've discovered that creating duplicate attributes is a big no-no should you ever decide to extract the attribute information. Turning on the Emphasize duplicate tags option displays any duplicate attribute tags in red. If it's not selected, duplicate tags appear. However, they're not emphasized in any way (so you can continue to live in denial).

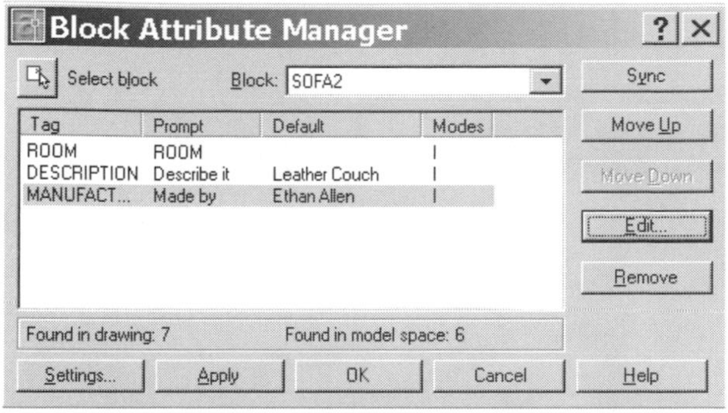

When using `battman` to change attribute information, you can choose to affect only those blocks inserted *after* exiting the Block Attribute Manager or all preexisting inserted blocks as well. Selecting the Apply

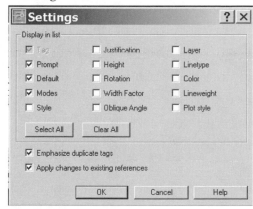

Figure 27.3 Use the Properties tab to change the layer, color, or linetype of the attribute.

changes to existing references option instructs AutoCAD to affect all those that came before and all that come after. I'll discuss this in more detail when I get to the Sync button. You're finished with the Settings dialog; now return to the main Battman dialog.

Do you remember the first time you put attribute information into a block? No doubt you discovered the hard way that the order in which you select the attributes later controls the order of the attributes when inserting. If you windowed the attributes when creating your block (which most do), then it was a total guess as to the final order. In most cases, you would have to completely redefine the block just to get the order correct. Notice that the right side of the Block Attribute manager contains the buttons Move Up and Move Down. Now it's easy to reorder the attribute information even after the block has been defined.

The Sync button is also key to your Attribute Happiness Factor (AHF). Allow me to set up a common scenario. You create a block with three attribute

Figure 27.4 Control the attribute list in the Settings dialog.

definitions, you insert the block a dozen times, then you realize that you need to add an additional attribute definition to the block. You explode the block, add the new attribute definition, and redefine the block. Do the original block instances update from three to four attributes? Not a chance. Any new blocks update to include all four attribute definitions, but the old ones remain as originally created. What's up with that? That's not the way blocks are supposed to work!

I hope over the years you discovered the attredef (attribute redefine) command. This command was archaic and clumsy, but effective nonetheless. Enter the magical Sync button. Hitting Sync takes a look at the latest update to the block definition and updates *all* instances of the block — hoorah! What used to take several steps has now been reduced to a simple pick of a button in AutoCAD 2002. The new attsync command does the exact same thing.

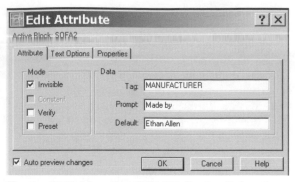

Figure 27.5 Use the Edit Attribute dialog to change the attribute settings.

The Remove option rips an attribute definition right out of a block — no questions asked. It's gone, so be careful. Of course a Cancel will put the attributes back. Incidentally, if a block only has one attribute, the Remove option is not available.

The Edit option takes you to an additional dialog that consists of the three tabs: Attribute, Text Options, and Properties (Figure 27.5). The Attribute tab is very similar to the attdef command you initially used to create your attributes. Here you can change the attribute mode, tag, prompt, and default. You'll also find that all three tabs allow you to turn Auto-preview on, so you can see the changes occurring as they're made. For example, if I change my attributes from invisible to visible, I should suddenly see them display in my drawing.

The Text Options tab changes such features as text height, style, and justification (Figure 27.6). The Properties tab makes it easy to change the layer, linetype, and color, to name just a few (Figure 27.7).

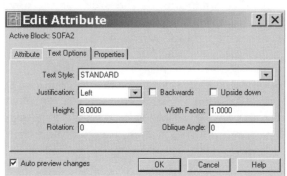

Figure 27.6 Use the Text Options tab to control such values as the height, style, and so on.

After making any changes necessary, hit OK to return to the main dialog. Apply the changes made to the block definition by hitting the Apply button (makes sense).

Sync or Apply? Hmmmmmmmmmmm — very confusing! If for some reason you only want the changes to affect future blocks, then you make sure Apply changes to existing references is *not* selected in the Settings dialog and use the Apply button. If you want all instances to be affected, use the Sync button. Make sense? You should also note that Syncing does not affect values assigned to preexisting blocks — that could be disastrous!

Previously, I mentioned another new attribute command, attsync. One nice advantage of this command over the Sync button in the Battman dialog is its ability to use wildcards. If you want to update all your block definitions in a drawing, you can use an asterisk to sync all attributes in all blocks.

What if you just want to edit one attribute in one block? Have you ever had to change the height of one attribute in one instance only? battman globally changes all of the blocks so that won't work. I used to use the painful attedit command (which was incorrectly mapped to Ddatte in AutoCAD 2000). Those of you in 2000i or 2000 need to use -attedit to change anything other than the attribute value of an individual block. attedit is an old, archaic command in desperate need of a face-lift. eattedit to the rescue!

Figure 27.8 shows the new Enhanced Attribute Editing dialog. Notice the same

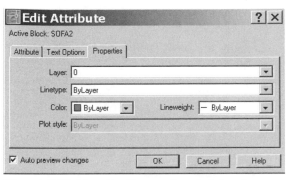

Figure 27.7 Use the Properties tab to change the layer, color, or linetype of the attribute.

three tabs found in battman along with the ability to change the attribute value. Simply select the block you want to modify and change the appropriate information. This affects one and only one attribute.

You'll still need the old attedit command to change multiple attribute values. For example, if you want to change all of the model numbers that read "X12345" to "L12345," you will spend a painfully long time changing them one at a time. attedit is still the easiest route to take here.

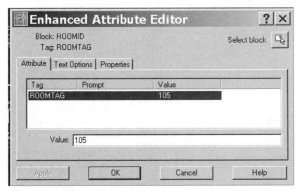

Figure 27.8 Use the new eattedit command to edit attributes individually.

CHAPTER 28

The Down-and-Dirty Basics of Customizing

You don't need to be a programmer to do some powerful customizing. Your job is to learn what you want to know; my job is to help you get there! Many sections of AutoCAD are worthy of customizing. The pull-down menus and toolbars are probably the easiest and most popular to work with. Most of you will start out modifying the ACAD menu file and move on to creating your own menus from scratch, followed by using the powerful partial menu load facility. I'll start by exploring the standard AutoCAD menu file.

Menu File Types

Those of you who have used AutoCAD since Release 13 might recall that Autodesk permitted loading both a DOS and a Windows version simultaneously. The DOS menu file and the Windows menu file were very different. Consequently, it was important not to get the two confused because they would only work in their corresponding platform. Hence, the birth of the MNC file. The MNC file equates to the MNX file in that it's the compiled version of the MNU file. The MNC file is Windows, whereas the MNX file is DOS.

You might also recall that Release 13 introduced the standard Windows interface for toolbars — a visual interface that was easily customizable because you could create your own icons, assign commands to them, rearrange them as you pleased, and so on. The bitmaps for these toolbars are stored in the MNR file (another compiled file). If you accidentally removed the MNR file from your search path, you were introduced to the friendly smiley faces on your toolbars. Many of you have written to me asking how to rid yourself of these friendly guys and get your toolbar icons back — read on!

With the added flexibility of being able to create your own toolbars came the ability to completely destroy your desktop! It was fairly easy to accidentally send toolbars into oblivion, never to be seen again. I can't tell you how many times I'd be moving a toolbar button from one toolbar to another only to accidentally drop it altogether. Autodesk in its infinite wisdom realized that there needed to be a method to restore your desktop; hence, the MNS file was created as an insurance marker. All toolbar modifications, additions, or subtractions were recorded in the MNS file. If you wanted to restore your original desktop, you would explicitly instruct AutoCAD to load the MNU file.

With this insurance came a price and a change in the procedure you'd been trained to follow for over a decade, in which you modified the MNU file and let AutoCAD automatically compile and create the MNX. This process no longer worked! If you added a new pull-down to your MNU file and reloaded it, AutoCAD would write over the MNS file and lose your precious custom toolbars. Ouch! To make your life simple, I suggest customizing the MNS file and staying away from the MNU file altogether. When you have the file set up the way you like, simply copy the MNS file over the MNU file and your custom toolbars remain safe for life.

Note   Always keep a clean copy of the out-of-the-box `acad.mnu` file safely tucked away in another directory, just in case!

For the record, the menu extensions were named with the following nomenclature in mind (should you be on AutoCAD Jeopardy).

MNU   Template File

MNS   Source File (keeper of the custom toolbars)

MNC   Compiled menu file

MNR   Resource file (keeper of the bitmaps)

By the way, if you were to compare the contents of the out-of-the-box MNS file to the MNU file, you wouldn't find much difference. The MNU file has a few more comments in it to help you understand the menu code, but other than that they're pretty much the same.

I think it's important that you realize the difference between all of these file types or all of your customizing will be for naught. With this background, take a look at the inner workings of the `acad.mns` file.

The Anatomy of a Menu File

Menu files comprise many small sections, using a modular approach. Each section controls a different part of the menu. All sections are delineated with three asterisks in front. Any of the following sections can be found within a valid AutoCAD menu (Release 13+).

```
***POP0-999
```
```
***screen
```
```
***buttons
```
1, 2, 3, or 4
```
***aux
```
1, 2, 3, or 4
```
***toolbars
```
```
***helpstrings
```
```
***tablet
```
1–4

```
***image
***accelerators
***menugroup
```

Although the above sections might appear scary, you'll find that the programming syntax remains fairly consistent throughout. Therefore, once you've learned the basics, they are transferable all sections. It would take an entire year to cover every section adequately, so I'll cover the more popular sections: toolbars, pop-ups, and my personal favorite, accelerators.

***POP0–999

The pull-down menus are defined in the POP sections. POP0 defines the cursor menu, whereas POP1 to POP16 define the standard pull-down menus that reside across the top of the screen. POP500 to POP999 define the shortcut menus that appear when you pick the second button on the input device (usually the right button). The cursor menu displays when you hit a <Shift>–right-click on your input device. You can have 999 menu items in a standard pull-down menu and 499 menu items in the cursor menu. Of course, it's highly doubtful that your display will accommodate that many, so they're truncated to fit the display. You should note — and this has got me a couple of times — that you must have at least one standard pull-down menu defined in order to use the cursor menu. In other words, ***POP0 all by itself is worthless and will never display.

***screen

Before the world of pull-down menus, users relied heavily on the screen menu that displayed on the right side of the screen. At one time, every single AutoCAD command resided in the screen menu (making it quite popular). Although you can still display and use this menu, you'll find it somewhat limited in functionality.

***buttons1–4 **and** ***aux1–4

Customizing the buttons on your input device can be a great time-saver. Many of you are still using input devices with as many as 25 buttons! This gives you plenty of leeway to set up the buttons in a way that complements your drawing style. Because the first button is always the pick or select button, only the remaining buttons are available for customizing. Therefore, if you are using a four-button input device, you have three buttons available for customizing; a 16-button input device has 15 buttons available.

If you're using a system mouse, you'll be customizing the aux sections. If you're using a tablet (or anything other than a system mouse), you'll be customizing the buttons sections. This, incidentally, used to be completely opposite in earlier releases. Both types of menus are programmed exactly the same. You will customize the one that works with your particular input device.

Assume you're using a tablet with four buttons on the input device. Programming the aux1 menu determines what happens if you do a simple pick of any of the three customizable buttons. Programming the aux2 menu determines what happens when you pair a simple pick with the <Shift> key. The aux3 menu controls what happens when you press the <Ctrl> key combined with a simple pick. Those of you who are incredibly coordinated can program the aux4 menu, which controls what occurs when you press the <Shift-Ctrl> key combination with a simple pick.

Confused yet? This means that if you have a four-button input device (three customizable buttons) you can assign 12 commands to your buttons. The same is true of the ***buttons menu. Here's a quick review.

***aux1 or

***buttons1: simple pick

***aux2 or

***buttons2: <Shift>-pick

***aux3 or

***buttons3: <Ctrl>-pick

***aux4 or

***buttons4: <Ctrl-Shift>-pick

Your input devices can be more powerful than you ever imagined!

***tablet1–4

Those of you with digitizing tablets will want to customize the top section of your menu, tablet1. The other sections are available for you to modify as well, but most users leave those sections alone. Tablet menus are among the easiest to customize. Figure 28.1 displays the standard ACAD tablet menu.

***helpstrings

This section contains the helpful text information that displays along the status line when you select a menu item (pull-down menu or toolbar).

***toolbars

You can create new toolbars easily via the user interface, or, if you're masochistic, you can hard code them in the

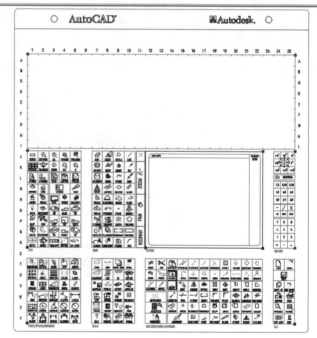

Figure 28.1 This is the standard AutoCAD digitizer tablet menu.

ACAD menu file (I strongly recommend the former). If you're having problems with smiley faces, you might consider touring this section to make sure the bitmap name that's stored in the MNS file is, in fact, the filename you stored in your support directory. Other than that, steer clear of this section.

***image

Before the new MFC-compliant dialog boxes were prevalent, you would create your own dialogs using Icon menus. These files required no LISP expertise to create and were very powerful. Nearly all of the old Icon menus have been replaced with the new, more polished looking dialogs, but don't discredit the power of these menus yet! If you've ever wanted to create a dialog box displaying a symbol library, this might be the ticket for you. You don't need to know DCL, DIESEL, or LISP — just some basic menu customizing. Release 13 renamed this section to ***image to avoid any confusion with the toolbar icons (although ***icon still works). Figure 28.2 displays one of the few remaining image menus still residing in AutoCAD. You'll notice that all image menus have exactly 20 boxes for picture representations and a column on the left for text strings. You might recall the old Font dialog that existed in this format.

***accelerators

Accelerators are my personal favorite! This section defines the keys on your keyboard. You can assign AutoCAD commands to Function Keys, <Ctrl> key combinations, <Shift> key combinations, arrow keys, <Ins>, <Del>, and <Esc> keys, as well as the number pad keys. Just imagine how dangerous you could become! All that power in one little section, which I'll delve into in Chapter 29.

***menugroup

This one opens a huge can of worms. It's used in partial menu loading, as well as in disabling and enabling individual menu commands. It's essential but somewhat difficult to comprehend. It also requires a fairly in-depth understanding of customization to understand its full benefits.

This chapter built the basic foundation needed for customization. In the next chapter, I dive into the programming codes and start you down the road to maximum productivity.

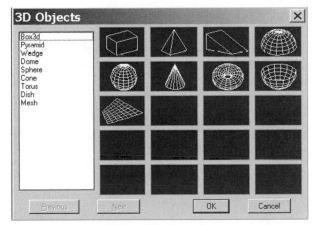

Figure 28.2 The Tiled Surface Layout is one of the few remaining image menus in AutoCAD.

CHAPTER 29

Button Menus and Accelerator Keys

Everyone uses some type of input device with AutoCAD (at least anyone who is sane does). Most prevalent nowadays is the mouse with two or three buttons, but many of you have stayed true to your digitizer and have as many as 25 buttons (Figure 29.1). Many of you no doubt have the awesome Intellimouse with all of its zoom and pan capabilities. As long as you have two buttons on an input device, you can do some rudimentary and simple customizing to meet your specific needs.

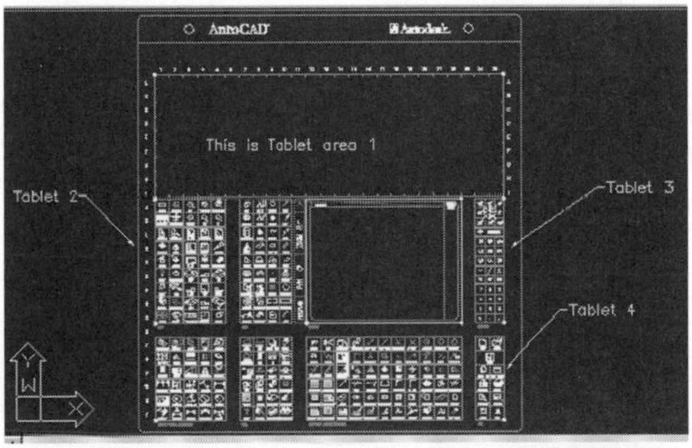

Button Menus

As a quick refresher: You cannot program the pick button on your input device. If you have a four-button input device, such as a digitizing puck, you can program three of the buttons. If you have a 16-button input device, 15 buttons are programmable, and so on. To customize the buttons on your input device, open your acad.mns file and find the ***buttons1 section. If you're using a system mouse, search for the ***aux1 section. If you aren't sure which one you have, feel free to duplicate the information in both (it can't hurt anything).

Figure 29.1 The Wacom Intuos 9x12 Digitizer Tablet, pen, and 4D mouse puck shown here are some of the newer offerings in digitizers and cutting-edge mice. The Digitizer 4D mouse puck offers five buttons for you to program; the mouse pen offers four.

Four sections control the buttons on your input device.

***aux1 or ***buttons1

***aux2 or ***buttons2

***aux3 or ***buttons3

***aux4 or ***buttons4

I'll refer to the buttons sections throughout this chapter, but keep in mind that everything I say for buttons is also true for the aux section.

***buttons1   programs a simple pick of the buttons on your input device.

***buttons2   programs a combination of the <Shift> key and a simple pick.

***buttons3   programs a combination of the <Ctrl> key and a simple pick.

***buttons4   programs a combination of the <Ctrl> key, the <Shift> key, and a simple pick (for those of you who are incredibly coordinated).

What does this mean to you? If you have a two-button input device, you can program your extra button to perform four different functions, and just think of the possibilities for those of you with a 16-button input device! You have 60 different functions you can assign to your buttons!

I'll start out by looking at some simple functions for your buttons.

***buttons1;

^C^C

'clayer

***buttons2

endp

int

cen

This function assumes you are using a four-button input device. The second button performs an <Enter> (;), the third button cancels out of any command (^C^C), and the fourth button allows you to set to a new current layer ('clayer). As was mentioned before, the apostrophe in front of clayer makes the command transparent, so you can use it from within an existing command. This is kind of nice because you can be within a command, realize you are on the wrong layer, and change it without leaving the command. (Someday Autodesk will make the layer drop-down list transparent.)

The above menu also assigns <Shift>–pick combinations. When you hold down the <Shift> key in conjunction with the second button, you get the Endpoint object snap (endp). Notice that I didn't just use end because in some versions of AutoCAD this could kick you out of your drawing file if you hit the button while at the command prompt. The <Shift> key combined with the third button executes the Intersection object snap (int). The <Shift> key combined with the fourth button executes the Center object snap (cen).

If you want to call a specific pull-down menu from a button, use the following syntax.

`$pn=*`

n is the number of the pull-down you want to display on the screen. Usually the Cursor menu displays with the <Shift> key is pressed in combination with the second button. The syntax for this situations follows.

`$p0=*`

For the record, the $ is a special character code telling AutoCAD to go get a menu area, the p indicates it's a pull-down menu, and the * tells AutoCAD to display the menu. If you want a button to pull down the first menu, for example, you'd use the syntax $p1=*. You can use the same syntax from anywhere to force a specific pull-down menu to drop.

In the AutoCAD menu, you find the following syntax for ***buttons2.

`***Buttons2`

`$p0=*`

If you're still in AutoCAD Release 14, here's a cool thing to know: you can get your button menus to perform double duty for you. When you pick a button on your input device, AutoCAD recognizes two different things: the menu macro you've assigned to that button and the coordinates of the current cursor location. You can use that coordinate information within your buttons menu. Here's how it works. I want to execute the Intersection object snap at the location of my cursor on the screen, and I don't want to have to hit my input device twice to do it. I can kill two birds with one stone if I program my buttons correctly. The backslash (\) tells AutoCAD to grab the current cursor coordinates and use them within the macro. It looks like this.

`***buttons1`

`int;\`

When you hit the second button on your input device, it does an intersection option snap at the location your cursor is sitting.

Perhaps you'd prefer it drew a circle using your cursor position as the center point, in which case, use this macro.

`^C^Ccircle;\`

All you have to do is select the radius (or diameter). Pretty cool, huh? This is not an easy concept to explain without demonstrating; I hope you're able to grasp it simply by reading about it.

Note   This functionality magically disappeared in AutoCAD 2000, never to be seen again. I'm not too sure what the deal is there but perhaps it has to do with the shortcut menus.

Table 29.1 Key assignments for the `***accelerators` **section.**

<Ctrl> key combinations
<Shift> key combinations
<Ctrl-Shift> key combinations
The Function keys <F1> through <F9>, <F11>, and <F12> (<F10> is reserved by Windows and not programmable)
<Esc> key (watch out!)
<Ins> and <Del> keys (in combination with <Ctrl>)
The arrow keys (defined as up, down, left, and right, also in combination with <Ctrl>)
The number pad keys (defined as `numpad1` through `numpad10`)

Another important system variable to know is `mbuttonpan`. If you have a three-button input device (and the third button isn't a wheel), AutoCAD will try to assign zoom and pan functions to that third button. Setting `mbuttonpan` to 0 tells AutoCAD to read in the assigned menu item instead.

The Awesome Accelerators

For years, it was difficult to assign your own commands to <Ctrl> key combinations, function keys, arrows, and so forth. You had to enter the cryptic world of DOSkey, and it just wasn't pretty. With the introduction of Release 13, you were given the ability to assign commands to a vast assortment of keys on the standard keyboard through the menu system. Not only that, it was also easy to do because it used the standard menu syntax. Open up the `acad.mnu` or `acad.mns` file and search for the following section.

`***accelerators`

Here, <Ctrl-C> is mapped to CopyClip, <Ctrl-V> is mapped to Paste, and so on. In fact, if you delete the <Ctrl-C> line, you'll get the old `cancel` command back while in AutoCAD (for those of you who haven't adapted to hitting the <Esc> key). See Table 29.1 for a list of keys that can be assigned through the `***accelerators` section.

At first look at the list in Table 29.1, you should realize that this information could make you very dangerous. For example, if you change the <Esc> key to execute the `line` command, you'll have a terrible time escaping out of your AutoCAD functions. However, just think of the new and improved ways you'll be able to torture your coworkers (and yourself)!

Some of the above keys are preassigned. For example, <F1> executes the Help function and <F2> performs a flip screen. You can change those settings, but do you really want to? You should also be wary of changing <Ctrl> key combinations. If you use <Ctrl-R> to move around from viewport to viewport, you may not want to override that capability.

Naturally, the <Del> key should be set to erase, and it would be nice if the <Ins> key executed the insert command. Take a look at Table 29.2 for some examples of key macros and the functions that they cause to occur.

If you open the acad.mns and look at the existing accelerators, you'll find that they use name tags to assign accelerators. Don't let this syntax intimidate you because you can also use the simple syntax outlined above.

For those of you in AutoCAD 2000i or 2002 you can take advantage of the new Customize dialog box for assigning your accelerators.

Table 29.2 Key macros and their functions.

Key Macro	Description of Function
[Shift+"E"]endp	<Shift-E> executes the Endpoint object snap.
[Shift+"I"]int	<Shift-I> executes the Intersection object snap.
[Shift+"C"]cen	<Shift-C> executes the Center object snap.
[Control+'F']*^C^Cfillet	<Ctrl-F> executes the fillet command over and over.
[Control+Shift+'U']^C^Cundo;2	Holding down the <Shift> and <Ctrl> and U keys undoes the last two commands (You need to be very coordinated for this!).
[Control+"INSERT"]^C^Cinsert	The <Ins> key executes the Insert dialog box.
[Control+"DELETE"]^C^Cerase	The <Del> key erases.
[Control+"LEFT"]^C^CU	The left-arrow key performs an Undo.
[Control+"RIGHT"]^C^Credo	The right-arrow key performs a Redo.
["F4"]'osmode;4095	<F4> turns on all of the object snaps.

CHAPTER 30

Toolbar Customization

It's probably easiest to start with programming your toolbars. Right-click once on any icon on a toolbar and pick Customize from the shortcut menu to display the Customize dialog box, as shown in Figure 30.1. Click again on a tool to display the Button Properties dialog, as shown in Figure 30.2.

Name   The tooltip name that appears when the cursor hovers over the button
Help   The user help string that appears along the status line
Edit   The property that sends you to another dialog box for editing the picture on the button
Macro   The programming that tells AutoCAD what you want a button to do when it's selected.

Now look at some basic macro syntax. As you know, you can't run a standard AutoCAD command unless you're at the command prompt (I'll address transparent commands later). For example, if you try to run the line command while still in the copy command, you will get an error message. To ensure that AutoCAD is at the command prompt before executing your toolbar command, you need to run a couple of cancels. This is done as follows.

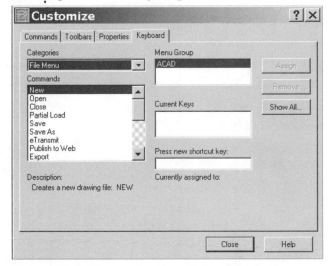

Figure 30.1 The customize dialog box is the place to start when programming your toolbars.

^C^C

This syntax executes two <Ctrl-C>s (or cancels). Why two? There are still some commands that require two cancels to get you all the way back to the command prompt. Selecting an option of the layer command, the old dim commands, or the change command all can put you in this particular situation. Just to make sure, always include two cancels (better safe than sorry!). I do know some overly paranoid programmers who include ^C^C^C in their macros, although it really is not necessary.

The following macro executes the line command.

```
^C^Cline
```

This macro executes the circle command.

```
^C^CCIRCLE
```

The two Cs next to each other look a bit strange, but it is correct.

Note It doesn't matter whether you use upper- or lowercase characters. I mixed it up in the two previous examples just to illustrate this.

The AutoCAD macros found in your existing toolbars include an underscore in front of the commands as displayed in the following example.

```
^C^C_MTEXT
```

Because AutoCAD is translated into so many different languages (19, I believe), it's important that it search for the English source command; hence, the underscore forces AutoCAD to do exactly that. If you have no intention of using your macros in any language other than English, you don't need to include the underscore. I'll leave it out.

Should you need to include an <Enter> in your macro, use a semicolon (;). The following syntax erases all of the objects in your drawing.

```
^C^CERASE;ALL;;
```

This is the same as entering the following syntax from the command prompt in AutoCAD,

```
<Esc><Esc>erase<Enter>all<Enter><Enter>
```

which yields the following results.

```
Command: erase
Select objects: all
34 found
Select objects: <Enter>
```

Because it takes two <Enter>s to get all the way out of the erase command, you press the additional <Enter> at the end. Without it, this macro leaves you in the erase command, which is bad programming manners!

You also might want to pause your macro and let the user answer a question. Perhaps you're writing a macro that inserts a block called Pulley. You probably want to pause when the insert command prompts for an insertion point and let the user answer that question. You can do this by placing a backslash in the macro to turn control over to the user. You might also want to let the user select a rotation angle for the block, as shown here.

```
^C^C-insert;pulley;\;;\
```

This is the same as entering the following syntax from the command prompt in AutoCAD,

<Esc><Esc>-insert<Enter>pulley<Enter>(*user input*)<Enter><Enter>(*user input*)

which yields the following results.

```
Command: -insert
Enter block name or [?]: pulley
Specify insertion point or [Scale/X/Y/Z/Rotate/PScale/PX/PY/PZ/PRotate]:
    pause for user input
Enter X scale factor, specify opposite corner, or [Corner/XYZ] <1>: <Enter>
Enter Y scale factor <use X scale factor>: <Enter>
Specify rotation angle <0>: pause for user input
```

Note Placing a dash in front of the insert command forces the command-line interface of the command.

You need to know the proper command sequence before coding your macro. If you've been using AutoCAD for years, you probably already know the various AutoCAD command sequences off the top of your head. If you are new to the program, you might have to key in the sequence within AutoCAD first, before coding your macro. Figure 30.2 shows the previous syntax placed in the macro area of a toolbar button. I also edited the picture to create an icon that resembles a simple pulley.

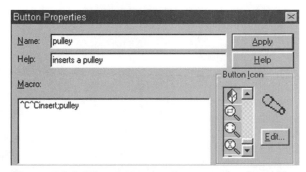

Figure 30.2 The command syntax is placed in the macro area of a toolbar button.

Even though you can execute a dialog box within a macro, you can't do anything else past that point; for example, you can't select any of the options within the dialog box. You can execute the Layer dialog box (layer), but you can't create any new layers, set a new current layer, and so on. There's no way to use a macro to select a button within a dialog, fill in a text box, and so forth. Hence, you'll have to resort to the old command line–driven commands. For example, instead of the layer command, use -layer; instead of mtext, use -mtext; instead of bhatch, use -bhatch.

```
^C^C-XREF
^C^C-LAYER
```

If you want to ensure that your users are on the dimension layer before they execute the dimlin command, you can use the following syntax.

```
^C^C-LAYER;S;dimension;;DIMLIN
```

This is the same as entering the following syntax from the command prompt in AutoCAD (the s is for Set).

<Esc><Esc>-layer<Enter>s<Enter>dimension<Enter><Enter>dimlin

```
Command: -layer
[?/Make/Set/New/ON/OFF/Color/Ltype/LWeight/Plot/PStyle/Freeze/Thaw/LOck/Unlock/stAte]
   : S
New current layer <0>: dimension
[?/Make/Set/New/ON/OFF/Color/Ltype/LWeight/Plot/PStyle/Freeze/Thaw/LOck/Unlock/stAte]
   :<Enter>
Command: DIMLIN
```

Transparent Commands

AutoCAD has many transparent command: zoom, pan, and vieware just a few that come to mind. A transparent command is a command that you can use within an existing command. To use a command transparently, place a single quote in front of it. When executing commands that can behave transparently, you probably won't want to include the usual cancels at the start of the macro, as in the following example.

```
^C^CZOOM
```

This macro cancels the user out of the existing command before executing the zoom command, which might upset the user that wants to perform the zoom without leaving the current command. 'zoom is a more versatile macro.

Macros are best used to increase your productivity, but they occasionally can be used to have a little fun with your coworkers. As I travel around the

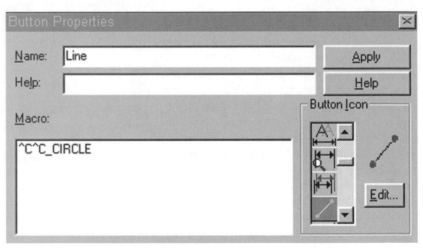

Figure 30.3 You can torture your coworkers by switching the line and circle command, as shown here.

world speaking on various AutoCAD topics, I am amazed to find the excitement generated when I share some clever ways to torture coworkers. You'll find that the more you learn about customizing, the more dangerous you become. With that disclaimer, I'll show you a clever trick you can perform using toolbars and your new-found knowledge.

A simple method of torture is to switch the toolbar macros around. For example, what's to keep you from switching the `line` command to the `circle` command, as shown in Figure 30.3. This is a mean trick, and one you probably shouldn't employ when your coworker is on a production deadline. However, if you understood this example, it tells me you understand the information presented in this chapter. Along with this knowledge comes the responsibility to use it wisely. Don't abuse it!

CHAPTER 31

Customizing Your Pull-Down Menus

Creating a Pull-Down Menu

In this chapter you create your own, very simple pull-down menu. You will not want to throw away the AutoCAD menu for your menu; it's primarily for practice. You can work in any text editor that outputs plain old ASCII text.

Your simple menu will use just one type of section: ***POP. Remember, use ***POP0 to customize the cursor menu and ***POP1–16 to customize the pull-down menus that reside across the top of your AutoCAD drawing area. You cannot create a menu with just a cursor menu (POP0); you must have at least one pull-down menu as well. If your menu file has no pull-down menu files defined, AutoCAD automatically inserts default file and edit menus, whether you like it or not!

Key the following syntax into your menu file. Save the file as sample.mnu.

```
***POP1
[&Misc]
[&Zap]^C^Cerase;all;;
[&Logo]^C^C-insert;logo
[&Square]^C^Cpolygon;4;e;\\
[&Filled Circle]^C^Cdonut;0;\
[&Cleanup]*^C^CFillet;r;0;\\
[--]
[z&Oom]'zoom
[&Pan]'pan
[&Annoying display items]^C^Cucsicon;off;+
blipmode;0
```

The first line of a pull-down menu (also known as a pop-up menu) contains the menu bar title, which is Misc in this example. The title goes within brackets; no macro is assigned to it as in other menu items. All pull down menus must have a menu title. Even though the cursor and shortcut menus don't display a title, you must include one (so go ahead and name it after your dog).

The ampersand indicates the mnemonic key, so place the ampersand in front of the character you want to be the mnemonic. Notice on all of your AutoCAD pull-down menus that one of the characters on each entry is underscored. This is the mnemonic key (also referred to as a menu accelerator key). For example, in this sample menu, <Alt-M> pulls down the Misc menu. In the AutoCAD menu, <Alt-F> pulls down the Files menu. Once you select a pull-down menu using the accelerator key, specific menu options are selected by entering the underscored character in the desired menu selection. <Alt-M>, followed by a Z executes the Zap menu item here.

Each pull-down menu and menu option should have a unique mnemonic character. If more than one option uses the same mnemonic, you'll cycle between them when using the keyboard. It's also bad customizing manners. Notice that two options start with Z in the sample menu: Zap and Zoom. Zap uses the Z as the mnemonic, whereas Zoom uses the first "O."

The lines of code beneath [&Misc] are options within your pull-down menu. The characters within brackets [] indicate the text you want to appear on the screen. The code outside of the brackets indicates the macro you want executed when the menu item is selected.

Consider the following line of code.

```
[&Zap]^C^Cerase;all;;
```

Zap is the first option available, and Z is the mnemonic key. When selected, AutoCAD issues two cancels, the erase command, an <Enter>, the All option, another <Enter>, and ends with an extra <Enter> to take the user all the way back to the command prompt.

Now skip to the third menu item.

```
[&Square]^C^Cpolygon;4;e;\\
```

The word Square will appear on the pull-down menu with the "S" underlined as the mnemonic. When selected, AutoCAD enters two cancels followed by the polygon command and an <Enter>. When prompted for number of sides, AutoCAD selects 4 and E for the Edge option, which is selected next, then adds an <Enter> and pauses twice so the user can select the two endpoints defining one edge of the square. If this sounds like Greek to you, execute the polygon command in AutoCAD and follow the steps.

You can repeat a command over and over by placing an asterisk in front of it.

```
*^C^Cfillet
```

This syntax repeats the fillet command over and over until you cancel the function. Because the fillet command kicks you out after one function (and you almost always need at least two), this is a handy modification to any menu. According to the customization manual, you cannot include command options, but that's incorrect. For example, the following syntax lets you draw squares over and over again.

```
*^C^Cpolygon;4;e;\\
```

Notice the line that contains [--]. This line draws a separator line in the pull-down menu the width of the longest title. Separators are typically used as dividers between different command categories or just to make it easy on the eyes. The user cannot select a separator line, and no macros are defined in conjunction with them.

Continuing on down the menu, the next item is Zoom.

```
[z&Oom]'zoom
```

The word Zoom appears on the screen, and "O" is the mnemonic. Notice that the cancels (^C^C) have been replaced with an apostrophe because Zoom is a transparent command. If you find yourself with an extra-long macro that needs to continue on to the next line, place a + at the end of the line of code; otherwise, AutoCAD assumes the next line of macro programming is intended for an entirely different menu item.

After you create the simple menu, save it and load it into AutoCAD. To use this menu, execute the menu command. As a reminder, once you load an MNU file, AutoCAD automatically creates an MNS file and compiles an MNC file. If you decide to make changes to the MNU file, reselect that specific file extension.

Note   AutoCAD issues an evil warning statement indicating that you will lose any of your custom toolbars. Not to worry. You don't have any custom toolbars in your sample menu.

Select the sample menu and you should see the pull-down menu in the upper left-hand corner of your screen. Try the different menu items to make sure they work. Figure 31.1 displays the sample menu created here.

To ensure I don't leave you out in limbo, you can always get back to the AutoCAD menu by loading the acad.mns file from the AutoCAD support directory. If you've created any custom toolbars, be sure you don't load the MNU by mistake (they will mysteriously disappear!).

As I pointed out earlier, I doubt you'd want to throw the AutoCAD menu by the wayside and use your own custom menu. More than likely, you'd prefer to (1) wedge your custom pull-down menu into the existing AutoCAD menu using the menuload command or (2) modify the acad.mns file, adding the commands into the existing pull-down menus or adding an entirely new pull-down menu.

If you select the second option, you'll need to show an

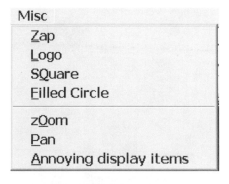

Figure 31.1 The pull-down menu in the top-left corner shows the sample menu that you created.

element of bravery as you open acad.mns. It's a huge file containing every menu type under the sun. Find the pull-down menus (***POP*n*) and go to it. If you have a favorite command you'd like to add to the cursor menu, simply find ***POP0 and add it using the information you've learned in the last two chapters. You should save a copy of the original acad.mns file just to make sure you don't botch anything up permanently. If worse comes to worst, reload acad.mnu for the out-of-the-box menu (but you will lose your custom toolbars). If you've safely set aside copies, you can feel free to experiment to your heart's content in the AutoCAD menus. I highly encourage it!

CHAPTER 32

The Long-Lost Image Tile Menus

An image tile menu is a simple dialog box populated with pictures. When these pictures or images are selected, a command is activated. I say image menus are simple only because you don't need to know LISP to create one. All you really need to know is basic menu syntax and how to create slide files. Image menus are often created by a resident CAD guru to display a company's library symbols. AutoCAD veterans might remember when they were called icon menus (pre-Release 13).

To see an example of an image menu, go to the Draw pull-down menu and select Surfaces and 3D Surfaces. Now, you may wonder why you'd go to the trouble to create an image menu when you can use DesignCenter. With an image menu, you can assign scale factors, rotation angles, layers, and so on.

Create the Slide File

First, decide what images you want to display in your image tile menu, then create a simple menu of several blocks using the following sequence of events for each block. Draw a block, take a picture of it with the `mslide` command, then make a block out of it with the `block` command.

The ratio of the image tile boxes (width to height) is 1.5 to 1. You want your picture to have the same ratio as the image displayed in the dialog box, so follow along with me.

- Switch to Paper Space.

- Turn `tilemode` off (`tilemode` = 0).

- Using the `mview` command, create a 3 × 2 viewport as follows.

  Command: MVIEW

  ON/OFF/Hideplot/Fit/2/3/4/Restore/<First Point>: (Pick in the lower left-hand corner of the screen.)

  Other corner: @3,2

- Zoom Extents.

- Switch back to Model Space.

Create your slide files in Paper Space. If you're not comfortable or familiar with the Paper Space world, feel free to draw the objects on your current display in Model Space.

Now look at Figure 32.1, and you'll see your goal — a very simple image tile menu. Start off by creating a simple pulley, as shown in Figure 32.2. It's just a combination of two circles and two lines.

The Pulley should fill the viewport. If you make it too small, it will be difficult to see in the dialog box. Now, you're ready to take a snapshot of it with the `mslide` command.

Using the `mslide` command, you're going to create a slide file in the AutoCAD `support` directory called `pulley.sld`. A slide file is just a simple vector image; no properties are attached to this

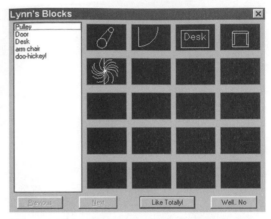

Figure 32.1 An example of the simple image tile menu created in the text.

small file. If you're in Model Space, `mslide` takes a picture of the current viewport. If you're in Paper Space, `mslide` takes a picture of the current Paper Space display, including all viewports. Objects off the screen display are not included within the slide file; it's pretty much what you see is what you get! (I'll go on record as saying that Flip Wilson coined this phrase way before Microsoft did!)

Keep in mind that image tiles show only the outlines of filled objects such as donuts, wide polylines, and solid fills.

Now that you have a slide file of the pulley, you need to make a block out of it. Using the `block` command, create a block (or a wblock if you plan to use it in other drawings) called Pulley. The pulley should disappear from the screen after creating the block. You now have one slide file and one block, both with the name Pulley.

Repeat the same process for the following five symbols shown in the dialog box. Here's a quick recap.

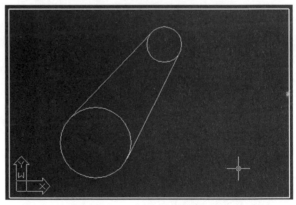

Figure 32.2 Use this simple pulley in your image tile menu.

1. Draw the object in the viewport.

2. Make a slide file out of the object.

3. Make a block out of the object.

The name for the following slides and blocks are Door, Desk, Chair, and Spiral. To create the spiral, I drew one arc and used grips to rotate/copy. The objects you draw do not need to match mine completely, but the names do in order to coincide with the menu syntax.

When all is finished, you should have five slides and five blocks. Now you're ready to create your menu.

Create the Image Menu

Image menus belong in the ***image section. Open acad.mns and search until you find this section. You will see several image menus. Each is preceded by two asterisks and the word image. For example, **image_3dobjects.

Make your own image menu called **IMAGE_BLOCKS and put it immediately after the **image_3dobjects section. Look at the syntax in Listing 32.1 and I'll explain it line by line.

**IMAGE_BLOCKS   The name of the image menu.

[Lynn's Blocks]   The title, which displays at the top of the image menu (see Figure 32.1).

[Pulley]^C^Cinsert;pulley   This line needs to be broken into two sections for proper explanation.

[Pulley] is the name of the slide file you want displayed in the first box. In this case, the word Pulley also displays in the left-hand column. It is case sensitive in that the case I use within the brackets will be the case displayed in the dialog.

^C^C-insert;pulley inserts the Pulley block into the drawing.

[Door]^C^C-insert;door   This line uses the slide file door as the image in the second box. When selected by the user, it inserts the Door block.

[Desk]^C^C-insert;desk   This line uses the slide file desk as the image in the third box. When selected by the user, it inserts the Desk block.

[chair,Arm chair]^C^C-insert;chair   This menu item has two elements within the brackets: chair and Arm chair. Suppose the name of the slide file and the text you want to display within the dialog are not the same. For example, although the slide file is called chair, I would prefer "Arm chair" to display in the dialog box. This is done by specifying the slide filename first and the text for the dialog second, separated by a comma. Notice the same syntax in the last menu item.

[spiral,Doo-hickey!]^C^C-insert; spiral   The name of the slide file is spiral, but "Doo-hickey!" displays within the dialog.

Listing 32.1 Image syntax.

```
***IMAGF
**IMAGE_3DOBJECTS
[3D Objects]
[acad(Box3d,Box3d)]^C^Cai_box
[acad(Pyramid,Pyramid)]^C^Cai_pyramid
[acad(Wedge,Wedge)]^C^Cai_wedge
[acad(Dome,Dome)]^C^Cai_dome
[acad(Sphere,Sphere)]^C^Cai_sphere
[acad(Cone,Cone)]^C^Cai_cone
[acad(Torus,Torus)]^C^Cai_torus
[acad(Dish,Dish)]^C^Cai_dish
[acad(Mesh,Mesh)]^C^Cai_mesh


**IMAGE_BLOCKS
[Lynn's Blocks]
[Pulley]^C^Cinsert;pulley
[Door]^C^Cinsert;door
[Desk]^C^Cinsert;desk
[chair,Arm chair]^C^Cinsert;chair
[spiral,Doo-hickey!]^C^Cinsert;spiral
```

Notice that the image tile menu accommodates 20 image tile boxes. If you were to create a menu with 25 blocks, 20 would go on the first page and five on the second. AutoCAD will create the second page for you, complete with buttons that permit you to switch between pages.

Now that you've written the code for the image menu, you need a way to get to the menu, such as a pull-down menu. I suggest you add your nifty new image menu to the end of the Insert pull-down menu. Search the acad.mns file for the ***pop4 menu and append the code shown in Listing 32.2.

[Personal &Symbol Library...] The text that displays at the end of the Insert pull-down menu, as shown in Figure 32.3. The ampersand in front of the S denotes the mnemonic key.

$I=image_BLOCKS This line tells AutoCAD to look for the image tile menu called image_BLOCKS.

$i=* This line tells AutoCAD to display the image tile menu

Listing 32.2 Add this code to the ***pop4 menu to add the image menu to the end of the Insert pull-down menu.

```
***POP4

**INSERT

ID_MnInsert    [&Insert]

ID_Ddinsert    [&Block...]^C^C_ddinsert

               [ — ]

ID_Xref        [E&xternal Reference...]^C^C_xref

ID_Image       [Raster &Image...]^C^C_image

               [ — ]

ID_3dsin       [&3D Studio...]^C^C_3dsin

ID_Acisin      [&ACIS Solid...]^C^C_acisin

ID_Dxbin       [Drawing &Exchange Binary...]^C^C_dxbin

ID_Wmfin       [&Windows Metafile...]^C^C_wmfin

ID_Psin        [Encapsulated &PostScript...]^C^C_psin

               [ — ]

ID_Insertobj   [&OLE Object...]^C^C_insertobj

[Personal &Symbol Library...]$I=image_BLOCKS $i=*
```

Without these components, the image menu won't display.

Save this to acad.mns (I hope you have a nice clean copy somewhere, just in case) and exit. Go back into AutoCAD and reload acad.mns. Pull down the Insert menu. You should find access to your Personal Symbol Library. Pick this option, and the dialog box should appear!

Now you can create dialog boxes to your heart's content using the instructions I've given you so far. If someone were to come along and delete one of the slide files that goes with your menu, you will have a vacancy in your image tile menu. The image tile will still work, but AutoCAD shows you a nasty message letting you know that the slide file wasn't found. In an effort to protect you slides from this situation, you can put them into a slide library using the old slidelib command. And when I say old, I mean old! It's a DOS function, and it requires you to be in DOS to use it. Here are the steps for creating a slide library.

Figure 32.3 The Insert pull-down menu with the added text, Personal Symbol Library.

Create a text file (such as myslides.txt) that contains the names of all of your slides. It should look like this.

```
Desk
Door
Pulley
Spiral
Chair
```

The order is unimportant, and you don't need to include the SLD extensions.

- Save this file and exit .

- Exit to DOS. Dust off your DOS brains, and make your way from the Windows directory to the AutoCAD support directory. Slidelib is hiding in there.

- Enter the following syntax at the DOS prompt from the support directory.

```
Slidelib blocks myslides.txt
```

Note   If you're completely ignorant of DOS, go to MS-DOS via Windows and open the Explorer dialog. Find slidelib.exe in the AutoCAD support directory. You can drag and drop this file to the command prompt at DOS.

Slidelib is the name of the program, blocks will be the name of the slide library, and myslides.txt is the name of the simple text file that contains the slide names. You now have a file called blocks.slb that contains all of your slides.

To use the slides from the slide library, you need to make changes to the original menu code of Listing 32.1. Precede each menu item with the name of the slide library (blocks) and enclose the name of each slide file in parentheses.

```
**IMAGE_BLOCK
[Lynn's Blocks]
[blocks (Pulley)]^C^C-insert;pulley
[blocks (Door)]^C^C-insert;door
[blocks (Desk)]^C^C-insert;desk
[blocks (chair),Arm chair]+
^C^C-insert;chair
[blocks (spiral),Doo-hickey!]+
^C^C-insert;spiral
```

You don't have to create a slide library to use your image tile menu; you might decide it's more trouble than it's worth. One Express Tools programmer, Randy Kintzley, was kind enough to write a quick AutoLISP routine that makes it easy for me to put my slides into a slide library.

Note   Do not delete your slides. If you ever want to add to your slide library, you'll need the original slides to recompile it.

As I come to the end of this chapter, I want to leave you with a few pointers about image tile menus.

1. Slide libraries don't support long filenames.

2. When creating slide files, keep them simple. Complicated slide files take more time to display in the dialog box.

3. Image tile menus aren't just for blocks; you can put any command inside an image tile menu.

4. Get your image menu to display text but no icon by putting a space in front of the text string.

   `[ Erase Everything]^C^Cerase;all;;`

5. You can launch another icon menu from within the image tile menu.

   `[ Electrical symbols]$I=ICON _ELEC $I=*`

6. The text that displays in the left column of the dialog box is limited to 17 characters.

Keep in mind that image tile menus can frustrate the most adept of users. I can't recommend enough that you keep copies of the original MNU files before you customize them. That said, have at them!

CHAPTER 33

Customizing Your Keyboard in AutoCAD 2002

What does <F12> do for you? Probably absolutely nothing! Why not assign your favorite AutoCAD command to it? Customizing the keyboard isn't nearly as cumbersome as it used to be now that you can use the new Customize dialog added to AutoCAD 2002. Keyboard customization has been possible for years in the Accelerator section in the ACAD menu, but few people have taken the time to tackle this feat. Customizing the accelerators required some basic menu macro knowledge, and many users just didn't have the time (or patience) to sort it all out.

There's no need to now because AutoCAD 2002 has made it easy to make some basic keyboard assignments.

Accelerator

The Accelerator section in the ACAD menu allows you to make some powerful keyboard assignments. You can set up the function keys and the <Ctrl>, <Shift>, and <Ctrl-Shift> key combinations to your liking. You also can configure the number pad, arrow, <Ins>, and <End> keys, and even the <Esc> key, to do as you please. The Accelerator section in the menu can make you powerful (and oh-so danger-

Figure 33.1 Enter the Customize dialog through the toolbar shortcut menu.

ous!). The new Customize dialog doesn't allow you to be quite so destructive as the old method (so all you CAD managers can relax). The Customize dialog permits you to customize the function keys and <Ctrl> and <Shift-Ctrl> key combinations only. There are just enough options to help you make your AutoCAD environment a little more comfortable.

Right-clicking on any toolbar in AutoCAD 2002 brings up the toolbar shortcut menu. At the bottom of this menu is the Customize option (Figure 33.1). The new Customize dialog box has four tabs: Commands, Toolbars, Properties, and Keyboard (Figure 33.2). The first three tabs are used to customize toolbars, but I'll focus on the fourth tab, Keyboard.

Figure 33.3 displays the Keyboard tab in the Customize dialog. The process here is simple; pick the command you want to assign first, then manually hit the function key or key combination to assign the keystroke(s) to the specified command. I will assign three commands: extend to <F11>, the Endpoint object snap to <F12>, and Zoom Previous to <Shift-Ctrl-Z>. I realize the last assignment is a pretty bad selection of keys, but I want to make sure you understand how to do key combinations.

Finding extend

Your first quest is to find the extend command. Drop the Categories list down from the upper left-hand corner of the dialog to display the various pull-down menus and toolbar titles. If you know which menu or toolbar the extend command resides in, you can select it from this drop-down list. I must confess, I find this too tedious for my liking. Also, and I'm not ashamed to admit this, I don't know all the menus and toolbars by heart. Frankly, if you do, you have too much time on your hands. Therefore, I opt for the low-stress option at the end of the Categories drop-down list, AutoCAD Commands. Here you'll find all the AutoCAD commands (and then

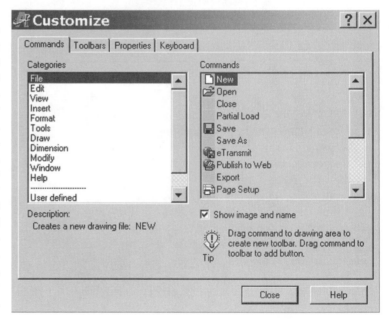

Figure 33.2 Customize toolbars and the keyboard in the Customize dialog.

some) in alphabetical order. I also prefer not bouncing around from toolbar to toolbar, searching for the various commands. My only complaint is that my customization life would be so much nicer if they'd placed this option at the top of the list, rather than at the end. I hate having to scroll allllllllllllllllllllll the way down.

In your continued search for the extend command, scroll through the alphabetized Commands list. You can also key in the first character of the command after picking in the Commands box to jump to that portion of the commands, so press E, and scroll to the extend command. After you've highlighted the command, you will be able to see whether it already has a keyboard assignment by looking at the right-hand side of the dialog box under Current Keys. (My guess is that extend probably hasn't been assigned yet to a keyboard combination on your system.)

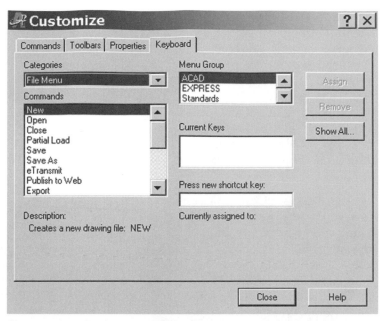

Figure 33.3 Set up your function keys and some basic key combinations in the Keyboard tab.

Next, place your cursor in the Press new shortcut key section on the right side of the dialog and hit the <F11> key. <F11> will display in this box, and any existing assignments for <F11> will display under the Currently assigned to section of the dialog. If you've managed to follow along this far, your dialog box should look like Figure 33.4.

Finally, simply hit the Assign key, and you've customized a function keys! Isn't that easy? To recap, perform the following steps.

1. Select the command you want to assign from the list on the left-hand side of the dialog.

2. Pick inside of the Press new shortcut key text box and hit the keyboard key or key combination to be assigned to the command.

3. Hit the Assign button in the upper right-hand corner of the dialog.

Next, I'll assign the Endpoint object snap to <F12>.

The Endpoint Object Snap

You won't find Endpoint under the obvious E section of the command list. Instead, you need to scroll down to the S section where you'll find all the object snaps listed under Snap to Intersection, Snap to Endpoint, and so forth. Choose a favorite object snap, move the cursor to the shortcut key box, hit <F12>, and press the Assign button, Now you've done two out of three.

Zoom Previous

After scrolling all the way down to Zoom Previous (a command I use frequently), move your cursor back to the Press new shortcut key text box. Now hold down the <Shift> and <Ctrl> keys and press Z. This combination should show up in the shortcut key box.

After assigning the final key, you're ready to exit the dialog and give it a go. Hitting <F11> should launch the extend command. Enter the line command and hit <F12> for the Endpoint object snap. Do a Zoom Window to zoom into a section of a drawing, then try the <Shift-Ctrl-Z> combination to zoom back to the previous display. If all three worked, pat yourself on the back!

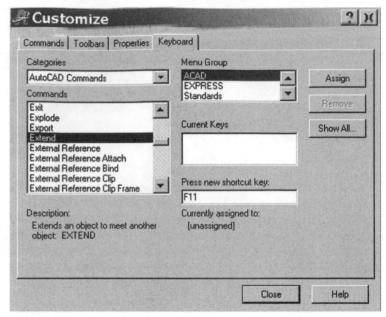

Figure 33.4 These settings assign <F11> to the extend **command.**

The Keyboard Tab

Return to the Keyboard tab, and I'll cover the rest of the dialog in detail. Notice that not only can you assign commands to the keyboard, but you can assign commands with a specific option. For example, you can assign the circle command to a key or a 3-Point Circle to a key. This is wonderful! Tour the list of commands to see the many possibilities available for assignment.

The right side of the dialog contains the various menu groups you've loaded into the current drawing. You will probably focus most of your efforts on the ACAD menu group. The Show All button takes you to a listing of all your currently defined keyboard settings, as shown in Figure 33.5.

Can you override the existing settings? You bet ya! If you don't like what <F3> does for you, feel free to change it to something that better suits your drawing style. You can't control the <F1> and <F10> function keys. Apparently Windows has custody of them and their assignments, but the others are up for grabs.

The Remove button removes a keyboard assignment. Note that some basic settings can't be removed; however, they can be changed. For example, you know that <Ctrl-C> copies to the Clipboard. You can't remove this assignment, but you can change it to something else, if desired.

You must have the Accelerators turned on to use any of your changes! This is controlled in the Options dialog under User Preferences in the upper left-hand corner. Make sure Windows standard accelerator keys is checked.

Where do keyboard settings go? Are they only good for one drawing session or one drawing, or do they stay set forever? These settings go directly to the AutoCAD menu; hence, they affect all drawings that use the standard ACAD menu. They work like toolbars (saved in the acad.mns file). If you override the MNS file with acad.mns, you'll lose your accelerator settings (just as you would your customized toolbars). I've been there, so be careful.

Wasn't that easy? After tackling basic keyboard customization, you might find yourself feeling adventurous and want to customize all of your keyboard. Taking it another step further will require learning more about the accelerators section in the ACAD menu and some basic macro information, which I covered in Chapter 30.

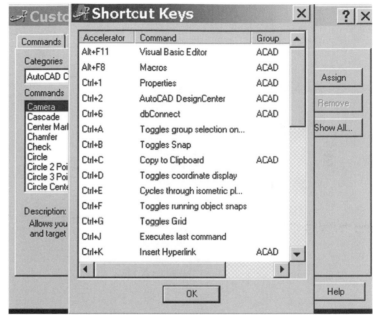

Figure 33.5 View the existing keyboard settings in the Shortcut Keys dialog.

CHAPTER 34

Limitless Linetypes

Linetypes are an integral part of nearly all CAD applications. To create simple linetypes, use the `linetype` command-line interface by placing a dash in front. Simple linetypes are made up of dashes, spaces, and dots only.

```
Command: -LINETYPE
```
```
?/Create/Load/Set: C
```
```
Name of linetype to create: sample
```

At this point, AutoCAD displays the Create or Append Linetype File dialog box. Create your own linetype file, `test`. The following will open a file called `test.lin` and ready it for storing information.

```
Descriptive text: first sample linetype
```
```
Enter pattern (on next line)
```
```
A,
```

All linetype pattern definitions begin with A, which signifies the pattern alignment. AutoCAD only supports A-type alignment, which ensures that all lines and arcs start and end with a dash. Because no options are available at this point, AutoCAD included A, so you can't make a mistake. The following define the rest of a basic linetype.

- A positive number is a vector.

- A negative number is a space.

- A zero is a dot.

AutoCAD uses a comma delimiter. A vector 1.5 units long, a gap of 0.25, a dot, and another space of 0.25 would be `1.5,-.25,0,-.25`. This definition can define an entire linetype. Add these values to your definition.

```
A,1.5,-.25,0,-.25
```

While you're still in the `linetype` command, you need to load the linetype into your drawing.

```
Linetype(s) to load: SAMPLE
```

After loading the linetype, set `test.lin` from the file dialog box as the current linetype.

```
?/Create/Load/Set: S
New object linetype (or ?): SAMPLE
```

Any new objects you draw should display the new linetype. If for some reason you do not see lines and dots on new objects, you might need to increase or decrease your `ltscale` factor.

The linetypes that come with AutoCAD are stored in the `acad.lin` file (support subdirectory). Feel free to open this file and look at the various linetype definitions. You'll see no surprises.

Complex linetypes fulfill a long-time need, for which many have resorted to third-party packages to satisfy. I'll create a simple linetype with the text "Fence" built in (Figure 34.1).

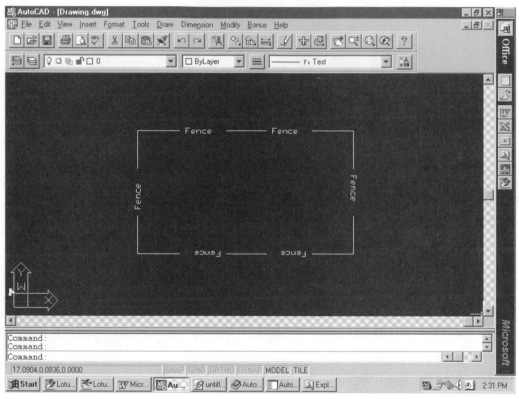

Figure 34.1 A simple linetype has text built in to it.

Complex linetypes cannot be constructed internally within the `linetype` command. Instead, you need to use an external text editor such as Notepad. Open the file `test.lin` and you'll see the original linetype definition (Sample) is already listed within. Notice that it consists of two lines. The first line starts with an asterisk and contains the name of the linetype followed by an optional description (maximum of 47 characters). The second line of code contains the coded definition, which must always begin with A. AutoCAD rejects any other character placed in the alignment field.

Name this new linetype Fence. The Fence linetype consists simply of a vector, the word Fence, followed by another vector. However, you need to include some extra information as well.

Text   The text string to include within the linetype. This string must be enclosed in double quotes. In this case, it will be the word Fence.

Text style   The text style in which AutoCAD displays the text. I'll use the Standard text style because all drawings include it. Be aware that this must be an existing text style, not a font. The text style is not enclosed in double quotes.

Text height   The text height when the linetype scale factor is 1. As the ltscale factor is modified, so is the text height. For example, if your text height is 0.2 and the ltscale factor is 3, the total text height is 0.6. This factor is often hit or miss and must be tried at several values to get the desired result. I'll set the height to 0.2 by including the phrase S = .2. (S is for scale factor.) The AutoCAD Customization Manual claims that this value is a multiplier of the text style height; however, this doesn't seem to be the case. The value appears to be absolute, regardless of the style setting for text height, so don't think of this value as a scale factor, think of it as a text height.

Rotation angle   The rotation angle for the text string. If you want the text to follow the same angle as the object you're drawing, set this value to 0. Any angle is acceptable. You can use two modifiers for setting the angle: A for absolute rotation and R for relative rotation. If you set A = 0, you would force the text to remain at 0 degrees regardless of the direction of the object drawn. R = 0 forces a rotation angle of zero relative or tangential to the direction of the object drawn. I'll use R = 0.

X and Y displacement   Displacement of the text from the last vector. If you want to place "Fence" slightly above the last vector, you can set the Y position to .1. To center the text, set Y to a negative number, which pulls the text downward. I will set the text displacement to y = -.1. If you want to modify the X displacement, you can, although it's usually not necessary. I'll leave X at zero.

Any zero value need not be entered. For practice, I'll specify x and r even though they are 0. Lines of code starting with a semicolon are ignored, in case you want to include comments. Now I'm ready to create the Linetype. Add the following to test.lin.

```
*Fence, sample complex linetype
A,1.5,-.25,["Fence", Standard,S=.2,R=0,X=0, Y=-.1],-1.5
```

Using A alignment, the linetype comprises a 1.5-unit vector, a 0.25-unit gap, the string "Fence," and a 1.5-unit gap, which allows enough space from the beginning of the string to the next vector — the reason the last value is so big.

Save this file and reenter the linetype command. Load and set the new linetype. As you draw new objects, you should see the newly created, complex linetype.

You can also use shape files within your custom linetype file. Remember how to create shape files? Unlike blocks, shape files are difficult and cumbersome to create. Years ago, AutoCAD users who were unhappy with the existing text fonts (there were only four) were forced to learn the ancient art of creating shape files to make their own text fonts. Some of those people who mastered the art went on to create multiple fonts and sell them to the AutoCAD masses. Even today, with the vast variety of fonts provided with AutoCAD software, many of you still use third-party fonts in your drawings.

Shape files are hard-coded ASCII text files. Using a combination of pen up/down, vector lengths, and angles, you explain to AutoCAD how to draw your shape. This explanation process is much more difficult than it appears. The Customization Manual includes explicit instructions on how to create shape files, if you feel up to the task. In the early days of AutoCAD, shape files were often used in place of blocks in a drawing. Shape files were believed to be faster and more compact. Working on an 8088 processor, a CAD user would do anything to save time. One of the best Express Tools is called shapemaker. You simply draw the shape, then Shapemaker does the hard work, magically creating a shape file from it.

Should you find yourself with an existing shape file that you want to place within a complex linetype, you'll notice only a slight difference between the complex linetype and text. You'll need to know the names of the shape and the compiled shape file (SHX extension).

A shape file called RR within the shape file demo.shx could be specified with the following linetype command.

```
*Railroad, sample linetype with a shape file
A,1.5,-.25,[RR, demo.shx,S=.5,A=0,X=0, Y=-.1],-1.0
```

AutoCAD knows RR is a shape file rather than text because it is not in double quotes.

AutoCAD allows multiple linetype scale factors per drawing. Previously, you had just the ltscale command, which controlled the linetype scale factor for the entire drawing. You often had to create multiple linetypes with various vector lengths to get the desired effect. Along came the great celtscale (current entity linetype scale) system variable, which controls the ltscale factor for individual entities. Set this value before you draw the intended objects. It can be set in the Linetype manager (linetype command) under the Details option. If you've already drawn some objects and want to change their ltscale factor, use the properties command.

If you have access to Express Tools, you'll find a Linetype maker, which simplifies this entire process. Nearly all CAD applications use linetypes in their drawings. These new improvements should speed up drawing time and eliminate the Band-Aids used in the past.

CHAPTER 35

Calculating Geometries

Precision is important to AutoCAD users, and AutoCAD provides many methods to ensure your drawings are geometrically and mathematically accurate. The underused and somewhat complex Geometric Calculator is one of the powerful tools AutoCAD has to define specific points and values in your drawing. I'll present the online Geometric Calculator capabilities in small, simple doses, and you'll wonder how you ever used AutoCAD without it!

Available since Release 11, the `cal` command came to AutoCAD as an AutoLISP routine. The `cal` command is used to solve mathematical problems or locate specific points in a drawing. The code the `cal` command uses is somewhat cryptic and tends to send the casual user running for cover. Power AutoCAD users know only too well how powerful the command is.

The `cal` command evaluates expressions. You can use the Geometric Calculator in much the same way as you use a hand-held calculator (although I wouldn't want to balance my checkbook with it!). By preceding the command with an apostrophe, `cal` is available transparently (from within other commands). I'll start with some simple mathematical expressions.

Mathematical Expressions

`cal` uses the standard mathematical rules of precedence. Do you remember the phrase "Please Excuse My Dear Aunt Sally"? No doubt one of your math teachers taught you this phrase to illustrate the abbreviation of parentheses, exponents, multiplication, division, addition, and subtraction. The `cal` command solves expressions using this order of precedence. The following mathematical symbols are used and understood by the Geometric Calculator.

( )	Parentheses group expressions (Please).
^	The caret indicates an exponent; for example, 5^3 is the same as 5 to the 3rd power or 5-cubed = 125 (Excuse).
*	An asterisk indicates multiplication; for example, $5*3$ is the same as $5 \times 3 = 15$ (My).
/	A forward slash indicates division; for example, $9/3$ is the same as $9 \div 3 = 3$ (Dear).
+	A plus sign indicates addition (Aunt).
–	A minus sign indicates subtraction (Sally).

Here's how it works using the calculator.

```
Command: CAL
Initializing...>> Expression: 5*3
15
Command: CAL >> Expression: 8*(4/2)
16.0
Command: CAL >> Expression: 5^3
125.0
```

Now you don't need to find your calculator to perform a mathematical function on the fly. (By the way, the geometric calculator uses pi = 3.14159.) Take a look at some of the more sophisticated numeric functions (those of you who are allergic to math can skip to the next section).

sin(*angle*)   returns the sine of the indicated angle; for example, sin(90) returns 1.

cos(*angle*)   returns the cosine of the indicated angle.

tang(*angle*) returns the tangent of the angle.

asin(*angle*) returns the arcsine of the indicated number, which must be between –1 and 1. For example, asin(1) returns 90 degrees; arcsine means the angle whose sine is 1.

acos(*angle*) returns the arccosine of the number (same restrictions as asin).

atan(*angle*) returns the arctangent of the number.

ln(*real*)   returns the natural log of a number (to the base *e*).

log(*real*)   returns the log (to the base 10) of the number indicated.

sqr(*real*)   returns the square of a number; for example, sqr(5) returns 25.

sqrt(*real*)   returns the square root of a number; for example, sqrt(100) returns 10.

r2d(*angle*)   (radians to degrees) returns the indicated angle (in radians) in degrees.

d2r(*angle*)   (degrees to radians) returns the indicated angle (in degrees) in radians.

Units and Angles Format

If you want to use feet and inches with the calculator, you need to use the proper syntax. The two acceptable formats are: feet'-inches" or feet'inches", or 2'-6" or 2'6".

The calculator converts these values to real numbers (based on inches). For example: 2'6" converts to 30 and 8" converts to 8.

cal also assumes you'll use degrees for input. You can, however, specify radians with an r and grads with a g. You can specify minutes and seconds (but you'll have to use a delimiter of d). For example, 130.2r = 130.2 radians; 15d10'25" = 15 degrees; 10 minutes, 25 seconds and 16g = 16 grads. Regardless of your input, the calculator converts the value to degrees.

Points

The Geometric Calculator can also handle points. Points, locations in space, are defined as x, y, z values, just as they are in AutoCAD. The Geometric Calculator expects points to be enclosed within brackets [ ].

```
Command: LINE From point: 'cal
>> Expression: [2,2]
to point: 'cal
>> Expression: [6,0]
```

AutoCAD assumes a value of 0 if it's not included; for example, [1,,3] is evaluated as (1, 0, 3); [,,2] is the same as (0, 0, 2). Wouldn't it be nice if AutoCAD accepted coordinate input the same way?

Polar, cylindrical, spherical, and relative coordinates are also accepted using the standard AutoCAD syntax.

```
>> Expression: [@2<45<30] (relative-spherical)
```

So why go to all this trouble? Stay tuned. I'll put this all together and you'll begin to see the true benefits.

Vectors

By definition, any two points define a vector. After defining a vector, you can find out the direction and length of that vector. See the following code as an example.

```
>>Expression: vec ([1,2],[3,4])
(2.0 2.0 0.0)
```

The value returned is the distance traveled in X from the first point followed by the distance in Y and Z. The following expression calculates the distance between two points.

```
>>Expression: dist ([1,2],[3,4])
```

Finding the Radius of an Arc or Circle

Perhaps you'd like to draw a circle that's one-third the size of an existing circle. Using the calculator, you can find the radius of an existing circle, then divide the result by three (or multiply by one-third).

```
Command: CIRCLE
3P/2P/TTR/<Center point>: cen
of Diameter/<Radius> <0.7910>: 'cal
>> Expression: rad/3
>> Select circle, arc or polyline segment for RAD function:
```

AutoCAD automatically draws another circle at the indicated point that's one-third the size of the original.

Object Snaps

The calculator can prompt for a particular object snap within an expression as well. Here's a list of the proper syntax.

end	Endpoint
ins	Insertion point
int	Intersection
mid	Midpoint
cen	Center
nea	Nearest
nod	Node (point)
qua	Quadrant
per	Perpendicular
tan	Tangent

Note From and Apparent Intersection object snaps are not accepted by the calculator.

These object snaps always return a point value (X, Y, Z). The result is saved under the AutoCAD `lastpoint` system variable. Also, use the @ to reference the result in the next drawing or editing command. To pick a point on the screen without using object snaps while in the Calculator command, use the `cur` function. It prompts you for a point.

Here is where the calculator becomes powerful. Say you want to find the midpoint between the center of a circle and the endpoint of a line.

`(cen+end)/2`

You will be prompted to select an arc or circle first (it records the coordinates for the center point; Figure 35.1). Then, it will prompt you to select an object with an endpoint (it records the coordinates for the endpoint). It takes those two coordinates and divides them by two to find the midpoint. Without the calculator, you'd probably create construction lines to find this value.

How about the center (centroid) of a triangle? Construct a triangle and try this great equation.

`(end+end+end)/3`

The Geometric Calculator prompts for the three corners of the triangle, divides those values by three, and finds the center for you (Figure 35.2).

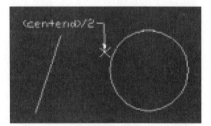

Figure 35.1 The calculator can find the midpoint between the center of a circle and the endpoint of a line.

Using Variables

The Geometric Calculator can also set and read variables, allowing you to temporarily store specific points, numeric values, or vectors for use later in the drawing session.

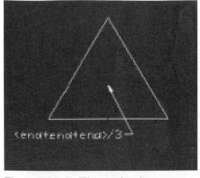

Figure 35.2 The calculator can find the centroid of a triangle.

- Set some simple variables.

```
Command:
CAL >> Expression: x=1
1     (AutoCAD returns the value)
Command:
CAL >> Expression: y=2
2
Command:
CAL >> Expression: x+y
3
```

- Assign points and vectors to variables.

```
Command: CAL
>> Expression: pt1=[2,3]
(2.0 3.0 0.0)
```

This expression sets pt1 to (2, 3).

- I'll make it more difficult. My goal is to create a tooling hole one unit over and up from the center of an existing circle. First, I'll use the calculator to set a variable of a point one unit up and one unit over from the center of my circle.

```
Command: cal
>> Expression: pt2=cen+[1,1]
>> Select entity for CEN snap:
(13.7172 7.19474 0.0)
```

Now, I'll use pt2 as the center of my new tooling hole.

```
Command: CIRCLE
3P/2P/TTR/<Center point>: 'cal
>> Expression: pt2
Diameter/<Radius> <3.6048>:
```

Incidentally, I could have performed this entire operation at once by accessing cal twice from within the circle command.

Shortcut Functions

The Geometric Calculator includes shortcut functions for some commonly used expressions. These functions provide information quickly and easily. I've included the ones I feel are the most valuable in everyday drafting:

DEE   (distance, end, end) returns the distance between two endpoints on one or two objects.

ILLE   (intersection, line, line, endpoint) finds the intersection point between two lines. You will be prompted for all four endpoints of the two lines.

MEE   (midpoint, end, end) finds the midpoint between any two endpoints (Figure 35.3).

I've covered about half of the capabilities of the `cal` command. You must practice and use it cleverly to increase productivity, but as you can see, it is well worth a little extra perspiration.

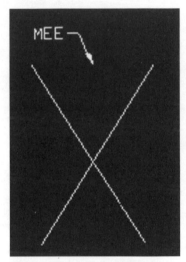

Figure 35.3 The MEE shortcut function can find the midpoint between the top ends of two crossed lines.

CHAPTER 36

The Top Secret Filter Command

Selecting objects is an everyday occurrence for CAD users. Shaving seconds off the selection set process can subtract minutes, possibly even hours, over the span of a project. In this chapter, I cover a command that helps you sift through your database of objects quickly, enabling you to grab only the ones you want. If you've ever wanted to get a specific type of object only (for example, text or dimensions) or find objects that share a specific property (layer, color, elevation), then the filter command will become your best friend.

AutoCAD 2000 introduced the new qselect command, which you can read about in Chapter 5, Modifying Object Properties. The qselect command is a low-stress version of the filter command, but not nearly as powerful.

filter is one of those top secret commands that's buried beneath the AutoCAD infrastructure. It's been around for many releases, and many an AutoCAD guru uses it when no one else is looking. You can use a filter search that selects something simple, such as all circles, or you can select a very specific filter that selects, for example, all circles with a radius of 2.3 that lie on the construction layer. Look at this treasure of a command so you too can select objects at lightning speed!

Since Release 14, the filter command has been banished from the pull-down menus and is nowhere to be found in the toolbars either. Don't let this dissuade you from using this cool, transparent command. You can always access it by keying in filter or its alias, fi, at the command prompt (it rated an alias but not a menu pick). If you find yourself wanting to use this command often, and you don't like to type, consider making a Filter toolbar button.

As a simple exercise, I've drawn three lines and three circles (Figure 36.1). I've placed these objects on two layers and assigned the color yellow to two of the objects. I've drawn them close together, making it difficult to select them manually (not uncommon in standard drawing practices).

Say your goal is to select just the yellow circles. The filter command makes this easy. Open the filter command and take a look (Figure 36.2).

Selecting the Filter

The first step in the process is to select the filter(s) you want AutoCAD to use to sift through the data. You want two. You want AutoCAD to search for circles (filter 1) that are the color yellow (filter 2). Filters fall into three categories: object (line, arc, pline, and so on), property (layer, color, linetype), or individual object characteristics (text height, block insertion angle). Select the drop-down list on the left side of the

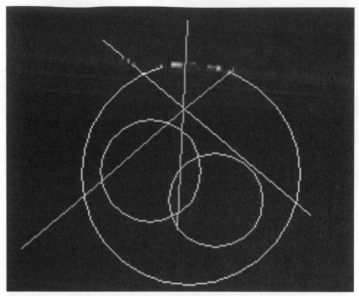

Figure 36.1 A simple drawing of circles and lines placed close together makes selection a challenge.

dialog box by the word Arc to see a substantial listing (Figure 36.3).

Select the Circle filter then select the Add to List button located in the lower left-hand corner of the Object Selection Filters (Filter) dialog. The line Object = Circle displayed at the top of the dialog indicates that you've chosen one filter. Some filters require additional information, such as layer name, size, hatch pattern type, and so forth. The second filter requires two bits of information. Select color first, then select exactly the color you're after. Notice the Select button located next to the word Color. Choose this button to display the color palette. After selecting yellow, reselect the Add to List button. Both filters should display, as shown in Figure 36.4. After selecting the appropriate filters, pick the Apply button to save the filter list and then exit the dialog box.

AutoCAD should be prompting you to Select objects. Put a window around all of the objects in your drawing and AutoCAD selects only those objects that pass the filter list; they must be yellow and they must be circles. In this case, two objects are selected. These are stored in the current selection set. To use these objects, enter a command; when prompted to select objects, enter P for previous. AutoCAD will use only the yellow circles in the command.

It often makes more sense to use the `filter` command transparently inside of the desired command.

`Command: ERASE`

`Select objects: 'filter`

Select your filters and pick Apply

`Select objects:` window all the objects

`6 found; 4 filtered out.`

This method eliminates the need to use the Previous option in the command.

Now, I'll look at the other options in the `filter` command.

You can select a filter that requires a numeric coordinate or a value, such as all circles with a radius of 4. Notice the drop-down list of opera-

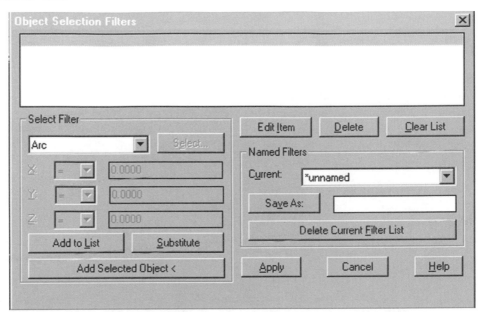

Figure 36.2 The Filter dialog box helps you select objects according to criteria defined by filters.

tors under the equals sign (Figure 36.5). These operators allow you to create a filter list that selects all the circles with a radius of less than 4, for example. The possible options are as follows.

!=	not equal to
<	less than
<=	less than or equal to
>	greater than
>=	greater than or equal to
*	all possibilities (standard wildcard)

Note that the != and * options are not documented. Test your local AutoCAD guru to see if he or she knows what these stand for!

I seldom use the asterisk because all possibilities are assumed. For example, why would I select circles of any radius, versus simply all circles? I suppose you might find yourself in a situation where you have specific X and Y coordinates but can accept any Z value. Is it just me, or is the Y filter box slightly off center? I remember this from previous releases, and it's apparently still not fixed.

If you choose a value such as Circle Center, the filter Object = Circle is automatically added to your list.

AND, OR, and NOT

You can make your filter list as simple or as complex as you desire. Those of you with some programming experience will immediately identify with the AND, OR, and NOT options. You'll find these operators at the end of the filter list (Figure 36.6).

For those of you who've successfully avoided the world of programming, I'll provide a brief and painless explanation.

Rule 1 You must have both Begin and End operators in your filter list. (If you do not follow this rule, AutoCAD calls you bad names.)

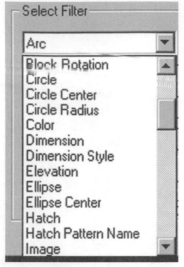

Figure 36.3 Use the Select Filter drop-down list of the Filter dialog box for access to more filter criteria.

Rule 2 You must begin and end with the same type of operator. `Begin NOT`, goes with `End NOT`, `Begin AND` goes with `End AND`, and so on. (Thou shalt not mix thy operators!)

Say you want to select all of the cyan polylines or all of the polylines that are on the floorplan layer.

`Object = Polyline`
`**Begin OR`
`Color = 4 - Cyan`
`Layer = FLOORPLAN`
`**End OR`

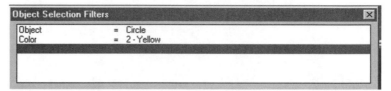

Figure 36.4 The two selected object filters are visible in the Object Selection Filters dialog box.

Notice how I diligently followed rules 1 and 2. The Not operator selects all objects that do not pertain to the filter list. XOR is still a mystery to me. I believe it's a combination of AND/OR and only accepts two operands.

The hottest button in the Filter dialog box is the Add Selected Object. This permits you to select an object with the characteristics and properties you're after, and it will be used to determine the filter set. From there, you can delete or modify the filter list to suit you. This dialog box still doesn't recognize the <Shift> or <Ctrl> keys as viable means to select multiple entries, so it can be a tad tedious.

To save a particular filter list, select the Save As option and provide a name. This name is saved to `filter.nfl` (named filter list — another good trivia question for your fellow AutoCAD gurus). You can also delete a filter list from the file with the Delete Current Filter List button, and you can Edit and Delete items. The Clear List button returns you to a clean slate by removing all of the entries in the filter list (don't hit it by accident or you could lose valuable time rebuilding your list). The Substitute button replaces one filter entry with another; to my mind, it's just as easy to delete and add an item.

Get creative with your filter lists and be sure to save those you use frequently. A filters is one of the best mechanisms you have to save valuable selection time.

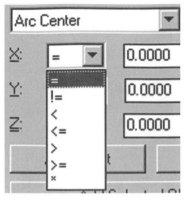

Figure 36.5 The specific operators for numeric values are available in a drop-down list.

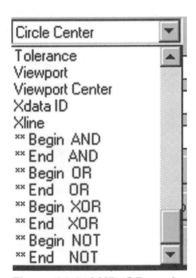

Figure 36.6 AND, OR, and NOT filter operators are available at the end of the filter list.

CHAPTER 37

The World of Raster

In today's world, it's not an uncommon practice to incorporate scanned documents, satellite photographs, digital photographs, or rendered images into an AutoCAD drawing. Before Release 14, AutoCAD's support of the raster world was limited, leading to a variety of comical workarounds. With the advent of the AutoCAD Image Support Module, the world of raster became much better!

What is a Raster Image?

A raster image is a compilation of a bunch of dots referred to as pixels. The word pixel is derived from the words "picture element" (a little raster trivia). These colorized pixels are put together in a rectangular grid that mysteriously creates an image. Think of the painter Georges Seurat creating his artwork from a variety of colored dots that magically come together to create a picture, and you have a primitive raster image. The specific color that a pixel depicts comes from a blending of the three components of the color spectrum: red, green, and blue. Up to three bytes of data specify a pixel's color — one byte for each color. All this information is stored in each little pixel, and it can add up to a fairly large file when you look at the entire image. Were it not for the clever method AutoCAD uses to store these graphic images with the drawing, you'd definitely notice your file size swelling with each inserted raster image.

The raster file is often referred to as a bitmap because it contains data directly mapped to the display grid. A bitmap is a file that contains the color information for each pixel along the horizontal axis (X coordinate), as well as the color for each pixel along the vertical axis (Y coordinate). Enough about the details, now I'll move on to the good stuff!

Table 37.1 lists the raster image file formats supported by AutoCAD. Notice that AutoCAD supports the most common raster image formats. These file formats are found in applications ranging anywhere from document management to geographic information systems (GIS).

Table 37.1 Raster image file formats supported by AutoCAD.

Type	Description and Version	File Extension
BMP	Windows and OS/2 Bitmap Format	BMP, DIP, RLE
CALS-I	Mil-R-Raster I	GP4, MIL, RST, CG4, CAL
GIF	CompuServe Graphics Interchange Format	GIF
JFIF	Joint Photographic Experts Group Format	JPG
FLIC	Animator FLIC	FLC, FLI
PCX	PC Paintbrush Exchange	PCX
PICT	Mac Image Format	PCT
PNG	Portable Network Graphics	PNG (patent-free replacement for the GIF)
TARGA	Truevision	TGA
TIFF	Tagged Image File	TIF

The AutoCAD Image Manager

The `image` command inserts a raster image into your AutoCAD drawing. You can also reach this command from the Insert pull-down menu–Raster Image. This command displays the dialog box shown in Figure 37.1.

If you've experimented with the External Reference Manager, you'll feel right at home in this dialog box. The Image Manager manages the image definitions and inserts each image. Similar to xrefs, the image definitions are referenced but not saved within the drawing file. This is great news because it keeps your drawing file size down.

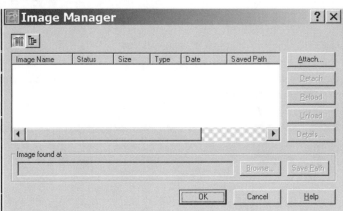

Figure 37.1 The `image` **command displays this dialog box.**

If you have set a project name (in Preferences), it displays at the top of the dialog. The two buttons in the upper left-hand corner control whether the attached images are shown in a list or a tree format. List format displays the status, size, file type, and date, as well as the physical location of the image file. You can sort the columns alphabetically or numerically by clicking on the column header. As with other MFC dialogs, hold down the <Shift> key to select multiple images, and the columns are completely adjustable.

The tree view displays the images and their respective nesting level. If you have an image attached from within an externally referenced drawing, the tree view makes it easy to visualize the nesting order. Should you feel the need to rename an image, double-click on the image name and hit the <F2> key. Although <F2> might seem natural to Windows users, it took me a while to sort it out.

> **Note**   Renaming the image does not affect the original filename. This works in both the tree and list views.

Attach

Selecting the Attach button sends you to the Select Image dialog box, as shown in Figure 37.2. Attaching an image creates an image definition, loads the image into memory, then displays the image. The image file is not saved within the drawing file, keeping the size of the drawing file down. The concept works exactly like external references. Each time you open the drawing file, AutoCAD searches for the attached images and loads them into your drawing.

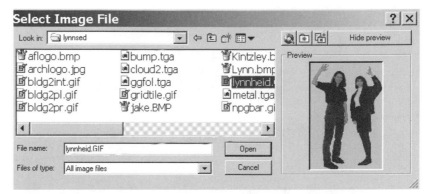

Figure 37.2 The Select Image File dialog box allows you to modify image parameters and is accessed by selecting the Attach button in the Image Manager.

There's nothing to keep you from attaching an image file multiple times within the same drawing. Each insertion will have its own unique clip boundary, as well as its own settings for brightness, contrast, fade, and transparency.

Selecting the image file to attach will send you to the Image dialog in Figure 37.3. Hitting the Browse button sends you to a standard file search dialog that helps you find your image file. After selecting the file, you can change some of the image parameters (similar to the standard `insert` command). You can key in a location, scale factor, and rotation angle, or you can manually specify these on the drawing screen. The Details button displays the information shown in Figure 37.3.

The Details section contains the information about the selected raster file. If resolution information is stored with the image file, you can set the units to millimeters, centimeters, meters, kilometers, inches, feet, yards, or miles. Unitless is the default setting when no such information is stored — image size will automatically be converted to the current AutoCAD units.

The resolution is measured relative to how many dots per AutoCAD Unit (e.g., 300 dots per inch). The actual image size is measured in pixels, as shown in Figure 37.3.

More than likely, you'll want to check the Retain Path box so AutoCAD can find the raster image in the future. If the box is not selected, the image name is saved, but without the path information, causing AutoCAD to search the Project File search paths and the AutoCAD Support Files search paths for the raster image. If you plan on playing musical directories with the raster files, it might not make sense to save the path information with the image file.

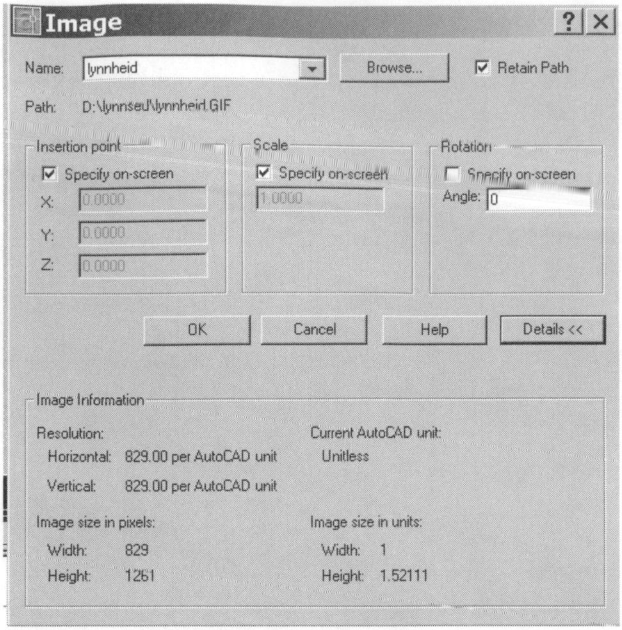

Figure 37.3 The Details section of the Image dialog box lets you set the units of measurement if the resolution information is stored with the image file.

Detach

If you no longer want to use a raster image in your drawing, you should use the Detach option in the Image Manager to remove the image references and to erase the associated objects in the drawing. Simply erasing the image won't remove the reference, so don't do that!

Unload and Reload

Too many raster images slowing you down? Although the images aren't stored with the drawing file, they take up precious memory to display within your drawing. Should you decide you don't need to view the images for the time being and could benefit from an increase in speed, unload your raster images. This doesn't actually detach the image, it just puts the raster image up on a shelf until you need it. The image frame or clipping boundary remains visible, so you'll know where the images reside within your drawing. You'll see the status of the raster image change within the Image Manager when you unload it.

If you need your raster image back in the drawing for plotting, simply reload the selected linked images. Reload also comes in handy should you find the raster image has changed and you want to make sure you've loaded the latest version of the file. This happens automatically when you leave and reenter the drawing.

Note   You can reload and unload a file easily by double-clicking on Load/Unload or Reload under the Status column.

The Details button provides you with all of the intimate details about your raster image (Figure 37.4). In the Image File Details dialog box, you'll find much the same information as is in the initial dialog, such as file type, size, date, path, and so on; you'll also find the color, such as RGB (red, green, blue), gray or palette, and a color depth value.

The value of color depth (also known as pixel depth) for a raster image varies depending on the number of colors the raster image can display. This is controlled by the number of bit planes or the number of bits of information available

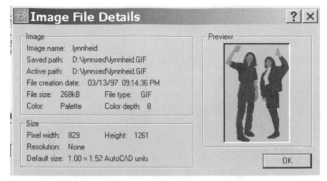

Figure 37.4 The Image File Details dialog gives you specific information about an image, including its size.

to define a pixel's color. If the color depth or bit plane value is set to 1, a pixel can be black or white only. As the bit plane or color depth jumps to 8, a pixel can be any of 256 shades of color. When the color depth is set to 24, a pixel can display nearly 16.8 million shades (wow!).

The bitmap in Figure 37.4 requires 8 bits of color depth because there are varying shades of gray, not just black and white. The bitmap in Figure 37.5, on the other hand, has a color depth of 24.

As you select each raster file within the Image Manager, you'll see that AutoCAD displays the directory in which the file was found. If you inadvertently move or delete this instance of the file, AutoCAD continues to hunt for the file using the standard search path set in Preferences and your current Profile. If AutoCAD still can't find the file, the words Not Found display in the Status column. Use the Browse button to reestablish a file's proper location and the Save Path button whenever you'd like to save new path information. If you browse to search for a raster file but do not use Save Path, AutoCAD searches the original search path the next time the drawing file is loaded.

You also can use the -image command with raster files. The command-line interface is especially efficient when you need to perform global functions, such as unloading or reloading all the attached images in your drawings.

Editing Those Raster Images

It's common practice to mix raster images with vectors in an AutoCAD drawing. Heretofore, this procedure didn't always yield desirable results. With the Image Manager, it's easy to attach, load, unload, and so on, any supported raster image. The Image Manager can be found in the Insert pull-down menu under Raster Image.

Modifying Your Image

Five commands affect your raster images in the Modify pull-down menu. Select Modify–Object–Image and you'll find four of these five commands: Adjust, Quality, Transparency, and Frame.

Adjust

This option executes the `imageadjust` command. After selecting the raster image you want to adjust, the dialog box shown in Figure 37.6 displays on the screen (I'm on the right!).

Figure 37.5 This raster image has a color depth of 24, so it can display nearly 16.8 million shades.

Use this dialog much as you would the adjust options on your television set (that doesn't mean kicking it!). Using the three controls of Brightness, Contrast, and Fade, you should be able to get the final picture you desire. Each property can have a value between 0 and 100. As you adjust the values, you see the changes to the preview image update immediately within the dialog box; any modifications you make to the image in your drawing do not affect the original image file.

Note   Bitonal images cannot be adjusted for brightness, contrast, or fade; a bitonal image consists of only a foreground and a background color.

Brightness works hand in hand with Contrast. The higher the value, the brighter the image becomes. Typically, you'll use Brightness to darken or lighten an image. Also, the higher the setting, the more pixels will become white as you increase the Contrast setting.

Contrast controls the contrast of colors within the image. Sometimes it can make poor-quality images easier to read. The higher the setting, the more each pixel is forced to take on its primary or secondary color.

Fade controls how much the image fades into the background color. A setting of 100 fades the image completely into the background. If you change the screen background color, the image automatically adapts to the new color. When plotting, AutoCAD uses white as the fading color. Some users use Fade to create a watermark effect on a drawing or to make it easier to see vectors over raster images.

The Reset button returns values to the standard defaults of 50 for Brightness, 50 for Contrast, and 0 for Fade. You can also access command line–driven prompts of imageadjust by putting a dash in front of the command (-imageadjust).

Quality

The next command on the list is imagequality, which can speed up or slow down your drawing performance. High-quality raster images take longer to display than those of draft quality. Note the imagequality command prompts.

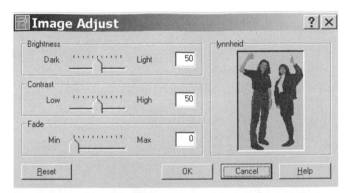

Command line: imagequality

High / Draft / <current> :

Setting the quality to Draft improves performance, and you'll notice the effect takes place immedi-

Figure 37.6 Modify Brightness, Contrast, and Fade in the Image Adjust dialog box.

ately (without a dreaded regeneration). AutoCAD always plots using High quality, so you don't need to worry about setting it back before plotting.

Transparency

The third command I'll discuss controls the transparency of your raster images. It comes in handy should you want other objects to display through the raster image or through those pixels set to transparent. Not all images support this capability. Transparency can be used on Bitonal and Alpha RGB or grayscale images; it is specified by object, and images are inserted with transparency set to off by default.

In order to select an image for modification or clipping, the image frame must be on (which brings in the frame command). Selecting Frame from the Modify–Object–Image pull-down menu executes the imageframe command, which is on by default. This setting affects all raster images. If you turn the frames off, the boundary edges are no longer visible, and your raster images are no longer select-

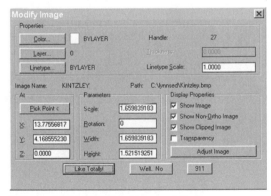

Figure 37.7 Edit images with the properties **command. The Modify Image dialog box lets you modify image properties, parameters, and display properties.**

able. You also can use the properties command Modify Images dialog (Figure 37.7).

The coolest of all the new image commands is `imageclip`. You now have the power to clip and keep only the portion of the raster image you desire. Clipping can be reversed or modified at any time, so there's no fear of incorrect clipping. `imageclip` is located in the Modify pull-down menu under Objects.

```
Command: IMAGECLIP
```

`Select image to clip:` pick the desired raster image

`ON/OFF/Delete/<New boundary>:`

The default option, New boundary, determines the clipping boundary. Accepting the default presents the following prompt.

`Polygonal/<Rectangular>:`

Polygonal/<Rectangular>

Rectangular prompts for two corners of a rectangle that is used to clip your raster image. Picking a point at the above prompt also assumes rectangular and prompts you for the second corner. The rectangle is always drawn parallel to the edges of the image frame. Polygonal gives you more control because you can select many straight-line segments. These segments are not allowed to cross each other or leave the image area. You can Undo, should you pick an incorrect point; the Close option has its usual function. Surprise, surprise; you must have at least three points to define a polygonal area.

You can have only one clipping area per image. If you try to create a second clipping edge, you will be asked if you want to discard the first clipping area. Answering No terminates the command.

Now jump back to the original options in the `imageclip` command.

`ON/OFF/Delete/<New boundary>:`

ON turns clipping on, and the clipped image (using the previously defined clipping frame) displays. OFF turns clipping off, and the entire raster image displays. If you create another clipping boundary, clipping automatically is turned back on.

Delete removes a previously defined clipping boundary; the full image again displays.

Bonus!

Introducing raster files into a vector environment is an amazing accomplishment. What used to be painful at best is now a simple process. If past experiences have caused you to shy away from using raster images in your drawings, I hope you'll give them another chance. I think you'll find them easy to use and modify.

You've Done It!

You've made it to the end, and I commend you! I hope you haven't taken too many tablets from the aspirin bottle and you've found some awesome tips and tricks that will increase your productivity. Be sure to stay tuned to my monthly columns in *CADENCE*, as I continue to provide insights into the most recent release of AutoCAD! Happy AutoCADing!

Index

- (dash) 14, 43, 219
– (minus sign) 16
$ (dollar sign) 43, 195, 213
%% (percent signs) 34
' (single quote) 212
* (asterisk) 213
+ (plus sign) 16
; (semicolon) 212, 218
@ (at sign) 9, 57, 128
[] (brackets) 224, 247
\ (backslash) 213
_ (underscore) 43

A

acad environment variable 85
ACAD menu group 235, 238
    Accelerator section 235
acad.lin 242
acad.lsp 183
acad.mln 60
acad.mns 225, 229
acad.mnu 206, 225
acad.psf 171
acad2002.cfg 171
acaddoc.lsp 183
acadlspasdoc 183
acadserver environment variable 171

accelerator key
    <Alt-F> 224
    <Alt-M> 224
accelerators, keyboard 209, 214–215
adcenter command 65
Add Control Point option 140
Add option 138
Add Vertex option 63
AI_Propchk 25
Align option, text 30
angle between items, hidden option 120
Angle option 54
Apparent Intersection (appint) object snap 10, 127
Arc option 157
array command 75–78, 120
array command, hidden option 120
Array dialog box 75
    Preview option 76
associative dimensioning 166, 185
asterisk (*) 213
at sign (@) 9, 57, 128
Attach option 82, 87
attdia system variable 142, 194, 196
attedit command 197–199
attredef command 199
attreq system variable 142
Attribute Definition dialog box 194

attributes
    duplicate 201
    edit 197–203
    edit globally 197–198
    edit individually 198
    order 201
    Sync button 201–202
attsync command 202
Auto option 72
AutoCAD 2002 129–133
    circular viewport 157
    closeall command 131
    dimensioning 99–103
    double-click to edit 132
    drawing file access 132
    edit attributes 200–203
    <Esc> to clear grips 131
    fillet command 130
    join noncontiguous polylines 131
    keyboard customization 235–239
    Layout Regen options 181
    Modify II toolbar 5
    new Customize dialog box 215
    new Layer Previous tool 5
    new Layout tabs 5
    new Model tab 5
    new Properties dialog box 25
    new Standard toolbar 5
    new text features 46
    nonrectangular viewport 157
    pedit command 130
    properties command 131
    pull-down menus 4
    Quick Select 132
    rememberfolders system variable 121
    speed 133
    startup options 183
    Status Bar 6
    trans-spatial dimensioning 165
    true associative dimensioning 103
AutoCAD LT, Group option 74
AutoCAPS 40
automatic object recognition 132

AutoSnap 12
    tab 13
    tooltip 12
autosnap system variable 186
AutoStack 38, 39

B

backslash (\) 213
Backwards option 44
base point
    determining 78
    grips 22
    polar array 77
    text 46
    xrefs 82
Base Point option 22, 77
baseline dimensions 100
battman command 200
bhatch command 49
Bind option 88
Bisect option 54
bitmap, create 69
block
    attribute 194–196
        default value 194
        prompt 194
        tag 194
    definitions, update 199
    drag and drop 69
    edit with attributes 96
    fade factor 98
    inserting 196
    mode 193–194
        Constant attribute 194
        Invisible attribute 193
        Preset attribute 194
        Verify attribute 194
    see all 65
    smart 193–196
    unnamed 83
    xref editing 98
Block Attribute Manager 200

block command 82
blockicon command 69
Boolean operators, filter command 254
Boundary Hatch dialog box 51
bounding box options 36
Box option 72
brackets ([]) 224, 247
B-splines 135
button menus 211–214

C

cal command 245
calculator, *See Geometric Calculator*
Caps option 61
case, changing 39
case, sensitivity 218
celtscale system variable 244
Center (cen) object snap 10, 13
chamfer command 130
change command 119
changing case 39
character control codes 33
circle command 6, 11, 57
Circular Array option 76
circular viewport 157
circular xrefs 83
clear grips 131
Clipped option 160
close all drawings 131
Close option 138–139
closeall command 131
Color option 60
Color Options dialog box 174
command
    3dorbit 5
    adcenter 65
    array 75–78, 120
    attedit 197–199
    attredef 199
    attsync 202
    battman 200
    bhatch 49

block 82
blockicon 69
cal 245
chamfer 130
change 119
circle 6, 11, 57
closeall 131
construction commands 53
copy 126
ddatte 197
ddim 101
dimdisassociate 103
dimlinear 126
dimstyle 101, 164
display commands 15–18
divide 11, 55–56
dtext 11, 29–33
eattedit 203
ellipse 135
erase 23
etransmit 85
extend 129
fillet 130
filter 28, 251–255
grips 19
GROUP ii
group 123
hatch 52
hatchedit 52
help 66
ID 9, 57
image 258
imageadjust 262
imageclip 264
imageframe 263
imagequality 263
insert 9, 69, 122, 196
justifytext 47
layer 166
lengthen 125
linetype 241
ltscale 244
measure 11, 55–57

menuload 225
minsert 95
mledit 63–64
mline 59, 62
mlstyle 59
move 126
mslide 228
mtext 35–41
mview 156–158, 167
offset 21
options 4
osnap 14
pan 16
pedit 21, 130
pline 157
plot 156
point 11
properties 131
propertiesclose 27
qdim 4, 99–101
ray 55
refclose 96
refedit 95–98
rtpan 15–16
rtzoom 15–16
scaletext 46
<Shift>ing 129
solid 10
spline 137
splinedit 137–140
text 33
tilemode 5
transparent commands 220–221
trim 129
ucsicon 7
units 69
vplayer 154, 166
vports 157
xbind 85
xclip 85, 91–94
xline 53
xref 81

zoom 4, 16, 158–160
command prompt 10
Compare Dimension Styles dialog box 102–103
concurrent engineering 85
configuration file, acad2002.cfg 171
construction commands 53
Construction Line menu option 53
Content Manager 65
Continuous option 100
control key
    <Ctrl-1> 26, 97
    <Ctrl-2> 65
    <Ctrl-A> 125
    <Ctrl-C> 214, 217
    <Ctrl-F> 215
    <Ctrl-R> 156, 214
    <Ctrl-V> 214
    and mouse wheel 15, 128
    object cycling 74
    object selection 120
    page forward and backward 128
    prevent toolbar docking 128
    select group member 125
coordinates, priority 185
copy command 126
copy command, Displacement option 126
cross-hatching, *See hatching* 49
Crossing option 71
Crossing Polygon (CP) 73
Current option 59
Cursor menu 9–14, 16
customization 205–209
    DesignCenter 67
    function keys 235
    keyboard 235–239
    menu file 206–209
    pull-down menus 223–225
    right-click 184
    toolbars 4, 217–221
Customize dialog box 236–239
    Keyboard tab 238
Cut Single option 64

D

dash (-) 14, 43, 219
datum dimensions 100
ddatte command 197
ddim command 101
default profile settings 121
Delete Vertex option 64
demand loading 180
demand-load options 93
demand-load xrefs 180
Description option 60, 69
DesignCenter 65–70
    adcenter command 65
    bitmap, create 69
    block scale factor 69
    blockicon command 69
    drag and drop 69
    Favorites folder 67
    Find 68
    help command 66
    insert command 69
    Load 68
    right-click 67
    toolbar 66–69
    tools list 66
    Treeview file display 66
    Treeview tool 66
    units command 69
    user preferences 185
DesignCenter dialog box 66
DesignCenter icon 65
Detach option 88
device driver file search path 170
diameter dimensions 101
digitizer tablet menu 208
dimdisassociate command 103
dimension style 101–103
    change 102
    child 102
    compare 102
    current 102
    import 65
    orphans 103

    parent 102
    trickle down effect, parent to child 103
Dimension Style dialog box 18, 101–102
    Alternate Units 115
        placement 116
        zero suppression 116
    Fit 109
        fine tuning 112
        options 109–110
        scale for dimension features 111
        text placement 111
    Lines and Arrows 105
        arrowheads 106
        center marks for circles 107
        dimension lines 105
        extension lines 106
    Primary Units 112
        angular dimensions 114
        linear dimensions 112
        measurement scale 114
        zero suppression 114
    Text 107
        alignment 109
        appearance 107
        placement 108
    Tolerances 116
        basic 117
        deviation 116
        limits 116
        precision 117
        symmetrical 116
        zero suppression 117
Dimension toolbar 5
dimension variable
    See also system variable
    dimadec 115
    dimaltd 115
    dimaltf 116
    dimaltrnd 116
    dimalttd 117
    dimaltu 115
    dimaltz 116
    dimapost 116

dimasz 106, 108
dimatfit 109
dimaunit 114
dimazin 115
dimblk1 106
dimblk2 106
dimcenter 107
dimclrd 105
dimclre 106
dimclrt 107
dimdec 112
dimdiameter 107
dimdle 106
dimdli 106
dimdsep 113
dimexe 106
dimexo 106
dimfrac 113
dimgap 108, 117
dimjust 108
dimlfac 114, 163
dimlim 116
dimlunit 112
dimlwd 105
dimlwe 106
dimpost 113, 116
dimradius 107
dimrnd 113
dimscale 108, 111, 114, 164
dimsd1 106
dimsd2 106
dimsoxd 110
dimtad 108
dimtdec 117
dimtfac 108, 112, 115, 117
dimtih 109
dimtix 110, 112
dimtm 117
dimtmove 111
dimtofl 112
dimtoh 109
dimtol 116

dimtolj 117
dimtp 117
dimtlz 117
dimtxsty 107
dimtxt 107
dimtzin 117
dimupt 108
dimzin 114
dimension variable settings 105–117
dimensioning
    associative 165–166
    automatic 126
    nonassociative 165
    standard associative 103
    true associative 103
dimensions
    baseline 100
    datum 100
    diameter 101
    Paper Space vs. Model Space 163
    quick 165
    smart 165
    staggered 100
    stupid 164
dimlfac dimension variable 163
dimlinear command 126
dimscale dimension variable 164
dimstyle command 101, 164
Displacement option 126
Display AutoSnap aperture box checkbox 13
display commands 15–18
Display Locked option 160
display resolution 175
dispsilh system variable 142
divide command 11, 55–56
docking, dialog 27
dollar sign ($) 43, 195, 213
Drafting Settings dialog box 12, 14
Drafting tab 13
drawings directory, search on open 121
drawings, externally referenced, See xrefs
dtext command 11, 29–33

E

eattedit command 203
edit attributes 197–203
Edit Attributes dialog box 197
    Attribute tab 202
    Properties tab 202
    Text Options tab 202
Edit option 101
Effects option 44
Element Properties dialog box 60
Element Properties option 60
Elevate Order option 140
ellipse 135–137
    Isocircle option 136
    offset 137
    Parameter option 136
ellipse command 135
Endpoint (endp) object snap 10
Enhanced Attribute Editor dialog box 203
environment variable
    acad 85
    acadserver 171
erase command 23
etransmit command 85
expert system variable 143
Express Tools 129
    exfillet command 130
    Linetype maker 244
    shapemaker command 244
extend command 129
Extension (ext) object snap 10
external references, *See xrefs*

F

facetres system variable 143
fade factor 98
Favorites folder 67
Fence option 73
file type 205–206
    FMP 46
    MLN 60
    MNC 205, 225

    MNR 206
    MNS 206, 225
    MNU 205, 225
    MNX 205
    PAT 50
    RTF 39
    SHX 43–44, 244
    TTF 43–44
files, location 170
Fill option 61
fillet command 130
filter
    Boolean operators 254
    operators 253
    selection 252
filter command 28, 251–255
filter.nfl 255
Find option 68
Find/Replace tab 39
Fit Data option 138
Fit option 156
Fit option, text 31
FMP file type 46
Font Name option 44
fontalt system variable 46
fontmap system variable 46
fonts
    See also text
    default alternative font 46
    mapping to alternative fonts (fontmap) 46
    TrueType 43–46
Fonts button 174
Format menu 11
freezing a layer 166
From (fro) object snap 9, 57
function keys 6–7
    <F1> 214, 238
    <F2> 214, 259
    <F3> 89
    <F4> 89, 215
    <F10> 238
    customizing 235
    reserved 214
    settings 7

Fuzz Distance option 130

G

geographic information systems 258
Geometric Calculator 245–250
    DEE shortcut function 250
    ILLE shortcut function 250
    MEE shortcut function 250
GIS 258
Grip mode 20
grips 19–23
    base point 22
    colors 19
    disappearing 20
    enabling 19, 22
    <Esc> to clear 131
    getting rid of 20
    hot 20
    hot to cold 21
    Multiple mode 21
    option
        keying 20
        Mirror 20
        Move 20
        Rotate 20
        Scale 20
        Stretch 20–21
    polyline 21
    right-click menu 20
    <Shift>key 21–22
grips command 19
Grips dialog box 19
GROUP ii
group command 123
group object selection 123–125
Group option 73

H

hatch command 52
Hatch Pattern Palette dialog box 50
hatchedit command 52

hatching 49–52
    and blocks 51
    and xrefs 51
    associative 49–50, 52
    Boundary Hatch dialog box 51
    changing (hatchedit) 52
    custom pattern (PAT file) 50
    disassociation 51
    flooding 49
    islands 49
    ISO patterns 50
    programming 52
    ray casting 49
    Remove Islands button 51
    Retain boundaries box warning 51
    style 51
    View Selections button 51
Height option 32, 36, 44
help command 66
Hide Plot option 160
Hideplot option 156
hideprecision system variable 144
hidetext system variable 144
Horizontal option 54
hot grip 20
hot grip, get multiple 128

I

ID command 9, 57
image command 258
Image Manager dialog box 258
image menu, create 229
image menu, text only 233
image tile menu 227–233
imageadjust command 262
imageclip command 264
imageframe command 263
imagequality command 263
images, *See also raster images*
import
    dimension styles 65
    layers 65
    text styles 65

Include Path option 87
inetlocation system variable 171
Inner arcs option 61
insert command 9, 69, 122, 196
Insert option 85, 88
Insertion (ins) object snap 11, 57
insertion parameters, viewing 122
insertion point 82
insunitsdefsource system variable 185
insunitsdeftarget system variable 185
Internet
    drag and drop from 65
Intersection (int) object snap 10
isavebak system variable 144
isavepercent system variable 144
Isocircle option 136
isolines system variable 145, 176
isometric drawing mode 136

J

Jointype option 130
justification abbreviations, horizontal 30
justification abbreviations, vertical 30
Justify option 30, 36
justifytext command 47

K

keyboard accelerators 209, 214–215
keyboard assignments 214, 235
keyboard customization 235–239
keyboard macros 215

L

Last option 74
layer
    create multiple 122
    Current VP Freeze 166
    drag and drop 69
    import 65
    naming 84
    New VP Freeze 166

Layer & Spatial index type 94
layer command 166
layers in layouts 166–167
Layout tabs 3–6, 151
Length option 157
lengthen command 125
Line Spacing tab 39
lines
    divide 55
    measure 55
    rays 53, 55
    xlines 53–55
linetype command 241
Linetype option 61
linetypes 241–244
    multiple scale factors 244
    pattern definitions 241
    shape file 244
    text 243
LISP routine 25
Load option 68
location of files 170
Lock option 156
locked layers 73
ltscale command 244

M

macro
    button 212
    pull-down menu 223
    syntax 217
    toolbar 217
Magnet option 13
markers
    place along an object 55
    snap to 57
mathematical expressions 245–249
    angles 246
    object snaps 248
    points 247
    precedence 245
    radius 247

units 246
variables 249
vectors 247
maxactvp system variable 145, 156
maxsort system variable 145
mbuttonpan system variable 146, 214
MDI, mutiple document interface functionality 4
measure command 11, 55–57
menu file 206–209
　accelerators section 209
　accelerators section, keyboard assignments 214
　aux section 207, 211
　buttons section 207
　helpstrings section 208
　icon section 209
　image section 209, 229
　menugroup section 209
　POP section 207, 223
　screen section 207
　tablet section 208
　toolbars section 208
menu, image tile 227–233
menuload command 225
Midpoint (mid) object snap 10
minimize all windows 121
minsert command 95
minus sign (–) 16
Mirror grip 20
mirrtext system variable 146
mledit command 63–64
mline command 59, 62
mline, See multiline
MLN file type 60
mlstyle command 59
MNC file type 205, 225
MNR file type 206
MNS file type 206, 225
MNU file type 205, 225
MNX file type 205
Model Space 5–6
　dimensioning 164

Model Space versus Paper Space 154
Modify II toolbar 5
modifying object properties 25–28
move command 126
move command, Displacement option 126
Move grip 20
Move option 139
Move Vertex option 139
mslide command 228
Mtext
　See also text
　bounding box 35–36
　bounding box abbreviations 36
　changing case 39
　edit text object (ddedit) 40
　fractions 38
　grips 40
　Height option 36
　Justify option 36
　line spacing 36–37
　Stack Properties dialog box 38–39
　stacking/unstacking 38
mtext command 35–41
Mtext Editor dialog box 37
multiline (mline) 59–64
multiline
　add 60
　caps 61
　closed cross 63
　corner joints 63
　create 62–64
　cut through 64
　delete 60
　element properties 60
　Element Properties dialog box 60
　fill 61
　list current style 59
　merged cross 63
　multiline properties 61
　Multiline Properties dialog box 61
　Multiline Styles dialog box 60
　negative offset value 62
　offset value 62

open cross 63
open, closed, and merged Ts 63
options 59
    Justification options 62
    Save option 62
scale factor 62
scale factor of 0 62
Select All option 64
styles 59–61
weld 64
multiline text, *See Mtext*
multiple document interface (MDI) functionality 4
Multiple mode 21
Multiple option 74
Mview
    Arc option 157
    Fit option 156
    Hideplot option 156
    Length option 157
    Lock option 156
    Object option 157
    Polygonal option 157
    Restore option 157
mview command 156–158, 167

N

Name option 59
Nearest (nea) object snap 11
nested xrefs 83, 89
Node (nod) object snap 11, 57
nomutt system variable 146
None (non) object snap 11
nonuniform rational basis splines (nurbs) 135
nurbs 135

O

object cycling 74
Object option 137, 157
Object Properties toolbar 3, 5
object properties, modifying 25–28

object snap 9, 13, 57
    Apparent Intersection (appint) 10, 127
    Center (cen) 10, 13
    cycling through 13, 128
    Endpoint (endp) 10
    Extension (ext) 10
    From (fro) 9, 57
    Insertion (ins) 11, 57
    Intersection (int) 10
    Midpoint (mid) 10
    Nearest (nea) 11
    Node (nod) 11, 57
    None (non) 11
    override 12
    Perpendicular (per) 11
    Quadrant (qua) 11, 13
    Tangent (tan) 11
    tooltip 12
Object Snap tab 12
ObjectARX applications 180
ObjectARX applications search path 172
Obliquing Angle option 44
offset command 21
offset ellipse 137
Offset option 54, 60
Open option 139
operators, Boolean 254
options command 4
Options dialog box 13, 169–190
    Display tab 172–177
    Drafting tab 185–187
    Files tab 169–172
    Open and Save tab 177–181
    Plotting tab 181
    Profiles tab 189–190
    Selection tab 187–189
    System tab 181–184
    User Preferences tab 184–185
Ordinate option 100
Ortho mode 20
osnap
    See object snap
    button 12
osnap command 14

Osnap Settings dialog box 14
Other Corner option 37
Outer arc option 61
Overlay option 84

P

Page Setup dialog box 152–153
Palette window, views 69
pan command 16
panning 6
Paper Space 5–6, 18, 151–161
    dimensioning 163–167
    scale factors 4, 158
    UCS icon 155
Paper Space versus Model Space 154
Paper Space viewport 155–156
parallel lines 59
    See also multiline
Parameter option 136
PAT file type 50
path, support 85, 87
pedit command 21, 130
pellipse system variable 146
percent signs (%%) 34
Perpendicular (per) object snap 11
Pick button 16–17
pick point, rules 128
pickadd system variable 28, 72, 131, 187
pickfirst system variable 187
pickstyle system variable 189
pline command 157
plinegen system variable 147
plot command 156
plquiet system variable 147
plus sign (+) 16
point command 11
Point Style dialog box 11, 56
pointer, xrefs 81
polar array 76
    base points 77
    Less option 77

methods 76
More option 77
rotation 77
Polar Array option 76
Polygonal option 157
polyline editing
    See also pedit *command*
    Fuzz Distance option 130
    joining noncontiguous polylines 131
    Jointype option 130
Preview option 44, 69, 76
Previous option 74
profile settings, controlling defaults 121
project files search path 170
Properties button 26
properties command 131
Properties dialog box 25–28
    keyboard navigation 27
    shortcut menu 28
Properties option 7
Properties tab 39
propertiesclose command 27
psltscale system variable 167
pull-down menus, customizing 223–225
Purge option 139

Q

Qdim 165
    Baseline option 100
    Continuous option 100
    datumPoint option 101
    Diameter option 101
    Edit option 101
    Ordinate option 100
    Staggered option 100
qdim command 4, 99–101
Quadrant (qua) object snap 11, 13
quick dimensions 165
    See also Qdim
Quick Select command icon 27
quotation mark, single (') 212

R

raster images 257–264
    attaching 259
    bitonal 262
    clipping 264
    color information 261
    detaching 260
    editing 262
    file formats 258
    image quality 263
    loading and reloading 260
    resolution 260
    transparency 263
rasterpreview system variable 147
ray command 55
rays 55
Rectangular Array option 76
redefine attributes 199
refclose command 96
refedit command 95–98
Refedit toolbar 95
Reference Edit dialog box 95
Refine option 140
regeneration speed 85
Reload option 88
rememberfolders system variable 148
remove objects from selection set 127
Restore option 157
Retain changes to Xref layers option 83
right-click customization 184
Rotate grip 20
Rotation Angle option 32
Rotation option 37
RTF file type 39
Rtpan button 15
rtpan command 15–16
Rtpan options 16
Rtpan right-click menu 16
Rtzoom button 15
rtzoom command 15–16

S

Saveas Options dialog box 94
scale factors 4, 7, 18
    XP decimal values 159
    XP standard values 159
Scale grip 20
Scale to Paper Space option 18
scaletext command 46
search drawings directory 121
search path
    device driver file 170
    ObjectARX applications 172
    project files 170
    support file 170
    working support file 170
search, filter command 251
Select All option 64
Select Objects
    Add 72
    All 73
    automatic windowing 72
    Crossing Polygon (CP) 73
    crossing window 71
    Fence option 73
    group command 123–125
    Group option 73
    individual selection 74
    Last option 74
    locked layers 73
    Multiple option 74
    nonrectangular area 73
    pickadd system variable 72
    Previous option 74
    Remove 72
    remove objects 127
    Shift to Remove 72
    Single option 74
    standard windowing 71
    Window Polygon (WP) 73
selection, filter command 251
semicolon (;) 212, 218
Settings dialog box 201
setvar, *See system variable*

Shade toolbar 5
<Shift> between commands 129
<Shift> key, and input device 212
shortcut functions 7
SHX file type 43–44, 244
Single option 74
slide files 227–233
slide library 231–233
    long filenames 233
solid command 10
special characters, text 33
speed, regeneration 85
splframe system variable 138, 148
spline 137–138
    Object option 137
spline command 137
spline edit
    Close option 139
    Fit Data option 138
        Add 138
        Close 138
        Move 139
        Purge 139
        Tangents 139
        Tolerance 139
    Move Vertex option 139
    Open option 139
    Refine option 140
        Add Control Point 140
        Elevate Order 140
        Weight 140
splinedit command 137–140
staggered dimensions 100
Standard toolbar 5
Status Bar 6, 12
Stretch grip 20–21
Style Name option 43
Style option 31, 37
support file search path 170
support path 85, 87
surftab1 system variable 148
surftab2 system variable 148
Sync button 201–202

system variable 141–150, 169–190
    See also dimension variable
    attdia 142, 194, 196
    attreq 142
    autosnap 186
    celtscale 244
    dispsilh 142
    expert 143
    facetres 143
    fontalt 46
    fontmap 46
    hideprecision 144
    hidetext 144
    inetlocation 171
    insunitsdefsource 185
    insunitsdeftarget 185
    isavebak 144
    isavepercent 144
    isolines 145, 176
    maxactvp 145, 156
    maxsort 145
    mbuttonpan 146, 214
    mirrtext 146
    nomutt 146
    pellipse 146
    pickadd 28, 72, 131, 187
    pickfirst 187
    pickstyle 189
    plinegen 147
    plquiet 147
    psltscale 167
    rasterpreview 147
    rememberfolders 121, 148
    splframe 138, 148
    surftab1 148
    surftab2 148
    textfill 45, 149
    textqlty 45, 149
    ucsfollow 149
    visretain 83, 149, 180
    vpvisdflt 166
    wmfbkgrnd 150
    xedit 98

xfadectl 98
zoomfactor 150

T

Tablet menu 11
Tangent (tan) object snap 11
Tangents option 139
text 29–34
    See also dtext *command*
    See also Mtext
    See also fonts
    See also text style
    Align option 30
    alternative font (fontalt) 46
    base point 46
    changing case 39
    character control codes 33
    double-clicking 40
    fill (textfill) 45
    Fit option 31
    height 32
    justification 30, 47
    justification abbreviations
        horizontal 30
        vertical 30
    losing 40
    multiline, *See Mtext*
    overscore 34
    regeneration speed 45–46
    resolution (textqlty) 45
    rotation angle 32
    scaling 46
    show bounding box (qtext) 46
    style 31
    styles 43–47
    underscore 34
text command 33
Text option 32
text style
    applying changes 45
    changing 45
    deleting 45
    direction 44

    font name 44
    height 44
    import 65
    obliquing angle 44
    renaming 45
    style name 43
    width factor 44
Text Style dialog box 44
textfill system variable 45, 149
textqlty system variable 45, 149
3dorbit command 5
tilemode command 5
Tolerance option 139
Toolbar dialog box 4
toolbars 4
    <Ctrl> to prevent docking 128
    customizing 4, 217–221
Tools menu 14
tracking 6
transparent commands 220–221
Treeview tool 66
trim command 129
TrueType fonts 133
TTF file type 43–44

U

UCS 9, 54, 154
UCS Per Viewport option 160
ucsfollow system variable 149
Ucsicon 151
ucsicon command 7
underscore (_) 43
units 184–185
units command 69
universal coordinate system (UCS) 9, 54
Unload option 88
unnamed blocks 83
Up option 69
Update command 164
Upside Down option 44
user preferences 190
User Preferences tab 166

V

Vertical option 45, 54
View menu 15
viewport 152–154
    3D 152
    aligned 167
    nonrectangular 160
    no-plot layer 167
    Paper Space 155–156
    scale factor 158
Viewports toolbar 5, 161
Views option 69
visretain system variable 83, 149, 180
vplayer command 154, 166
vports command 157
vpvisdflt system variable 166

W

Weight option 140
Weld All option 64
Width Factor option 44
Width option 37
Window option 71
Window Polygon (WP) 73
wmfbkgrnd system variable 150
word processing, *See text*
working support file search path 170

X

xbind command 85
xclip command 85, 91–94
Xclip tool 91
xedit system variable 98
xfadectl system variable 98
xline command 53
xlines 53–55
xref command 81
Xref Manager 82, 85–89
    list view 86

tree view 89
xrefs 81–89
    and hatching 51
    Attach option 82, 87
    Bind option 88
    binding 84
    block editing 98
    circular 83
    clip 91–94
    clipping boundary 93
    concurrent engineering 85
    Detach option 88
    detaching 82, 84
    edit 94–98
    fade factor 98
    Include Path option 87
    Insert option 85, 88
    insertion point 82
    Layer & Spatial index type 94
    minsert command 95
    missing 84–85
    nested 83, 89
    Overlay option 84
    overlaying 84
    path 85
    pointer 81
    refclose command 96
    refedit command 95–98
    Refedit toolbar 95
    Reference Edit dialog box 95
    reference name 88
    regeneration speed 85
    Reload option 88
    Retain changes to Xref layers option 83
    scale factor 82
    support path 85, 87
    Unload option 88
    visretain system variable 83
    wblock 84
    xbind command 85
    xclip command 85, 91–94

Z

zoom
  All option 17
  Center option 17
  Clipped option 160
  defaults 17
  Display Locked option 160
  Dynamic option 17
  Extents option 17
  Hide Plot option 160
  Previous option 17
  Scale option 17
  UCS Per Viewport option 160
  XP option 18, 158
zoom command 4, 16, 158–160
zoomfactor system variable 150
zooming 15–18

Design with Authority

Tools for your success

Cadenceweb.com

Your daily resource for:

- CAD news
- Searchable database of CADENCE magazine features and reviews
- Discussion forums for CAD Managers and Technical Questions
- Links
- Downloads
- And more CAD community resources...

CADENCE Newsletters

Delivered directly to your desktop – bi-weekly or monthly sources of professional information about your CAD specialty, from the experts at CADENCE magazine. Sign up now – FREE – at www.cadenceweb.com.

AEC Newsletter

Author and researcher Lachmi Khemlani writes about the impact of CAD on architecture, engineering and construction.

CAD Manager's Newsletter

Robert Green, noted expert and management consultant, explores the ins and outs of both the finanacial and technical aspects of managing a CAD group.

MCAD Newsletter

Joe Greco, an MCAD consultant and contributor to CADENCE magazine, reports on software, hardware and industry developments that impact MCAD professionals.

Sheerin Hardware Report

CADENCE Senior Technical Editor Peter Sheerin, known for his stringent benchmark testing and hard-hitting reviews, talks about the latest hardware products and the CAD standards that your hardware should meet.

CMP
United Business Media

CADENCE